REFLECTING HIS GLORY

Revivals Call

A call of the Lord to believers
and the Church of today.

Courtney A. Laird

Copyright © – Courtney Laird – 2022
All rights reserved

ISBN: 978-0-6488463-2-1

All rights reserved. No part of this publication may be reproduced, stored in a retrieval system, or transmitted in any form or by any means mechanical, electronic, photocopying or otherwise without the express written permission of the author.

The author can be contacted at:
courtney.a.laird@gmail.com

All scripture references, unless otherwise indicated, are taken from the Authorised King James version of the Bible.

Words of scripture written in bold are used by the writer for specific emphasis.

DEDICATION

To my amazing, incredible, wonderful wife, Bethany.

I cannot thank you enough for your continual support and encouragement throughout this endeavour. I so value everything that you have done to help me get this finished. This book would simply not be possible without you.

You are such an incredible person, mother, wife, friend and woman of God and I am so blessed to share this life with you. I so admire the fire of God that is upon your life and the passion that you have for worshipping in His presence. You constantly inspire me to press deeper into Him.

With my utmost gratitude and all my love,

Court.

FORWARD

This study was prompted by a thought laid on the heart of the writer during a time of corporate prayer in 2020. Prior to this time of prayer, the group had been discussing the call for the people of God, and the Church, to shine in the days that we are in. The discussion covered thoughts on how this occurs, why it occurs and why sometimes the light doesn't seem to be as bright as it needs to be.

In meditating upon this discussion and seeking the Lord, the writer felt quickened by the Lord to a passage of scripture which at the time didn't quite make sense. As the writer went home and began to look into the Word about what the Lord had impressed upon his heart, the Lord started to speak a message to the writer's heart which forms the basis for this study.

Within the Word of God there is indeed a call for the Church, and believers, to reflect His glory. As we progress through this text, we will begin to see that this call is tied to the call of revival that the Lord is stirring in these days.

The aim of this study is to look at what it means to shine, how it is enacted in each of our lives and churches and what its purpose is. It is the writer's prayer that as the reader considers the thoughts laid out in this study, that they will be both encouraged and challenged to shine brightly in the areas where God has placed them.

The world around us changes when His glory is reflected.

Blessings in Christ,

Courtney A Laird.

CONTENTS

DEDICATION i
FORWARD iii
PART A THE PREMISE 1
    Part A Introduction 3
    Considering 2 Kings 3 5
    Are We Called To Shine? 21
    Understanding the Tabernacle 27
    The Call to the Individual 33
    The Call to the Church 55
    Part A Summary 77
PART B THE PROCESS 83
    Part B Introduction 85
    Digging 87
    Infilling 169
    Reflection 197
    Victory 231
    Part B Summary 237
PART C REVIVALS CALL 241
    Part C Introduction 243
    The Parable of the 10 Virgins 247
    The Early and Latter Rains 257
    Correlation of The Virgins and The Rains 277
    Part C Summary 281
FINAL THOUGHTS 283
SUPPLEMENTAL 287
OTHER BOOKS BY THE AUTHOR 295

PART A
THE PREMISE

PART A INTRODUCTION

The basic premise of this text is that we as believers and churches are called to reflect the glory of the Lord to the world around us. This, in a nutshell, is what the Lord put on the writer's heart. It was in dwelling upon this thought that the writer was directed to a passage of scripture in 2 Kings 3, and from here the Lord slowly put together the pieces of the puzzle which have resulted in this text.

This section will cover an overview of this 2 Kings chapter, breaking down the verses before considering the message that the Lord impressed upon the writer's heart. As was mentioned in the forward to this study, though the passage did not initially make sense to the writer, after meditating upon it and seeking the Lord about it, the writer felt that the Lord started to speak a message to the heart of the writer. Though what was revealed was not a profound revelation, it is a message that the writer has felt time and time again is for believers and the Church today.

Once we have looked at out the points that the writer felt the Lord impress upon his heart, we will then turn our attention to see whether these thoughts are confirmed in the Word of God. It is one thing to have a thought, it is another altogether to have that thought be confirmed by scripture. The Bible is the divine standard by which we measure all else. Any revelation or word we receive from the Lord must always be weighed against the truth of scripture. This was an act that the people of Berea were commended for by the writer of Acts when they listened to Paul and Silas (Acts 17:11). In weighing the thought that was impressed upon the writers heart by the Lord we will consider how it aligns with the Word of God by following the scriptural law of witness:

> ....., that in the mouth of two or three witnesses every word may be established. (Mat 18:16)

We never just take one verse or one reference. We always follow the Word of God and weigh it against the fulness of scripture where we will either receive confirmation or

Part A Introduction

correction. With the right attitude, both are equally as valuable. We will seek to do that here and present to the reader scriptural consideration that would confirm the message that the writer received.

Having looked at the message impressed on the writers heart and how it is confirmed in scripture, we will then move onto Part B of this text where we will consider what application this message has to us as believers and New Testament churches.

CONSIDERING 2 KINGS 3

At the start of 2 Kings 3 we read that Jehoram the son of Ahab had begun to reign in Israel, during the time that Jehoshaphat was king over Judah. Jehoram was a king recorded as being evil in the sight of the Lord. As one reads over the accounts of the books of Kings and Chronicles, we read that there were either good kings or bad kings, there was no middle ground. Scripture is fairly black and white on this issue. Jehoram was a bad king, but, and it is a small but, he was not as bad as his father and mother, king Ahab and his wife Jezebel.

Under Ahab's rule (Jehoram's father) the king of Moab had been put under forced tribute to the nation of Israel. The king of Moab was their sheep master and would bring unto king Ahab one hundred thousand lambs and one hundred thousand rams with their wool. No small tribute! After the death of Ahab though, Mesha king of Moab saw a chance to withdraw from this enforced tribute while the new, younger king was still settling in. Mesha did not hesitate on taking up this opportunity, rebelling against the nation of Israel and ceasing to provide the previously imposed tribute. When Jehoram king of Israel learned of this, he went out in battle against Moab in order to reinforce the tribute that had been imposed upon Moab by his father.

Jehoram started by numbering all of Israel to ascertain the size of his army. Possibly believing he didn't have the numbers, or maybe just wanting a bigger army, Jehoram then approached Jehoshaphat king of Judah to see if he would join him on his quest. King Jehoshaphat agreed and they set off through the wilderness of Edom toward Moab.

From here we will turn to a more expository approach to 2 Kings 3 and break down the verses, so the reader sees the fulness of what was happening in this passage. Before we move forward, the reader is encouraged to spend some time reading over 2 Kings chapter 3 before proceeding.

So the king of Israel went, and the king of Judah, and the king of Edom: and they fetched a compass of seven days' journey: and there was no water for the host, and for the cattle that followed them. (2Ki 3:9)

What started out as a journey of two kings now had three. Going out to battle against Moab were the king of Judah, the king of Israel and the king of Edom. Their journey to Moab had taken them seven days and they were at a point of being too committed to simply withdraw. It was here that they found themselves in a predicament that was not favourable. The three kings found themselves in a situation where they had run out of water and there was no available supply around them to draw from. There was no water for the host and there was no water for their cattle. Their supplies had dried up and there was seemingly nowhere around them where they could seek water out. They were in a dry, arid area and the prognosis wasn't good. They had possibly continued on in their expedition expecting to find water on the way, but their path was a dry one and they were now seven days into their journey and completely out of water.

Water is essential for life. Man can go for a period without food, but water is a necessity for life to continue. Life cannot be sustained without water. Water rejuvenates the body. Water provides energy and nourishment for the body to function. Water helps brain function. Water helps regulate our body temperature. Water helps maintain and regulate our bodily functions. Water improves our blood oxygen circulation. Without water natural man will die. Whilst the kings weren't quite at this crossroads, going into a battle in a dehydrated and weakened state would result in the same outcome. The three kings, their armies and their cattle were in dire straits.

And the king of Israel said, Alas! that the LORD hath called these three kings together, to deliver them into the hand of Moab! (2Ki 3:10)

Jehoram's response to this situation shows exactly where his relationship with the Lord was at. Jehoram had absolutely no faith in the Lord. He surmised from the situation that doom and destruction would be the outcome, and that this was the will of the Lord. At the start of 2 Kings 3 we are told that Jehoram in no way honoured the Lord and yet as soon as things looked bad in his life, he was ready to blame Him. Jehoram had no reverence for the Lord and would not once have thanked Him for the blessings in his life, but as soon as things started to look bad, he was ready to attribute the fault to God. This behaviour would possibly suggest that Jehoram knew he was living in a wrong way. He had a knowledge that the way he was living and leading was wrong and at some point, there would be consequences for it.

Jehoram was an individual who didn't have an active relationship with the Lord and certainly didn't have any faith in the Lord to deliver him. He saw but one outcome from the situation that was before him. His declaration of doom was certainly not something that would have inspired hope amongst the men of his army!

But Jehoshaphat said, Is there not here a prophet of the LORD, that we may enquire of the LORD by him? (2Ki 3:11)

But Jehoshaphat! In contrast to the words of Jehoram we now read of the response of king Jehoshaphat of Judah to the same situation. It is this marked difference that makes their alliance a little unusual. Jehoshaphat was a king who, unlike Jehoram, walked according to the ways of the Lord. Rather than blaming the Lord for the situation, Jehoshaphat's response was that they should be seeking Him.

Whilst Jehoram was ready to simply blame God for their circumstances, Jehoshaphat's mindset was to seek the Lord in their circumstances. The two men here sum up the two responses that we often have to the events of life that unfold. We either blame God for them for or we seek Him in them. One draws us close to the Lord and the other pushes us away.

Jehoshaphat's response here was that they should seek a prophet of the Lord. In the Old Testament the prophets were recognised as the ones who heard the voice of God and communicated the will of the Lord to man. Here Jehoshaphat asked whether there was a prophet of the Lord that the three kings could enquire of. Note the clear distinction Jehoshaphat laid out. They were not to seek an oracle, fortune teller or a false prophet. They were to find a prophet of the Lord. Jehoshaphat was uncompromising in his beliefs, even in the midst of unbelievers. Whilst Jehoram was looking to blame the Lord, Jehoshaphat was looking to seek Him out.

And one of the king of Israel's servants answered and said, Here is Elisha the son of Shaphat, which poured water on the hands of Elijah. (2Ki 3:11)

Whilst the king of Israel was ungodly, his servants had knowledge of not only Elisha, but also where he resided. They knew who he was, they knew where he lived, they knew his heritage and they knew without a doubt that he was a prophet of the Lord. Whilst the king was ungodly, godliness still existed within Israel. The Lord always has a faithful remnant!

The reference here in regard to Elisha pouring water in the hand of Elijah points to the close relationship that Elisha and Elijah had, where Elisha learned from being a servant to Elijah. Elisha had been called by God to train up under Elijah and it was a call Elisha chased after with all his heart. When it came time for Elijah to be taken to heaven, Elisha dared not part from his side. Elisha wanted to fulfil his call and receive not only Elijah's mantle but also a double portion of his spirit (2 Kings 2:9).

Given the context that the kings found themselves in, it is interesting that the water they lacked for themselves and their army had been in abundance for Elisha when he washed Elijah's hands.

And Jehoshaphat said, The word of the LORD is with him. So the king of Israel and Jehoshaphat and the king of Edom went down to him. (2Ki 3:12)

Jehoshaphat was clearly satisfied with the servant's suggestion, immediately recognising the gifting and calling upon Elisha. Elisha had the Word of God within him and he would be able to enquire of the Lord on behalf of the three kings. Elisha would be able to act as an intermediary for the kings and seek the Lord in regard to the predicament that they were in.

And Elisha said unto the king of Israel, What have I to do with thee? get thee to the prophets of thy father, and to the prophets of thy mother. And the king of Israel said unto him, Nay: for the LORD hath called these three kings together, to deliver them into the hand of Moab. (2Ki 3:13)

As the kings arrived, the king of Israel received a welcome that wasn't exactly warm by Elisha. Jehoram's father and mother were wicked rulers and sought at times to kill Elisha's master Elijah. They wanted nothing to do with the Lord and pursued everything that was contrary to Him. It would seem that their son had followed in a similar vein, but perhaps not quite as badly.

Elisha's words here were pretty clear. He said in essence to Jehoram, you have never wanted anything to do with the Lord, why come now? Why don't you pursue those ungodly ways that have been the crux for your life? Like most prophets Elisha was very black and white. He wasn't there to give a feel-good message, he was there to speak the truth of the Lord into the situation.

Despite the sternness of Elisha's greeting, Jehoram still had the gumption to reply, though possibly somewhat humbled. He responded that if the Lord had allowed all this to happen, then they needed to seek the voice of the Lord for direction.

And Elisha said, As the LORD of hosts liveth, before whom I stand, surely, were it not that I regard the presence of Jehoshaphat the king of Judah, I would not look toward thee, nor see thee. (2Ki 3:14)

But for Jehoshaphat, Elisha would not have given Jehoram the time of day. Jehoshaphat was a godly king and one for whom Elisha had respect. What was an unlikely venture between the righteous and unrighteous going out to battle, saw the unrighteous blessed through the favour of the righteous here. One would wonder if Jehoram ever looked back on this fact. But for Jehoshaphat, Jehoram would have been lost!

But now bring me a minstrel. And it came to pass, when the minstrel played, that the hand of the LORD came upon him. (2Ki 3:15)

Interesting to note here is the link between worship and the spirit moving and bringing revelation to man. Elisha requested music before he went and sought the Lord. The Word then tells us that as the music was played the hand of the Lord came upon him. As the worship resounded, the Lord moved and spoke to Elisha. Here we see the Word and the Spirit operate in a harmonious balance.

The Spirit and the Word are constantly linked throughout the Word of God. Both are equally important, and both are equally needed in the lives of believers and the Church. One should never be emphasised to the detriment of the other.

The Word of the Lord that came to Elisha covers the next 4 verses of chapter 3.

And he said, Thus saith the LORD, Make this valley full of ditches. (2Ki 3:16)

The Word of the Lord first of all consisted of an action that the kings would have to fulfil. There was an onus upon them to do this part before God did His part. The Lord spoke through Elisha and told the kings to make the valley full of ditches.

The Hebrew word for ditches as used here is "gabe". Its emphasis is on the effort to either cut out, used in relation to a log, or to dig, as with a well or cistern. The kings here were called to dig and make the valley full of ditches. They were not to dig one, or two ditches. The valley was to be dug full of ditches for that which the Lord would do next.

The question that could be asked is why dig? Why couldn't God just provide a ready flowing stream or simply refill their water stores? Often with the things of God there is first of all a condition laid out on the part of man before the blessing comes. The condition is a requirement that upon being met, sees the fulness of the blessing received. If man can be obedient to the Word of God, then the Lord responds and blessing flows. That is exactly what we see here. There was a faith step that the kings had to take. They had to be prepared to ask their armies to dig ditches throughout the valley. We need to remember that this was an army without water, drained and already tired, yet they were going to be asked to commit what energy they had left to dig ditches.

We also need to remember here that this was a united army that had set out prepared for battle. They would have been armed with swords, shields, spears and bows. Shovels would not have been high on the inventory list. Despite all of this, the Word of the Lord to the three kings was to dig. The valley was to be made full of ditches. If they wanted to receive the blessing they so desperately needed, they had to dig. The kings and the men had to make do with what they had and find a way to dig the ditches that the Lord asked them to.

For thus saith the LORD, Ye shall not see wind, neither shall ye see rain; yet that valley shall be filled with water, that ye may drink, both ye, and your cattle, and your beasts. (2Ki 3:17)

The Word of the Lord continued through Elisha and in this verse we have the promise of obedience. If the kings of Israel would fill the valley full of ditches, then the Lord would fill those ditches with water. The act of faith on behalf of the kings would be met with the provision of supernatural blessing. The required action by the men in the natural, i.e. digging, would prepare the way for the Lord to supernaturally provide. Man does the natural, God does the supernatural! Time and time again this proves to be true.

The blessing that would come would be an absolute miracle of God. There would be no wind and there would be no rain and yet water would be provided by the Lord in the ditches that the kings had dug. There is absolutely no way that this miracle of the Lord could have been reasoned away by man. Ungodly Jehoram would be in no way able to deny that what would happen was anything but a supernatural intervention of the Lord. This would be a supernatural provision from the Lord.

Note the extent of the provision here. It was not just water for the kings. It was not just water for their armies. This was water for the kings, their armies, their cattle and their beasts. There was an abundance of provision, more than met their needs. There would be an overabundance of water.

And this is but a light thing in the sight of the LORD: he will deliver the Moabites also into your hand. (2Ki 3:18)

Elisha continued his discourse, telling the kings that though this may seem like an incredible thing in their minds, this was but a small thing in the sight of the Lord. The Lord would not only provide water for the armies, but He would also deliver Moab into their hands. Only a few verses ago Jehoram was resigned to being delivered into the hands of Moab because of their situation. Now the Word of the Lord to him was that not only would the Lord deliver him out of the situation he had gotten himself into, but the Lord would also deliver Moab into his hands. This was a complete juxta position. The circumstances of the kings would be completely flipped. They would go from scarcity and defeat to abundance and victory.

And ye shall smite every fenced city, and every choice city, and shall fell every good tree, and stop all wells of water, and mar every good piece of land with stones.(2Ki 3:19)

The Word continued. The kings would not only defeat Moab, but they would also completely conquer their land. In battles, armies would often retreat to the safety of their fenced cities where they could hold off the opposition, but this would not be the case here. The Word of the Lord through Elisha was that the kings would defeat the army and they would smite every fenced city, even the choicest ones. Nothing would stop the victory that the Lord was working through the three kings. Moab would be completely defeated.

The kings would not only conquer the people of Moab, they would also conquer their land. They would fell every good tree. They would stop up all the wells and they would mar every good piece of the land that could be used for crops and grazing. Moab's defeat was to be total. The country of Moab would be physically and economically defeated at the hands of the three kings.

And it came to pass in the morning, when the meat offering was offered, that, behold, there came water by the way of Edom, and the country was filled with water. (2Ki 3:20)

Between verse 19 and 20 we have a jump in time. We are not told exactly when the three kings presented themselves before Elisha, but from the language of verse 20 it would seem implied that it was the day before the events of verse 20.

What this means is that there was a very small window of time for the three kings to heed the words of the Lord through Eisha and fill the valley with ditches. If they were to receive the blessing that they needed, they had to act upon the Word of the Lord to them immediately.

In verse 20 we are told that it was now morning. Not just any time of morning though, it was the time of the morning sacrifice when the meat was offered. There is a link seen here between sacrifice and blessing. The Lord could have acted at any time of day, but He chose to act at the time of the morning sacrifice. We see similar occurrences of this link between sacrifice and provision happening with Israel being sustained in the morning and the evening with manna and quail (Ex 16:12), and also with the raven sustaining Elijah in the morning and evening (1 Ki 17:6).

We need to remember here that Jehoshaphat was the only Godly king in the group and that this was an expedition that ungodly Jehoram was leading. It would seem though, as so often happens, that the needs of the people of Israel brought them back to seeking their God. Time and time again is this pattern repeated, not just with natural Israel, but with spiritual Israel. We wander after our own ways but when life presents obstacles, we re-realise our great need of the Lord and start seeking Him afresh.

Here the people were in need of water. They had sought the Word of the Lord through Elisha and then they sacrificed to the Lord their God according to the Old Covenant economy. A change of heart had occurred. They sought, they heard and they acted.

Having been faithful to the Word of the Lord, and having offered the morning sacrifice, the Lord then moved. We are told that water came from the way of Edom, the home country of one of the three kings. This was no trickle or stream though, this was a volume of water that flowed from the direction of Edom and filled the valley where the three kings and the army were.

It would seem implied here from scripture that this was a body of water that was moving and flowing. This water flowed through the land and filled it as it went. This was not a body of water that stopped, but one that passed through the land. The purpose of digging the ditches was so that this water could be caught. The promised water of the Lord came as a flowing river, but the Word of the Lord was to fill the valley with ditches so that the water could be caught. As the water flowed through, it filled the ditches that had been dug and the valley was literally full of wells of water. Through digging the kings had prepared room to receive the blessing of the Lord.

If the three kings hadn't acted in faith, they may have been able to get some water and may have had temporary provision for themselves, their men and their beasts. The Lord though, through His Word, had told them to dig ditches in order to catch the water so that they would have sustained provision. The provision of the Lord was coming but the three kings and their armies had to make room to receive it. They had to dig to be able to receive the fulness of what the Lord had for them. The Lord had more than enough for their needs, but their faith determined what they received.

The Word of the Lord was to prepare, but they had to act before the Lord moved. In acting in faith, the armies dug in hope to receive that which they couldn't naturally see. In response to this the Lord supernaturally provided a blessing that was more than could be fathomed. The actions of the kings determined what they received. Through their faith in the Word of the Lord, their circumstances were changed in the blink of the eye. What a testimony this must have been to the kings of Israel and Edom.

And when all the Moabites heard that the kings were come up to fight against them, they gathered all that were able to put on armour, and upward, and stood in the border. And they rose up early in the morning, and the sun shone upon the water, and the Moabites saw the water on the other side as red as blood: (2Ki 3:21-22)

Moab had heard that the three kings were coming out against them to battle, and the people of Moab weren't going to surrender easily. Moab gathered all that they had, all that could put on armour and set out to the border of their land in preparation to meet the three kings and their armies.

From a reading of verses 21 and 22 it would seem that the army of Moab arrived at their border at the same time that the three kings were seeking the Word of the Lord through Elisha. The enemy had arrived at a point when the three kings were at their weakest. The three kings had no water, Jehoram was already conceding defeat and the armies had used what little energy they had left digging holes in the ground. Digging a hole manually, let alone in dry ground, is long tiring, work. It is not easy and when you have no water to replenish your strength it becomes even harder. The armies of the three kings would have literally been on their last legs.

As things were at their most dire and when the need of a miracle was at its highest, the enemy showed up in force. The enemy came at a time when the kings and their armies were at their weakest. How often does the enemy try and scare us away from continuing in faith and receiving the fulness of what the Lord has for us? He constantly tries to intimidate, and it is always a bluff. He comes in our weak moments in the hope that in our depleted strength, we will not be able to stand against his intimidation.

Moab rose early to prepare for battle, but the Lord had already moved! By the time Moab rose the water had already flowed and filled the ditches that the armies of the three kings had dug. Moab didn't see the intervention of the Lord, they just saw the result. Moab didn't see the water flow, all they saw was the sun reflecting off the water that had been caught in the ditches dug by the three kings.

What is interesting to note though, and this is something we will discuss further as we look at the next verse, is that when Moab saw the sun reflecting off the water they didn't see light, they saw blood. Usually when the sun is reflecting off water it is fairly readily identifiable. There is a shining and almost blinding affect that occurs. In this case though, we see the second supernatural act of the Lord in 2 Kings 3. The reflecting of the sun off the water looked as blood to Moab. They did not see a blinding reflection; they saw blood.

And they said, This is blood: the kings are surely slain, and they have smitten one another: now therefore, Moab, to the spoil. And when they came to the camp of Israel, the Israelites rose up and smote the Moabites, so that they fled before them: but they went forward smiting the Moabites, even in their country. (2Ki 3:23-24)

As we noted above, when Moab saw the sun reflecting upon the water, they saw blood. When they looked across to the valley that had been filled with ditches instead of seeing the reality, they saw blood. From this the people of Moab then wrongly concluded that this was in fact the blood of the armies of the three kings. They thought that division must have arisen between the kings, and that they had turned on each other and fought out a bloody battle. Moab assumed that they wouldn't have to fight because the battle had been taken care of for them. So rather than charging into battle, Moab's mindset instantly changed, and they ran in to collect the spoils. What had been a united army was now every man for himself seeking to gain as much spoil as he could for himself.

We see here that God had more in mind through the working of His miracle of provision for the three kings. The words of Elisha were that it was only a small thing for the Lord to provide water for the three kings and their armies and that He would also ensure the defeat of Moab. What was probably not foreseen at the time was how these two were interconnected. The Lord used the water to not only save and sustain the three kings, He also used it to ensure Moab's defeat. There was more to the digging than just self-sufficiency. As the water poured down into the valley from the way of Edom it filled the ditches that had been dug in faith. These ditches provided for the three kings and their men more than they could have imagined or hoped for. This was the inner working of the Lord's provision.

But there was also an outworking received from the infilling. The infilling wasn't just meant for the people who were receiving it. The people received the infilling, but the purpose of God was to do more with it than what man could have foreseen. It was the infilling of the ditches that allowed Moab to wrongly see the valley filled with blood, and it was this outworking that ultimately brought about the victory for the three kings. As Moab ran to the plunder, wrongly perceiving the valley to be full of blood, the armies of Israel rose ready for battle and smote down the Moabites. Victory came through the infilling that had occurred! When Moab looked out on the sun shining upon the water provided by the Lord, they saw blood. When they saw this their demeanour was instantly changed, and it was this change, brought about through what they saw, that brought about victory for the armies of Israel. Israel took the ground of Moab as the enemy retreated before them.

And they beat down the cities, and on every good piece of land cast every man his stone, and filled it; and they stopped all the wells of water, and felled all the good trees: only in

Kirharaseth left they the stones thereof; howbeit the slingers went about it, and smote it. And when the king of Moab saw that the battle was too sore for him, he took with him seven hundred men that drew swords, to break through even unto the king of Edom: but they could not. (2Ki 3:25-26)

The armies of Israel had a full and complete victory over the Moabites. As the kings and the armies were faithful to the Words of the Lord through Elisha, as detailed in verse 19, the Lord worked with them to bring about total and complete victory. The armies went forth beating down the cities, destroying the good land, stopping the wells and felling all the good trees. This was all done to drive the enemy back and ensure that they couldn't quickly regain the territory that had been lost.

The wells in the land of Moab were filled in to cut off a readily available supply of water. The three kings had just experienced what it was like to go without water and how without it defeat would come quickly. In filling up the wells the Moabites no longer had ready access to a source of life and sustenance.

As every man passed by a field, he would throw a stone onto it. By the time the whole army had done this, the field was left marred and unusable. This was not an uncommon practice in Biblical times. This essentially prohibited crops from being easily sown. The good fields were rendered as bad and in order for them to ever be able to produce again a lot of work would be required to clear and prepare them.

Finally, the trees for building, refuge and fruit were chopped down. Trees take time to grow and mature. As the armies chopped these trees down, it literally reset the productivity of the land.

This, as we have said, was all done to stop the Moabites returning. It cut off sources of supply and the necessities by which life is maintained. God moved with the united armies to push the enemy back. This was not just a battle that saw Moab defeated, it was one that saw the enemy pushed back.

THE PROCESS REVEALED

As we have gone through the account of 2 Kings 3, we have discussed the deliverance that the Lord provided to the three kings and their armies against the nation of Moab. As the united armies found themselves without water seven days into their journey, they sought the Lord afresh and as they followed His Word, they received not only deliverance, but also the promised victory of the Lord.

Within this working of the Lord there are four points of application that have particular significance to this text. It was in fact what the Lord spoke to the writer here that birthed this study.

Within this account we can observe four stages that were involved for the armies of Israel to receive the victory of the Lord and drive the enemy back. From the time they returned to seek the Word of the Lord through the prophet Elisha to the time that the Lord's Word was fulfilled there are four distinct stages. These are:

A. Digging

    The Word of the Lord to the three kings through the prophet Elisha was to dig! This was a step of faith for the kings, to trust the Word of the Lord and have their armies dig ditches throughout the valley. There was no evidence for what they were doing, they had to step out in faith and dig. It did not make sense in the natural.

    The Lord had promised to honour their efforts but there was an initial responsibility that was laid upon man. Before the Lord would move, the kings had to dig. Man had to make the first move and prepare for that which the Lord said He would do.

    The first thing we see is that there was digging!

B. Infilling

    The second thing that happened was the infilling. As the water flowed from the way of Edom and through the valley it filled the ditches that had been dug. The valley had been dug full of ditches and the water that flowed filled each and every one of them.

    The ditches were dug because the Lord had a purpose for them. As the armies were faithful in digging, the Lord was faithful in filling. The promise of the Lord was that if they would dig, He would fill, and that is exactly what happened. As man fulfilled his part, the Lord fulfilled His.

    The second thing we see is infilling.

C. Reflection

    The third thing to happen was that the sun reflected off the wells of water that had been filled. As the sun reflected off the water there was an affect that couldn't be ignored. It was this reflection that caught the attention of the people of Moab.

    The infilling was used for more than just those who received it. The Lord used it to catch the attention of those around them as well. The reflection occurred as the sun shone on that which had been infilled. As the glory of the sun shone upon the wells that had been infilled with water, there was a resulting reflection that occurred.

    The third thing we see is reflection.

D. Victory

The final thing that happened was that the armies of Israel were victorious in their battle. As the sun shone upon the waters, the Lord used the reflection to bring about victory for the people. The victory had started with a return to the Lord and an adherence to His Word. Here the victory was completed as the enemies of Israel were driven back.

The fourth and final thing we see is victory.

And so we see here, that there are four stages to this process: digging, infilling, reflection and victory. As the reader looks over each of these steps, they will notice the progressive nature of each. i.e. one leads to two, two leads to three etc, etc. Each step is unique, and each step is absolutely vital for that which is to follow.

You cannot jump from digging to reflecting, because the reflection is dependent upon the infilling. Nor can you jump from infilling to victory, for the victory is dependent upon the reflection. Each step is progressive, and each step is absolutely vital for the whole to work. The reflection can only occur when the wells have been infilled and the infilling can only occur when the wells have been dug. In 2 Kings 3 we see that the victory came because the world saw the reflection. The reflection occurred because of the water that was there. The water was there through the infilling of the Lord. The water infilled because the people had dug ditches to hold it. There is a progressive nature in the process and each step is absolutely dependant on the one that precedes it. The promised victory could only occur if the people were obedient to the first step of digging.

THE MESSAGE

From 2 Kings 3 we observed the deliverance of the armies of Israel and her allies from certain destruction. This deliverance only came as the people not only sought the Word of the Lord through the prophet Elisha, but as they were obedient to it. It was obedience to the Word that was the critical part for the kings to grasp hold of. What seemed like foolishness in the eyes of man and the natural proved to be absolute wisdom in the eyes of God. The kings challenge was not to question but rather to obey.

As the kings obeyed the Word of the Lord, we saw that there were four steps revealed.

   A. Digging.
   B. Infilling.
   C. Reflection.
   D. Victory.

These four steps started with obedience to the Word and resulted in total and utter victory according to the Word. These were the four successive steps that we observed from 2

Kings 3. As the armies of Israel were obedient to the Word of the Lord, we saw each of these steps occur and we saw the promised deliverance of the Lord attained.

It is these four steps that form the basis of the message that the Lord impressed upon the writer's heart. As the writer originally considered the above process, he felt the Lord prompt him to write down what he was hearing. The following is what was written and shared with the others who were at the time of corporate prayer referred to at the start of this study:

"As we were praying on Sunday, I felt the Lord prompt me on something, but I needed to look into it to understand a bit clearer. There is still more that I need to study in regard to this as I feel there is more here, but just wanted to share it with you guys as I feel it very much ties in with what we were discussing in regard to reflecting the glory of the Lord and shining like lights in our areas of influence.

The Lord prompted me on 2 Kings 3, specifically verses 9-24 In the passage we read that the king of Israel joined forces with the king of Judah and king of Edom to go out into battle against Moab. Seven days into their journey to Moab the company ran out of water. Jehoshaphat King of Judah suggested that they seek a prophet of the Lord and they then went to Elisha to seek a word from the Lord. In seeking the Lord Elisha told the Kings.

And he said, Thus saith the LORD, Make this valley full of ditches. For thus saith the LORD, Ye shall not see wind, neither shall ye see rain; yet that valley shall be filled with water, that ye may drink, both ye, and your cattle, and your beasts. And this is but a light thing in the sight of the LORD: he will deliver the Moabites also into your hand. (2Ki 3:16-18)

The kings obeyed the word of the Lord here and filled the valley with ditches. Scripture goes on to say that the next morning at the time of the morning sacrifice the valley was full of water. The holes that the kings had been instructed to dig were filled by the working of the Lord. We then read that:

And they rose up early in the morning, and the sun shone upon the water, and the Moabites saw the water on the other side as red as blood: And they said, This is blood: the kings are surely slain, and they have smitten one another: now therefore, Moab, to the spoil. And when they came to the camp of Israel, the Israelites rose up and smote the Moabites, so that they fled before them: but they went forward smiting the Moabites, even in their country. (2Ki 3:22-24)

In this I believe that the Lord was speaking to me four things.

Considering 2 Kings 3

1. Digging

    Digging takes time, effort, energy, purpose, deliberate action, perseverance, dedication.

    The people of Israel dug according to the Word of the Lord.

    Now is the time for His people, the Church, to dig ditches. It is a time for His people to purposefully press into the Lord in prayer, worship, the Word and relationship. It is time to dig deeper in Him corporately and individually.

2. Infilling

    The digging we do creates the room for Him to be able to infill us. The valley couldn't have been filled with water if ditches hadn't been dug to hold it. Likewise, the amount of water held was directly linked to how deep the holes were dug.

    There is an infilling on offer from the Lord, but there is a responsibility upon His people to be able to receive it. As we press into Him and deepen our relationship, we allow more of His presence to be poured into our lives.

    As we dig into Him, His promise is to fill us.

3. Reflection

    As the sun reflected upon the water, so the glory of the Lord is reflected by His glory within us. The water reflected the greater glory and so do we.

    We are able to shine through the measure of His Spirit within us. By digging into our relationship with Him we allow ourselves to be filled and to be vessels that reflect His glory. As we are filled, we are able to reflect the glory of the Father.

4. Victory

    The victory came for Israel after they had been obedient to the Word of the Lord and had dug down. The victory came when the glory of the sun was reflected off their ditches.

    Likewise, for us, the world is impacted when they witness the reflection of His glory through our lives. What is interesting though is that it is not the brightness of the light but the message of the blood that brings the victory. To Moab the reflection looked as blood!

> When we reflect the Father's glory to the world, we show them Jesus. Victory comes when the world sees Jesus reflected through us. The reflection of the blood brings the victory.
>
> The victory came because the world saw the reflection.
> The reflection occurred because of the water that was there.
> The water was there because the people had dug ditches to hold it.
>
> It is a time to dig deeper in the Lord. The outworking power of each of us as Christians is directly linked to the depth of our wells. As we are filled with Him, we are able to reflect Him to the world around us. As we shine forth the world sees Jesus through us. When this occurs, we impact the world around us."

It is these thoughts that have been the instigation for this study. As the writer considered these thoughts, he felt the Lord cause him to focus in on the process of shining or reflecting. The outworking of the miracle in 2 Kings 3 was the sun reflecting upon the water. The victory for the three kings came as the sun shone upon that which had been filled. The shining was the outworking of what had preceded it. It was only because of the digging and infilling that the shining could occur. Similarly the victory only came because of the same shining. Without the shining, there was no victory.

As the writer pondered the account of 2 Kings 3 and its application to believers and the Church, if any, he felt the Lord direct his thoughts. If that which we have so far examined has application, then there must be within scripture a call for believers to shine. The shining or reflection was the undeniable outworking of the process from 2 Kings. It was visible and clear for the world to see. Now, if digging and infilling have an application to New Testament believers, then there must exist a call in scripture for them to reflect the glory of the Lord and shine visibly to the world around them. Shining or reflection is the central and pivotal piece of the narrative. It is completely dependent on the steps before it and the victory for the people of Israel was based solely on the reflection occurring. The reflection or shining occurred because of what preceded it and it subsequently caused the victory for the people of God. The reflection or shining ties the process together. If we can establish the truth of the outworking, then we determine the necessity of the steps before and the promise of the victory that follows.

As we continue here in Part A, we will seek to find if that which the writer felt from 2 Kings 3 lines up with the Word of God, as we look at whether we are called to shine. Before proceeding though, the reader is encouraged to read over 2 Kings 3 several times and ponder the thoughts of digging, infilling, reflection and victory that we have discussed in relation to this.

ARE WE CALLED TO SHINE?

The purpose of this section is to examine the premise that within scripture there is a call for believers, and the Church, to shine forth. As we have said in our previous point, if we can establish this truth then suddenly the process discovered in 2 Kings 3 is more than a thought, it is a message that the Lord is wanting His people to hear. It shows us that the process seen in 2 Kings has application to believers today.

Whilst this text has been written on the belief that there is a call to each and every believer, especially in the days we are in, to shine, our purpose here is to examine whether or not this is confirmed in scripture. As we move forward in this section, we will not only highlight the existence of this call but show how it applies to New Testament believers.

LIGHT

As we read over the Word of God it becomes evident that there is an unmistakable call in scripture for the people of God to stand out from the world in the places in which they live. It is not so much a divisionary issue, but rather a point of difference that should be noticeable in the lives of His people and one that should be a testimony of that which we believe. Throughout the Word, this difference is referred to as believers being as light in a dark place. The point of difference is the light, and it comes into being when the people of God shine forth.

Let us consider some passages of scripture which attest to this fact:

Are We Called to Shine?

A. In Matthew Chapter 5, Jesus gave a clear example of this when He gave His sermon on the Mount. Jesus said in verses 14-16 in reference to believers that:

> *Ye are the **light** of the world. A city that is set on an hill cannot be hid. Neither do men **light** a candle, and put it under a bushel, but on a candlestick; and it **giveth light** unto all that are in the house. Let **your light** so shine before men, that they **may see** your good works, and glorify your Father which is in heaven. (Mat 5:14-16)*

Jesus stated, in this passage, that ye, that is you, are the light of the world. Jesus referred to this distinction as believers being as light. As we consider the words of Jesus in these verses it becomes evident that believers are not just to be as light, but they are to be as light that is visible to all who would be in their vicinity. His followers are to be as distinctive as a light that is clearly seen.

Jesus then stated that believers are to be as a city on a hill. A city on a hill is a beacon to all that surrounds it. Its light shines forth and can be readily observed from the lower vantage points. It acts as a light house on land, clearly displaying the path to any who would gaze upon it.

Jesus then further expanded on this thought and said that believers are also to be as a candle that is not hidden, but rather displayed in such a way that its light fills the whole house. Believers are not to be tucked away, masked lights with the dimmer switch turned all the way down. They are to shine forth fully so that their light fills the entirety of the area where God has placed them. Believers are to be beacons of light to all those that would come into the reach of their glow.

The light of believers is to shine forth before those that are in darkness so that they may see. The call of Jesus is for His followers to shine forth. To be the light of the world.

B. In 1 Thessalonians Paul said that:

> *Ye are all the children of **light**, and the children of the **day**: we are not of the night, nor of darkness. (1Th 5:5)*

There is a double emphasis here used by Paul. He refers to believers as children of light and children of the day. This is immediately contrasted to the night and darkness. Paul's words are that having been born again we are now children of light. Believers are as the day or light and are distinct from the night or darkness. That is the point of difference that Paul is referring to, it is as day and night. Believers are to literally stand out from the darkness that is around them and they do that by shining forth as children of light. That is the call to each one of us, to shine as the light of day.

C. Paul also states in Ephesians:

> *For ye were sometimes darkness, but now are ye **light** in the Lord: walk as children of light:(Eph 5:8)*

We are not only children of light, but we are called to walk as children of the light too. A walk describes the way in which an individual lives and conducts their life. Having come to Christ we have left the ways of darkness behind and now walk as children of the light. The difference in our lives should be evident and shown through our actions. The way we live in Christ should stand in stark contrast to how we lived formerly. We are called to shine as light within our world. Believers are to be distinct, and this distinction is shown through believers being and walking as children of the light.

Whilst we have looked at only a few passages here, there is no mistaking the call that exists in scripture for believers to shine. Time and time again the Word calls us to be vessels of light that shine in places that otherwise would be in darkness. We are indeed called to shine.

As we move forward in this section, we are going to investigate the call to shine on an individual and corporate (Church) level. For the purposes of this chapter though we will spend a little time having a look at what light is and how it affects the environment around it. If we are called to be children of light it is beneficial to have an understanding of what light is.

WHAT IS LIGHT?

Light is an agent or medium that allows vision or sight. It is an energy form that makes it possible to see things. Throughout scripture there are numerous Hebrew and Greek words used to describe light. In the Matthew 5:14-16 alone, which we have quoted above, there are three different Greek words used which are translated to the English word light.

In scripture we see that light is used in both a natural and a spiritual sense. In the natural light is seen through both elements of creation and manmade elements. For example:

- Light of the sun, moon and stars – Jer 31:35
- Light of a lamp – Ps 119:105
- Light given by fire – Ex 13:12

In the spiritual sense light is used to describe:

- God's Word – Ps 119:105
- The countenance of the Lord – Mat 17:2, Rev 21:23, 1 John 1:5
- Jesus – Joh 1:7

- Believers – Eph 5:8, 1 Thess 5:5

The overall theme of light is of illumination that allows things to be visible and changes the environment around it.

LIGHT AND DARKNESS

As we begin to study the thought of light in scripture it is interesting that light is often used in conjunction or comparison with darkness. Whilst the two are often described as opposites, and that is how we generally tend to view them, they are also intrinsically linked.

One of the first creative acts of God when He made the world was to create natural light. In Genesis 1:2-5 we read:

> *And God said, Let there be light: and there was light. And God saw the light, that it was good: **and God divided the light from the darkness**. And God called the light Day, and the darkness he called Night. And the evening and the morning were the first day. (Gen 1:3-5)*

At the very beginning of creation God created light and He divided the light from the darkness. Both were in existence naturally at the very beginning. They co-existed and yet they were divided. The Hebrew word for divide as used here means to separate, to distinguish, to differ and carries the thought of distinction between the day and night. The light was called day and the darkness was called night. There was a God ordained division placed between the two. In the beginning there was light and there was darkness and whilst the two are linked they are also divided and distinct.

We see the same truth when we look at God's judgement upon the nation of Egypt during the time of Moses. The ninth plague that the Lord used in an attempt to soften Pharaoh's heart was a plague of darkness. According to Strong's the word for darkness in the Hebrew as used here means: dark, darkness, figuratively misery, destruction, death, ignorance, sorrow, wickedness. As Moses stretched out his hands in accordance to the Word of the Lord a thick darkness fell upon the nation of Egypt. Upon all those of Egypt was a plague of darkness. None could see and none dare venture out. The nation of Israel though was spared from this darkness. There was a distinction or divide between the nation of Israel and the nation of Egypt.

> *Exo 10:22-23 And Moses stretched forth his hand toward heaven; and there was a **thick darkness in all the land of Egypt three days**: (23) They saw not one another, neither rose any from his place for three days: **but all the children of Israel had light** in their dwellings.*

Egypt had darkness, but Israel had light. Light and darkness were in existence at the same time, in the same area, but there was a divide and a distinction between the two.
When we come to the New Testament, we see this theme of light and darkness carried through to have a spiritual application. That which had truth in the natural now takes on spiritual significance. In 2 Corinthians Paul writes:

> *Be ye not unequally yoked together with unbelievers: for what fellowship hath righteousness with unrighteousness? And what communion hath light with darkness? (2Co 6:14)*

Here Paul compares the light to righteousness and darkness to unrighteousness. His message here is that the two are opposite and can't coexist at the same time. Just as there is separation in the natural so too is there to be separation in the spiritual. The natural truths have spiritual application. Whilst light and darkness are related, they are distinct.

Throughout scripture this is the running theme. Light and darkness are opposites. Whilst they both exist, they can't co-exist. Light can't have fellowship with darkness and darkness can't have fellowship with light. They are polar opposites and there is a distinction and divide between the two. It was true in creation, it was true in Egypt and it remains true spiritually today.

MEASURING LIGHT AND DARKNESS

What becomes interesting is when we look at how light and darkness are measured. We have all experienced different degrees of light, from light that is just visible to light that is blinding to behold. The same is true of darkness. We have all experienced mild darkness through to pitch blackness. The question remains though, how do we measure this? How do we measure how light something is and how do we measure how dark something is?

Light can be measured a few different ways. One of the most common though is through a light meter which measures light in a unit called lux. This method basically describes how much light is emitted over a certain area. This measurement will differ given the proximity the light meter has to the light source. The closer you are to the light source the higher the lux number will be. The further away you move from the light source the smaller the lux number will be. This is a truth we witness in the natural constantly. The closer in proximity we get to any light source the brighter it becomes.

Darkness though, in terms of being the opposite of light, does not have a measurement. There is not as it were, a darkness meter. In order to be able to tell how dark something is, you use a light meter to find how low the light level is or how little light is present. Darkness is produced from an absence of light and it is measured in the same way. You are not actually measuring the darkness, you are measuring how low the light is or how much light there isn't in a given area. Darkness is measured by how low the light is.

If we think about that and take that same natural truth and apply it spiritually, we see something that should challenge all of us in our Christian walks. Just as in the natural darkness is measured by the absence of light so too could we say that spiritual darkness is measured by the absence of spiritual light. The less spiritual light that there is in a given area, suburb, state or nation the greater the spiritual darkness will be. The lower the light the greater the darkness.

There is a division between light and darkness and this division is determined by how bright the light source shines. When we have this understanding that darkness only exists when there is an absence of light, suddenly the words of Jesus in Matthew 5 that we considered at the start of this section take on new magnitude. The brightness that we shine with has direct spiritual implications on those areas where the Lord has called us. The challenge to be a city on a hill and a candle that is not hidden under a bushel takes on a whole new context. We are to shine as cities on a hill so that we illuminate all that are in the valleys and low places that are around us. A light is to shine forth as a beacon of hope and show unto the people the way to salvation. We are to shine as candles that are not hidden because anytime we turn the dimmer switch down, we allow the spiritual darkness around us to increase. There is an onus of call on believers to spiritually shine in order that darkness would be pushed back.

Darkness cannot overcome light. Darkness can only exist and increase when the light doesn't shine as brightly as it is created to. We live in days where there is a vital necessity for believers to shine as brightly as we have been called to. It is only as we do this that we will see spiritual darkness pushed back and our cities, lands and nations changed.

God is light and we have been created by Him to reflect His glory. The purpose of this study is to help believers understand how vital it is that they shine as brightly as God would have them to. Darkness increases when Christians have the dimmer switch turned down. We are living in days when God is calling to His people to shine as brightly as they are called in the areas where He has placed them. Darkness flees at the sight of light, and it can only increase when the light decreases. We are in the days when we need to shine brighter than ever before. The call of the Lord is for His people to shine and as we shine forth, we will see radical changes to our families, workplaces, towns, states and countries.

In the next parts of this section, we are going to look at scriptural examples that show forth the call and need for believers to shine as individuals and corporately as the Church. Before we get there though we are going to spend a little time considering the Tabernacle of Moses. The Tabernacle of Moses is one of the great structures of the Bible that contains many truths applicable to believers today. Whilst this initially may seem out of place, it will be seen as we progress how this ties in with the application to shine for individuals and the Church as a whole. The call to the individual and to the Church have their truths rooted in the Tabernacle and it would be impossible to truly understand the fullness of what the Word of God is telling us without first having a basic understanding of the Tabernacle.

UNDERSTANDING THE TABERNACLE

The Tabernacle of Moses was the first Tabernacle structure, built by man, that God dwelt within. It is an amazing study in itself and our purpose here is not to give a discourse on it, but to look at an overview of its structure and function. For those wanting to dive deeper into the Tabernacle the reader is recommended to look at "The Tabernacle of Moses" by Kevin J Conner. This is a great resource which forms an invaluable part of the writer's library and is one that is constantly referred to.

The Tabernacle of Moses was actually a design given to Moses by the Lord. Moses oversaw its construction, but all was built according to the plan and pattern that the Lord revealed to Moses upon Mount Sinai. This was a blueprint given to Moses during his first period of spending forty days and forty nights before the Lord, at the same time that Moses was given the ten commandments by the Lord.

In Exodus 25:9 we read the Lord instructed Moses to build everything according to the pattern he had seen.

> *According to all that **I shew thee**, after the **pattern** of the tabernacle, and the **pattern** of all the instruments thereof, even so shall ye make it.(Exo 25:9)*

The Lord showed Moses a pattern of what he was to build. Moses was shown a pattern for the Tabernacle, and he was shown patterns for each of the individual pieces of Tabernacle furniture that the Lord wanted him to build. It was not just a case of instructions being given to Moses but was also a case of Moses seeing a vision of what he was to replicate. Moses saw with his eyes all that the Lord had outlined to him regarding the Tabernacle.

Understanding The Tabernacle

The writer of Hebrews takes this truth one step further and expands on just what Moses was shown. In regard to the Tabernacle and its furnishing we read in Hebrews 8:5:

> *Heb 8:5 Who serve unto the **example and shadow** of heavenly things, as Moses was admonished of God when he was about to make the tabernacle: for, See, saith he, that thou make all things according to **the pattern shewed** to thee in the mount.*

The writer of Hebrews tells us that Moses was shown a pattern on Mount Sinai when the Lord revealed the Tabernacle to him and that this pattern was an example and shadow of the heavenly realities. Moses literally saw heavenly examples of what he was to copy. What Moses made were a shadow of their heavenly counterparts. The only way to ever understand the truth of a shadow is to follow it back to see what is actually creating the shadow. A shadow is a representation of truth, but not the full truth in and of itself. In order to understand the full truth of the shadow one has to look at the source. When one does that with the Tabernacle of Moses one ends up in the book of Revelation where the examples that Moses saw are shown to have heavenly realities. One only has to read through Revelation to see the countless Tabernacle references described in the heavenly realm.

- The Golden Lampstand – Rev 1
- The Golden Altar – Rev 8, 9
- The Golden Censer with incense – Rev 8
- The Ark of His Covenant – Rev 11

The list could go on, but the truth of the matter is that which was given to Moses was a shadow of the heavenly realities. What Moses saw when he received the pattern was the heavenly source of which the Tabernacle shadowed.

When we understand that the Tabernacle was a revelation from God and not a manmade design, we start to see the fulness of truth contained within it. Whilst it was a revelation given at the same time as the Old Covenant it holds truth that transcends through to the New Covenant. It is more than just a tent, it is a Tabernacle of truth for the Church to grasp hold of. This is an important truth for the reader to keep in mind as we progress through this section.

In the pattern given to Moses upon Mount Sinai the Tabernacle centred around three distinct yet interrelated areas of the Outer Court, The Holy Place and the Most Holy Place.

The Outer Court was an open area measuring one hundred cubits by fifty cubits. Its perimeter was separated from the camp of Israel by a linen curtain that stood five cubits high. At the front of Tabernacle, the area facing east, was the entrance to the Tabernacle known as the Gate of the Door. This was a curtain measuring twenty cubits in length and five cubits in height. It was made of needlework of blue, purple, scarlet and fine twined linen. It was clearly marked as the entry point of the Tabernacle and for all who sought to enter, this was the one and only entry point. There was no other way in than through the

Gate. As one entered the Outer Court, they would first of all see the Brazen Altar. This was the largest piece of Tabernacle furniture and was the place where all sacrifice occurred. Immediately behind the Brazen Altar was the Brazen Laver. The Brazen Laver was the place of washing and cleansing. These were the only two pieces of furniture within the Outer Court and both were made of brass. Brass is symbolic of judgement and that is exactly what occurred in the Outer Court. Sin was judged and dealt with here through the sacrificial system of the Old Covenant.

Still within the Outer Court and behind the Brazen Laver stood the Tent of Meeting. The Tent of Meeting measured thirty cubits in length, ten cubits in width and ten cubits in height. The two sides and rear of this structure consisted of wooden boards overlaid with gold. The roof was compromised of four layers of curtains which not only formed the roof but flowed down to cover the two sides and rear of the tabernacle. It was a completely covered tent. This structure was twice the height of the Outer Court fence and was tall enough to be seen from the camp of Israel. Only the priests though were able to enter within this tent and see its interior. Within this structure were the areas known as the Holy Place and the Most Holy Place.

The Holy Place formed the first part of the Tabernacle tent. Its area measured twenty cubits by ten cubits by ten cubits. It comprised two thirds of the Tabernacle space. The entry to the Tabernacle tent and the Holy Place was a curtain knows as the Door. This curtain was made in the exact same fashion as the curtain that marked the entry way to the Outer Court. Whilst the Holy Place curtain was smaller than the Outer Court curtain, the fact that these were replicated designs made it obvious to anyone which direction they were to follow when moving forward in the Tabernacle.

Within the Holy Place were three pieces of furniture. On the right-hand side stood the Golden Table of Shewbread. On the left-hand side stood the Golden Lampstand. At the far end, standing before the entrance to the Most Holy Place, stood the Golden Altar of Incense. As one entered the Holy Place one would immediately notice the change in furniture construction. The furniture of brass was left behind in the Outer Court. Brass is symbolic of judgement whereas Gold is symbolic of God, the Divine, that which is completely pure. In the Holy Place stood only instruments of gold.

As we noted earlier the Tabernacle was a structure with wooden walls overlaid with gold and four layers of covering that formed the roof and covered the sides of the Tabernacle. Whilst the Outer Court had the sun to provide light for the ministry that needed to occur there, within the Holy Place the only thing providing light was the Golden Lampstand. This instrument was to burn continually, and it was by its light that the priests were able to perform their ministrations as mandated by the Lord in the Holy Place. Without the light of the Golden Lampstand the Holy Place would have been in darkness.

The final area of the Tabernacle was the Most Holy Place. This area measured ten cubits by ten cubits by ten cubits. It was a cube shape and formed the final third of the Tabernacle tent. This area was separated from the Holy Place by a curtain known as the Veil. This curtain was again made in the exact same way as the Gate of the Outer Court and the Door of the Holy Place. There really was no mistaking which way one progressed in the Tabernacle. The Lord laid a clear path of progression out in the Tabernacles design.

Within the Most Holy Place resided one piece of furniture, the Ark of the Covenant. The Ark was made of pure gold and was the most holy of all the tabernacle furniture. The Ark represented the throne of God on the earth, and it was upon its lid, the blood-stained mercy seat, that the presence of the Lord dwelt. This presence came upon the Ark on the day of the dedication of the Temple. In Exodus 40 we read that the cloud descended upon the Tabernacle and the glory of the Lord rested above the blood-stained mercy seat in the Most Holy Place. Here the glory of God resided. The only time it moved was when it was time for the camp of Israel to move. The glory would rise, and the cloud would lift and lead the people of Israel in their wilderness wanderings. When it came time to set up the camp again the cloud would stop and as the Tabernacle was re-setup the cloud would again descend upon the Tabernacle and the glory of the Lord would again fill the Most Holy Place.

This presence was known as the Shekinah glory of the Lord. This was the visible glory and brightness of the Lord and from this, the voice of the Lord would speak. John tells us that God is light (1 John 1:5) and it was this tangible presence of the Lord above the Ark that provided the light for the Most Holy Place. By this light the High Priest would enter once a year, going past the Veil, to fulfil the Great Day of Atonement ceremonies. By this light the High Priest was able to see and fulfil his priestly ministrations.

In summary, there were three distinct sections of the Tabernacle. Each was distinct and separate from the other, yet there was unity within them. Each of these areas had their own furniture, and each was distinguished by their entry point and source of light. The Outer Court had the Gate and ministry occurred here through the provision of the light of the sun. The Holy Place had the Door and light was provided through the Golden Lampstand that was tended to daily. The Most Holy Place had the Veil and the light in this room was provided by the Lord himself. It was the glorious presence of the Lord that filled this room with light and caused it to be the brightest of all the Tabernacle areas. These thoughts are condensed in the table below:

OUTER COURT	HOLY PLACE	MOST HOLY PLACE
Light of the Sun	Light of the Golden Lampstand	Light of the Lord
Natural light	The fire was divinely provided, but it was the Priests responsibility to maintain	Divine light
Open area	Closed area	Closed area
Enter via the Gate	Enter via the Door	Enter through the Veil
Frequent entry	Daily entry	Restricted entry

These truths are also depicted on the diagram on the next page:

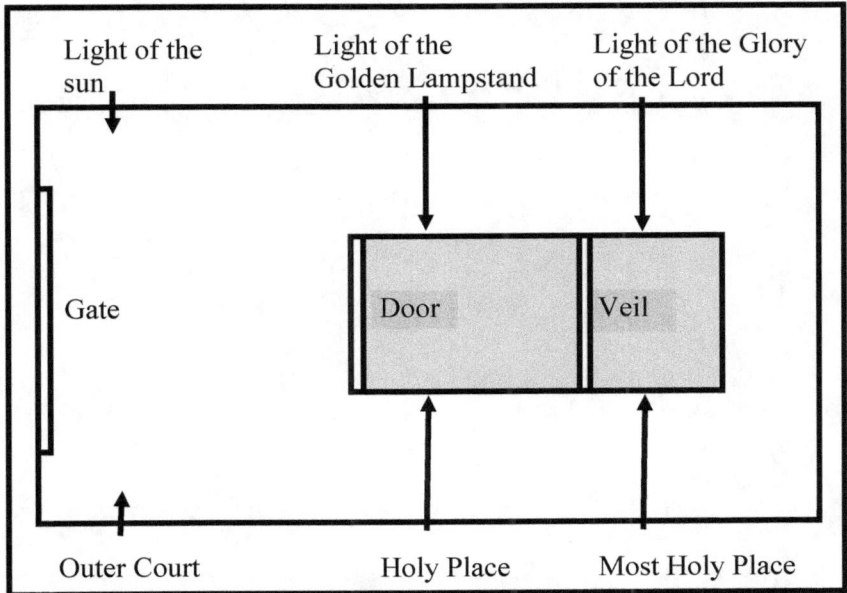

Having looked at a brief overview of the Tabernacle of Moses and considered its layout and light sources, we'll now turn our attention to looking at the call to the individual and to the Church to shine. Whilst this overview may initially seem out of place, it will begin to make sense as we move through the next parts of our study.

As we progress through The Call to the Individual and The Call to the Church, we will constantly be making reference back to the Tabernacle of Moses and to this section. In doing this we will see just how the truths of the Tabernacle apply to New Testament believers and their call to shine.

Whilst our overview has been brief, the reader is encouraged to make sure they are familiar with what has been discussed in this section as a sound understanding will provide the foundation for the Spirit to build upon with the truths of scripture that we will consider.

THE CALL TO THE INDIVIDUAL

2Co 3:18 But we all, with open face beholding as in a glass the glory of the Lord, are changed into the same image from glory to glory, even as by the Spirit of the Lord.

Having established that within scripture there exists a call for the people of God to shine and be distinct from their surroundings, we now look a little more specifically at this thought and just how it applies to us as New Testament believers. Our purpose here is to focus in on the call to the individual to shine and reflect the glory of the Lord.

In the 3rd Chapter of 2 Corinthians, Paul draws on an example from the Old Testament which can be found in Exodus 34. As Paul works through this discourse, he takes the truths from Exodus and expounds upon them to bring revelation and understanding to the Corinthian Church. Throughout this chapter of Corinthians, Paul compares and contrasts the Old Covenant to the New Covenant. This same writing approach can be seen in the book of Hebrews where the writer brings in Old Testament examples and constantly affirms and reaffirms that the Lord Jesus Christ is the greater one, who supersedes the Old Testament types and shadows. Throughout the New Testament, the writers constantly refer to the Old Testament to show how Christ has come to not only fulfil the type but how He succeeds it and surpasses it.

As we look at 2 Corinthians 3, we see that Paul takes us through a comparison and contrast of the Old Covenant and the New Covenant and those who minister in them respectively. As he does this, he is constantly affirming the supremacy of Christ, the New Covenant and the call that exists to the people of the Lord.

The Call To The Individual

Paul starts by outlining Moses as a minister of the Old Covenant and goes on to compare his function to that of believers as ministers of the New Covenant. In doing this, Paul brings out a number of truths applicable to the people of God especially in relation to them shining as the Lord has called them to. This is something we will see as we begin to break down the verses and look at what Paul is saying.

Before we start to investigate this passage though, we must first have an understanding of Moses and his interactions with the Tabernacle. Having an understanding of these that will provide us with the keys needed to understand the truths that Paul has exhorted and how they apply to the Church and to us as believers.

MOSES

Having looked at a brief overview of the Tabernacle of Moses in the previous section, we now turn our attention to the man himself. Our purpose here is not to do an in-depth character study, but just bring back to the reader's mind some information about Moses that is pertinent to our passage in 2 Corinthians 3.

It is clear from the very beginning that Moses was born with a God ordained purpose for his life. Despite the efforts of Satan to destroy this deliverer of Israel as a child as described in Exodus 1 (much the same approach that he used around the birth of Christ!), Moses survived and grew up not with his brethren, but as a member of Pharaohs' household. Despite this separation from his native people, it is clear from the book of Acts that Moses as a younger man felt a sense of what the call of God was for his life (Acts 7:25).

At the spritely age of eighty the Lord appeared to Moses in the burning bush and announced that it was now time for him to deliver the nation of Israel and fulfil the call that was upon His life. As Moses steps into this, he grows not in pride, but in a godly confidence of who the Lord has called him to be. Moses leads the nation of Israel, taking them out of the bondage of Egypt and to the border of the Promised Land of the Lord.

Moses as the mediator of the Old Covenant operated in the roles of prophet, priest and pastor to the nation of Israel:

- As a priest he oversaw the construction, dedication and functioning of the Aaronic and Levitical Priesthoods. It was Moses who anointed and offered the sacrifices at the dedication of Aaron and his sons as priests (Exodus 40, Leviticus 8)

- As a pastor Moses shepherded the flock of Israel from their exodus and throughout their forty years of wandering in the dessert.

- As a prophet Moses was the mouthpiece of the Lord for the nation of Israel. Moses was the intermediary. The Lord spoke to Moses and Moses spoke the Lords' words to the nation.

Whilst other Old Testament individuals touched on the same offices, Moses was set apart from the other Old Testament prophets in that the Lord would speak to Moses face to face as a man would speak to a friend. This was a distinction made by and defended by the Lord. In Numbers 12 we read that Aaron and Miriam spoke against Moses and seemingly challenged his position as leader of Israel because he had taken an Ethiopian wife. Their challenge to Moses' leadership was based upon the fact that they too heard the voice of the Lord, and that Moses in essence was just a prophet as they were. It was a judgemental attitude of Aaron and Miriam that sought to bring Moses down. Upon hearing this the Lord summoned Moses, Aaron and Miriam to the door of the Tabernacle and said:

> *And he said, Hear now my words: If there be a prophet among you, I the LORD will make myself known unto him in a vision, and will speak unto him in a dream. My servant Moses is not so, who is faithful in all mine house.* **With him will I speak mouth to mouth, even apparently, and not in dark speeches; and the similitude of the LORD shall he behold**: *wherefore then were ye not afraid to speak against my servant Moses? (Num 12:6-8)*

Moses was not like any other prophet; he was set apart by the Lord. When the Lord spoke to Moses, He did it face to face. Moses would literally stand in the very presence of the Lord, beholding his glory and communicate with Him. It was not through vision or dream, but through literally interacting, one standing before the other, that the Lord communicated with Moses. This was a call and a privilege unique to Moses. The other prophets did not experience this. Aaron and Miriam didn't experience this. Moses alone was one who repeatedly came into the very presence of the Lord and had the Lord communicate openly with him.

Moses truly filled the mediator role for the nation of Israel. He stood before the Lord for them and communicated the message of the Lord to them. He was the go between. Moses would enter into the presence of the Lord and come out with the Lords' commands for Israel. He did what no one else could do. The High Priest would go once a year into the presence of the Lord, but Moses frequented His presence. He was given the unique blessing of standing in the very presence of God.

INVESTIGATING THE PASSAGE

Having done a very brief background on Moses, we are now ready to look at our passage from 2 Corinthians 3. We will quote the passage in full to start, before breaking down and examining its parts and the truths revealed therein. The reader is encouraged to read over this passage several times before moving forward in this section. It is as we read and meditate upon the Word of the Lord that we allow the Spirit of the Lord time to minister to us and give us wisdom and understanding into His inexhaustible Word.

> *Do we begin again to commend ourselves? or need we, as some others, epistles of commendation to you, or letters of commendation from you? Ye are our epistle written in our hearts, known and read of all men: Forasmuch as ye are manifestly declared to be the epistle of Christ ministered by us, written not with ink, but with the Spirit of the living God; not in tables of stone, but in fleshy tables of the heart. And such trust have we through Christ to God-ward: Not that we are sufficient of ourselves to think any thing as of ourselves; but our sufficiency is of God; Who also hath made us able ministers of the new testament; not of the letter, but of the spirit: for the letter killeth, but the spirit giveth life. But if the ministration of death, written and engraven in stones, was glorious, so that the children of Israel could not stedfastly behold the face of Moses for the glory of his countenance; which glory was to be done away: How shall not the ministration of the spirit be rather glorious? For if the ministration of condemnation be glory, much more doth the ministration of righteousness exceed in glory. For even that which was made glorious had no glory in this respect, by reason of the glory that excelleth. For if that which is done away was glorious, much more that which remaineth is glorious. Seeing then that we have such hope, we use great plainness of speech: And not as Moses, which put a vail over his face, that the children of Israel could not stedfastly look to the end of that which is abolished: But their minds were blinded: for until this day remaineth the same vail untaken away in the reading of the old testament; which vail is done away in Christ. But even unto this day, when Moses is read, the vail is upon their heart. Nevertheless when it shall turn to the Lord, the vail shall be taken away. Now the Lord is that Spirit: and where the Spirit of the Lord is, there is liberty. But we all, with open face beholding as in a glass the glory of the Lord, are changed into the same image from glory to glory, even as by the Spirit of the Lord. (2Co 3:1-18)*

The purpose of this chapter from Paul is to reveal to believers the truths that surround them as ministers of the New Covenant. Paul was unique and distinct from the other Apostles of Jesus. Most of the Apostles were unschooled, ordinary men which is what baffled the religious leaders of the day. Paul though, was an expert in the law. From a young age he grew up being taught the Old Testament. Acts 22:3 tells us that he sat at the feet of Gamaliel and "was taught according to the perfect manner of the law of the fathers". Paul grew up as one versed in the law of the Lord and it was with this vast knowledge that Paul could pull truths from the Old Testament and preach them to New Testament believers. Paul truly was an individual for such a time as this.

Paul, through the Holy Spirit, was able to bridge the gap between the Old Covenant and the New Covenant. And that is exactly what he does here. Paul takes the truths of scripture from the Old Testament and uses these truths to build and expound a message to the New Testament Church. As we move through these verses, we will clearly see the compare and contrast method used by Paul to establish scriptural truth applicable to believers today.

Do we begin again to commend ourselves? or need we, as some others, epistles of commendation to you, or letters of commendation from you? (2Co 3:1)

Paul started this chapter by posing a question to the Corinthian believers. The question Paul posed to them was whether he needed credentials. A common practice in early times was for ministers to take letters of recommendation with them when they went to minister. Once they had finished ministering in a certain location they would ask to be provided with letters of recommendation to take to their next place of ministry.

A letter of recommendation was a testimony from a group of people/believers and essentially provided an individual with the credentials to be able to minister.

Pauls' question here is three-fold. He asks:
A. Whether he needed to commend himself?
B. Whether he needed to provide letters of recommendation?
C. Whether he should be asking for letters of recommendation?

Paul was challenging the thinking and standard of operation at the time. Whilst this was not necessarily a wrong concept, it had the potential for division and was possibly part of the cause of division Paul talks about in 1 Corinthians 1:12 where some claimed to be of Paul, some Apollos and some Cephas.

Ye are our epistle written in our hearts, known and read of all men: (2Co 3:2)

In Jeremiah 31:31-34 the prophet declared under inspiration of the Holy Spirit that the time would come when the Lord would make a New Covenant with the House of Israel. This would be different to the Covenant of their fathers and that the Lord would put His laws in their inward parts and write it in their hearts. The Lord declared that there would come a time when His laws would be written upon the hearts of His people. That which was once head knowledge would then be a matter of the heart.

Paul had received and experienced such from the Lord. Paul had come out of the Old Covenant and received the revelation of Jesus. The Lord had written His laws on the heart of Paul. It was from this revelation that Paul preached wherever he went. The Corinthian believers had received the message of Paul and walked according to it. They were the embodiment of the what the Lord had written on the heart of Paul and having received such also had the same laws written upon their hearts.

The Corinthian believers were themselves the letter of commendation for Paul and his companions. There was no need for a written letter for proof of Paul's credentials. The Corinthian believers were a living testimony of the ministry of Paul. The way they lived, who they were, their character gave a greater reference than any letter of commendation ever could. As those around them witnessed and observed the Corinthian believers, they saw the truths of the message that the Lord had placed on Pauls' heart. The Corinthian believers were the proof of the ministry of Paul and his associates. They were living examples of the New Covenant.

Forasmuch as ye are manifestly declared to be the epistle of Christ ministered by us, (2Co 3:3)

Paul preached one thing, Jesus Christ. Since his conversion on the Damascus Road, Paul's life was dedicated to preaching and sharing the good news of the Gospel of Christ. This was a message he had shared with the Corinthian Church, and it was one they had taken to heart. Paul was not concerned with making disciples of Paul, his mission was to fulfil the call the Lord had placed upon him and share the good news of the Gospel of Christ. The Corinthian believers had received this message and were living epistles of the doctrine of Christ

The lives of the Corinthian believers were a testimony unto Christ. Paul in telling them this was actually writing an Epistle of Christ to the Corinthian believers and informing them that they were the living examples of these truths.

It is important to note here that Paul's writings, which forms a large part of the New Testament, were built upon the truths of the Old Testament. Paul brought the truths of the Old Testament through the cross and applied them to New Testament believers. The Corinthian believers, as epistles of Christ, were examples of the truth of Christ revealed throughout the entirety of the Word of God.

written not with ink, but with the Spirit of the living God; not in tables of stone, but in fleshy tables of the heart. (2Co 3:3)

In these verses we see that Paul brought in two ideas that form the basis for his comparison and contrast in the verses that follow. In verses two and three Paul described the Corinthian believers as epistles of Christ. Having done this, he then went on to compare and contrast the Old Covenant and the New Covenant.

When we are talking about covenants it is important for the reader to understand two key points:

A. To be aware that within the Bible there is more than just two covenants and
B. That the two prominent Covenants, The Old and the New, are not just mere opposites.

In the beginning God made a covenant with Adam. This was known as the Adamic covenant. This was a covenant that was broken when man sinned and partook of the tree of the knowledge of good and evil. Since then, the Lord has introduced a number of covenants to man as a means of restoring man to his original intended relationship. Each progressive covenant does not necessarily abolish the previous. The Covenants are best looked at as rungs on an ascending ladder. Each covenant builds upon the last, and each new rung is made possible by the one below it. The New Testament believers had moved onto the rung of the New Covenant, and this is a message that Paul was communicating to them.

Having established the Corinthian believers as epistles of Christ, Paul then moved on to explain to them that they were also under a New Covenant. This particularly comes into light in the above passage. Paul takes the language of the Old to establish the truths of the New.

written not with ink
When Moses received the Old Covenant, he met with the Lord on Mount Sinai. It was here that the Lord communicated with him all the specifics of the Old Testament economy. Whilst God wrote the ten commandments on the two tables of stone, it was Moses that transcribed all of the ordinances, directions and law for the nation of Israel. This was a covenant written with ink.

but with the Spirit of the living God
The Old Covenant was transcribed by Moses, but the New Covenant is transcribed by the Holy Spirit. It is first the natural and then the spiritual. That which was once done by man is now done by the Spirit.

not in tables of stone,
As the ten commandments were written by the finger of God

but in fleshy tables of the heart
*Behold, the days come, saith the LORD, that I will make a new covenant with the house of Israel, and with the house of Judah: .... But this shall be the covenant that I will make with the house of Israel; After those days, saith the LORD, I will put my law in their inward parts, **and write it in their hearts**; and will be their God, and they shall be my people. (Jer 31:31, 33)*

That which was once external to man is now done internally. It is in the heart of man that the New Testament is engraved. When we come to Christ and accept the Lord Jesus Christ as our Lord and Saviour and walk in the truths of the Word of God, submitting ourselves to Him, His Word becomes written on our hearts. This is what the Corinthian believers had experienced, and this is the call to all believers.

That which Paul had received and ministered from was to be the same experience for all believers. Paul was the one to minister the Covenantal truths, but it is the Holy Spirit who engraves the truths of the New Covenant upon the hearts of believers. The Corinthian believers were a testimony of Christ having the truths of God written upon their hearts by the Holy Spirit.

And such trust have we through Christ to God-ward: Not that we are sufficient of ourselves to think any thing as of ourselves; but our sufficiency is of God; (2Co 3:4-5)

Paul had an absolute assurance of the call of God upon his life. He was not proud and did not see himself as self-sufficient, but nor did he look to men to provide his sufficiency. Paul's sufficiency was of God. The fruits of his ministry reinforced to Paul the call of the

Lord upon His life. His absolute trust in the Lord was strengthened through the fruit of his labours and in the lives of those he reached, such as the Corinthian believers. This was greater than any letter of commendation.

Who also hath made us able ministers of the new testament; (2Co 3:6)

Paul's sufficiency was of God and it was God who had made him an able minister of the New Covenant. There are two things to note in this verse:

A. It was the Lord who enabled/qualified Paul to minister. Paul's revelation didn't come from his own thoughts and knowledge, it was imputed to him through revelation by the Lord.

B. The Lord had called Paul to be a minister of the New Covenant. He was not a self-appointed, self-anointed preacher. Paul was called by the Lord to minister the New Testament.

Jesus had introduced the New Testament or Covenant to His disciples, and it was the Lord who had called Paul and enabled and qualified him to minister it. Paul had been brought up and raised with the Old Covenant but on the Damascus Road he was called by the Lord to minister the New. It was Pauls' understanding of the Old Testament and the previous Covenants that allowed him to comprehend and explain the New Covenant as the next rung on the covenantal ladder. He was the perfect vessel to bridge the understanding gap and explain how the Old leads to the New.

not of the letter,: for the letter killeth,. (2Co 3:6)

Paul again is clear to make a distinction between the Old and New Covenants. Having announced that he was a minister of the New Covenant, he now clearly outlines and confirms the difference between the Old and the New. Paul here refers to the letter of the law as the Old Covenant and clearly outlines to the Corinthian believers that this was not the covenant that the Lord had called and equipped him to minister. The Old Covenant was of the letter and the letter produced death. The Greek word for killeth as used here literally means "to kill outright, to destroy".

Paul discusses this same sentiment in Romans Chapter 7. There Paul stated that whilst the law was in fact good, sin takes occasion by the commandments and deceives man into sinning. The law sets the benchmark, it makes us aware of what we are supposed to do and how we are supposed to live. But sin sees this benchmark and works against it and man, causing him to fall short and suffer the consequences of sin. Sin uses the law as its starting to point to separate man from God. It seeks to drive a divide and separate man from God. Sin did this with the one commandment given to Adam and Eve in the garden of Eden and it did it with the ten commandments given to the nation of Israel.

Just like with Adam and Eve the result of any transgression against the law of God results in death. The law of the Lord to Adam and Eve was that in the day you eat of it you will die. Spiritually on that day in the garden of Eden Adam and Eve died. Natural death followed, but their spiritual death was immediate. Their connection with the Lord was broken, there was a great divide, and death was introduced to the world.

Under the Old Covenant Moses brought the law of the Lord to the nation of Israel. These were laws that history shows the nation of Israel were never able to live up to. Time and again the nation of Israel would have to present sacrifices unto the Lord to atone for their sins. The letter of the law brought death to the nation of Israel because man of his own efforts could never fulfil the law of God.

The letter of the law brought death to man, because man could never of his own volition fulfil the requirements of the law. This is the point Paul is making, the letter kills.

but of the spirit but the spirit giveth life. (2Co 3:6)

On the other hand though is the New Covenant. Not of the letter but of the Spirit and the Spirit brings life. When Jesus hung upon the cross of cavalry, He didn't abolish the law, He fulfilled it! Death was defeated, sacrifice was completed, and the law was fulfilled. Through Jesus we are now able to experience the fulness of life because the requirements of the law have been fulfilled. What man could never do, Jesus did and by doing such ushered in the New Covenant. Now for any that accept Jesus as their Lord and Saviour, they get to experience eternal life.

> *For God so loved the world, that he gave his only begotten Son, that whosoever believeth in him should **not perish, but have everlasting life**. (Joh 3:16)*

> ***He will swallow up death in victory**; and the Lord GOD will wipe away tears from off all faces; and the rebuke of his people shall he take away from off all the earth: for the LORD hath spoken it. (Isa 25:8)*

The Old Testament showed that no matter the efforts, good works etc of man, death was the result. The letter of the law lead to death, for man of himself was never able to fulfil the requirements of the letter. The law pointed to the fact that man needed a saviour. Man needed someone to mediate between God and himself. This was the cry of Job (Job 9:32-33). The blood of bulls and goats could never atone for the sin of man. It required more than this. Then in the fulness of time the Lord Jesus Christ came, and through His perfect sacrifice brought in the New Covenant through which we may have life by the Spirit (Gal 4:4-5).

The letter kills, but the Spirit gives life. The Old Covenant brought death but the New Covenant, the Covenant that Paul was an able minister of, equipped by the Lord to minister, was a Covenant of life through the Spirit. Between the Old and the New is the great dividing line of the cross. On one side is death, on the other is life.

It is important to note that as we move forward here the reader needs to remember that the Old and the New are not polar opposites or diametrically opposed, but rather the New builds from the Old and is the next rung on the covenantal ladder of man's restoration.

But if the ministry of death, written and engraven in stones, was glorious, (2Co 3:7)

Notice here that Paul starts this sentence with a 'but'. He has just stated to the Corinthian believers how the Old Covenant was a covenant of death but the New was a covenant of life by the Spirit. And he has also affirmed to them that his calling was to preach the New Covenant, for God had equipped and called him to this. He then affirmed that the Corinthian believers were living examples of this epistle that the Lord had written upon his heart. Having gone through all this and clearly establishing the difference between the Old and the New and emphasising how the New is greater than the Old, he then says 'but'.

Paul says 'but' if this Old Covenant, the ministration of death, that which killeth. And just to make sure we understand exactly what he is referring to, he adds that "was written and engraven in stones". There is really no mistaking this to be the Ten Commandments that the Lord gave to Moses. This is a clear reference back to the giving of the Old Covenant when Moses ascended the mount of God, received the Ten Commandments on the two tables of stone then descended with the Ten Commandments and presented them to the nation of Israel. This is the Covenant Paul is referring to, in essence saying, but if this Old Covenant.

Having put in this clause and make sure his readers knew what he was referring too, Paul then adds something unexpected. At first glance what he says seems to be a statement that contradicts his previous discourse. He states that this Old Covenant, the ministration of death, that which has been surpassed was in fact glorious. Having just outlined how the Old Covenant was a ministration of death and how the letter killed, Paul then stated that this same Covenant was glorious. It seems like such a juxtaposition. As New Covenant believers it is not something we readily associate with the Old Covenant, but the Word of the Lord through Paul is that the Old Covenant was in fact glorious. How readily do we dismiss it now days and consider the Old Testament of little value? But the Lord said through Paul that it was indeed glorious. The Old Covenant was a glorious covenant. What a prompt this should be to believers of today, to highlight the importance of the Old Covenant and the Old Testament. They are glorious. Literally touched by the glory of God and given to man. They are not to be belittled or thought of as having no value.

The Old Covenant was glorious!

so that the children of Israel could not stedfastly behold the face of Moses for the glory of his countenance; which glory was to be done away: (2Co 3:7)

When Moses first received the Ten Commandments, he descended from Mount Sinai and found that the nation of Israel had fallen into idolatry and revelry. Having come back to the camp after spending forty days and nights with the Lord on Mount Sinai, Moses found the nation worshipping the golden calf that Aaron had made. Upon seeing this Moses threw the tables of stone to the ground, shattering them both to pieces.

In Exodus 34 we then read of Moses ascending Mount Sinai for another forty days and nights and receiving the commandments afresh from the Lord. It is after this period that Moses again descended to the nation with the tables of the law within his hands. For the sake of this point we will quote from Exodus 34 so that the reader can clearly understand what Paul is conveying to the Corinthian believers.

> *And it came to pass, when Moses came down from mount Sinai with the two tables of testimony in Moses' hand, when he came down from the mount, that Moses wist not that the skin of his face shone while he talked with him. And when Aaron and all the children of Israel saw Moses, behold, the skin of his face shone; and they were afraid to come nigh him. And Moses called unto them; and Aaron and all the rulers of the congregation returned unto him: and Moses talked with them. And afterward all the children of Israel came nigh: and he gave them in commandment all that the LORD had spoken with him in mount Sinai. And till Moses had done speaking with them, he put a vail on his face. (Exo 34:29-33)*

Moses face literally shone from the time that he had spent in the presence of the Lord. As the Lord renewed the covenant with Moses and wrote out for him the ten commandments on the two tables of stone, Moses' face was filled with the glory of the Lord just as the moon reflects the light of the sun. As Moses stayed in His presence, his face literally absorbed and reflected the glory of God.

When he descended the mount, Moses was unaware of the physical manifestation from his time of spiritual impartation. He was unaware that the skin of his face shone, that his countenance was changed and that his appearance was altered. The nation of Israel though saw it and were afraid. Paul expands upon this point and infers that so great was the brightness that shone from Moses that the nation of Israel could not steadfastly look at his face. This glory, that was upon the face of Moses, was too bright. This impartation occurred as Moses received the Old Covenant from the Lord.

This is the crux of what Paul is saying. This Old Covenant, whilst it was a ministration of death, was glorious. It was given as Moses stood before the glory of the Lord and the glory of the Lord was imparted upon him. Moses received the covenant and went back to the camp of Israel as a beacon of the glory of the Lord. What a glorious encounter and representation of being in the presence of the Lord. And all this whilst under the ministration of death!

How shall not the ministration of the spirit be rather glorious? (2Co 3:8)

If the ministration of death was so glorious and had such a profound effect on Moses that the nation of Israel could not behold him fully, how much greater shall the ministration of the Spirit be. If that which lead to death had a glory that lit up the countenance of a man, how much greater the glory from a ministration of life. This is the message that Paul is conveying to the Corinthian believers. The New Covenant is indeed greater than the Old, but if the Old attracted such a glory, how much greater should the glory be exhibited in the lives of New Covenant believers.

If a Covenant of death could cause the face of Moses to shine so brightly that the nation of Israel had to look away, what should a Covenant of life do to New Covenant believers?

The word for rather as used here means "more, better, in a greater degree". If the Old Covenant had such a gloriousness attached to it, how much "more, better, in a greater degree" is the gloriousness of the New Covenant.

Paul's message to the Corinthian believers is that they are under a covenant that is even more glorious than that which Moses experienced. The ministry of the Spirit is greater and more glorious than the ministration of death.

For if the ministration of condemnation be glory, much more doth the ministration of righteousness exceed in glory. (2Co 3:9)

Another comparison and contrast is made by Paul here. This time it is the ministration of condemnation compared to the ministration of righteousness.

The Greek word for condemnation in this verse means "sentencing adversely" whereas the Greek word for righteousness means "justification". The Old Covenant was one that brought condemnation to man because man on his own could never fulfil its requirements. Man was condemned by the rule of law that he couldn't keep. Under the New Covenant though, man is justified through the precious blood of Jesus Christ. Man is able to live in a state of righteousness because of the atoning work of Christ.

Paul's point is continued here. If a ministry that saw man condemned was glorious how much more glorious is the ministry that sets man in a place of righteousness. Paul's words are that the New Covenant exceeds in glory compared to the Old.

According to Strong's, the Greek word for exceed in this verse is "Perisseuo" and it means "to *superabound* (in quantity or quality), *be in excess, be superfluous*; also (transitively) to *cause to superabound* or *excel*". The Old Covenant was glorious but the New, in comparison to the Old, has an overabundance of glory. The ministration of righteousness superabounds in glory compared to that of the Old Covenant and what Moses experienced.

For even that which was made glorious had no glory in this respect, by reason of the glory that excelleth. (2Co 3:10)

Paul's words here are that so great is the glory of the New that the Old pales in comparison to it. That which once was glorious looks to be inglorious when seen in the light of the New. It is like comparing the light of the moon to the light of the sun. If the first light you see is the moon it looks incredibly glorious compared to the stars around it, but when you see the light of the sun. the glory of the moon appears as nothing.

That is the message of Paul here. So great is the glory of the New that the Old does not even come close to it. The glory of the New excels far beyond what the Old ever did. They are as night and day.

For if that which is done away was glorious, much more that which remaineth is glorious. (2Co 3:11)

The law was never the permanent solution. It was always temporary, and its ministry would pass when Christ ushered in the New Covenant. If the temporary had such a glory though, how much greater is the glory of that which is to remain.

Paul continued his comparison and contrast to the Corinthian believers to get them to understand how much greater the glory of the New is compared to the glory of the Old. His whole approach is to provoke the minds of the readers and get them to understand the message he is communicating.

The New Testament believers are under a New Covenant that in every way is more glorious than the Old Covenant.

Seeing then that we have such hope, we use great plainness of speech: And not as Moses, which put a vail over his face, (2Co 3:12-13a)

Here Paul links back to his earlier quote from verse 7 in reference to when Moses descended from Mount Sinai, and his face was literally glowing from his encounter with the Lord. In Exodus 34 we are told in regard to this quote by Paul that:

> *And when Aaron and all the children of Israel saw Moses, behold, the skin of his face shone; and they were afraid to come nigh him. And Moses called unto them; and Aaron and all the rulers of the congregation returned unto him: and Moses talked with them. And afterward all the children of Israel came nigh: and he gave them in commandment all that the LORD had spoken with him in mount Sinai. And till Moses had done speaking with them, **he put a vail on his face**. But when Moses **went in before the LORD to speak with him, he took the vail off**, until he came out. And he came out, and spake unto the children of Israel that which he was commanded. And the children of Israel saw the face of Moses, that the skin of Moses' face shone: **and Moses put the vail upon his face again**, until he went in to speak with him (Exo 34:30-35)*

When Moses was on the mount he received not only the law, but the revelation of the Tabernacle. After spending forty days with the Lord, Moses descended the mount. As we have learned Moses was unaware of any physical change until the people of Israel brought it to his attention. Because of the reactions of the people, after Moses had given the revelation of the Lord to the Israelites, he put a veil over his face.

As we learned from a brief look at Moses at the start of this section, Moses was not like any other prophet. The Lord would speak to him face to face. Moses encounter upon

Mount Sinai was not a once off event. Moses would frequent the presence of the Lord. We go on to read in Exodus that after coming down the mount Moses had a tent erected outside of the congregation and there he would go to speak to the Lord up until the time that the Tabernacle was finished. Once the Tabernacle was completed, Moses would then go into the Most Holy Place and there, he would communicate with the Lord as a man talks with his friend, face to face.

Regardless of the place where Moses communicated with the Lord, we are told in the above quoted passage that Moses' modus operandi was the same. After coming out from the presence of the Lord Moses would let the nation of Israel see his face. The glory of his countenance was the evidence of his time with the Lord. There was no way of faking this. After Israel had seen this, Moses would speak to them the words of the Lord and upon finishing he would then cover his face with a veil. This veil remained in place until the next time Moses went before the Lord. As Moses went in before the presence of the Lord, he would lift the veil and speak face to face with the Lord God Almighty. His face was uncovered in the presence of the Lord but veiled when away from it.

In many ways Moses' face was a literal representation of the Most Holy Place. At the start of this study we noted that the Most Holy Place was the inner most part of the Tabernacle and it was here that the glory of the Lord resided and it was the glory of the Lord that provided the light in this space. The Most Holy Place was spiritually illuminated. We also noted that whilst the Tabernacle had three progressive entrances, all made of the exact same material, the entrance to the Most Holy Place was called the Veil. It was the Veil that separated the Most Holy Place from the Holy Place and was a light barrier if you will between the two. The only time that anyone entered into this (apart from Moses) was the High Priest once a year on the Great Day of Atonement. On this day the High Priest got to go through the Veil and experience the glory of the Lord. For the rest of the year though this glory was sealed off by the Veil.

Whilst Moses' face was lit by the glory of being in the presence of the Lord, his face was veiled and hidden from the congregation of Israel. It was a glory hidden behind the veil in the same way as the Most Holy Place. In both cases the glory of the Lord was in the camp of Israel, but it was veiled form their sight. It was present and yet hidden.

that the children of Israel could not stedfastly look to the end of that which is abolished: (2Co 3:13b)

The Israelites could not initially look upon the countenance of Moses because it was too bright, they were then prohibited from seeing it through the veil that Moses wore. In the writer's mind there are two reasons for this:

A. When we looked at the layout of the Tabernacle of Moses, we saw that there were three distinct sections. These being the Outer Court, the Holy Place and the Most Holy Place. These three sections relate and are prophetic of three ages of time in relation to man.

The nation of Israel was under the Old Covenant and the Age of the Outer Court. This age covers the period of time from Adam up until Calvary. This was the period of sacrifice. It covers the period from Adam and the sacrifice at Eden up until the sacrifice of Christ at Calvary. Just as the Outer Court was the largest area of the Tabernacle so too does the age of the Outer Court cover the largest period of time. It covers a period of approximately four thousand years.

Sacrifice occurred in the Outer Court, but the glory of the Lord was within the Most Holy Place behind the veil. The glory was in Israel, but Israel did not have access to it, the way had not yet been opened. Just as in the Tabernacle the glory was present but hidden, so too it was with the face of Moses. The glory was on the face of Moses, but it was hidden from the nation of Israel. It was kept behind the veil. It was not the right time for the people of God to be gazing upon the glory of the Lord. They were under the age of the Outer Court.

B. Moses' countenance was changed from the time he spent with the Lord. When Moses was back in the camp attending to the needs of the nation, it is the writer's opinion that this glory would have begun to fade. It is this sense conveyed by Paul when he says that Moses wore a veil so that the children of Israel could not look upon the end of that which is abolished. The glory of Moses' face was a glory that would have faded during the times he was away from the presence of the Lord. When he went back into the presence there would be a fresh impartation and recharging if you will, but while he was away from the presence of the Lord the imputed glory would have faded in his countenance. Part of the reason for the veil was to hide this fading from the nation of Israel. It would have been a massive distraction and hindrance to Moses and the people. One can imagine all of the murmurings that would have occurred had the nation of Israel witnessed the fading glory upon Moses' face.

But their minds were blinded: for until this day remaineth the same vail untaken away in the reading of the old testament; which vail is done away in Christ. But even unto this day, when Moses is read, the vail is upon their heart. Nevertheless when it shall turn to the Lord, the vail shall be taken away.(2Co 3:14-16)

Israel was kept from seeing the glory of the Lord. The veil upon Moses' face and the Veil in the Tabernacle kept the glory hidden away. Pauls describes how there still remains a veil over the eyes of the Israelites in the reading of the Old Testament and it prevents them from seeing the fullness of the glory of the Lord. The Veil of the Old Covenant is still in place for those who are under it.

When Christ gave Himself upon the cross of Calvary and breathed His last, the earth shook, the rocks were rent and the Veil of the Temple was rent from top to bottom (Matt 27:51, Mark 15:38, Luke 23:45). At this time the Veil was in the rebuilt Temple and it was much larger than the original Veil in the Tabernacle of Moses, but still contained the same truths.

There is no mistaking that the Veil was rent as Christ gave Himself as the ultimate sacrifice, fulfilling the obligations of the Law. The curtain was ripped as Christ's sacrifice was complete. As the body of Christ was ripped in death so the Veil was ripped in half. The fact that the curtain was ripped from top to bottom shows that this was of the Lord, it was ripped from Heaven to earth. It was not ripped from the bottom, where man would start, but from the top, that which pointed to Heaven, and torn down to the earth, that which points to man. The ripped curtain signified open access to the Most Holy Place. The curtain which had divided the people of God off from the presence of the Lord had been removed.

Paul notes that it is only though Christ that this Veil is removed. The cross of Christ is the dividing line between the Outer Court and the Holy Place of the Tabernacle of Moses. The Outer Court is the place of sacrifice and represents the Old Covenant. For any that would accept Christ as their Lord and Saviour, they move from the Outer Court into the Holy Place and into the New Covenant. The cross is the dividing line between the two. Once we come to Christ and dwell in the Holy Place, we can now experience the joy of the removed Veil. We do not yet dwell in the fulness of the Most Holy Place, but we have access to the presence of the Lord permanently. The Veil has been removed, the divider has gone and for any who accept Christ and enter into the New Covenant and dispensation of the Holy Place, they have continual access to the presence of the Lord.

For any who haven't come to Christ and for those who are still under the Old Covenant the Veil still remains. They cannot see the fulness of the glory of the Lord. They do not see His presence, they do not see the fulness of His glory in His Word, their eyes are veiled. This Veil remains for any that have not come to Christ.

Through Christ though, the New Testament believers get to experience both. We have access to the presence of the Lord and through Christ we see the fulness of the glory of the Word of the Lord. The Veil is lifted and we experience the blessed glory of the Lord.

The apostle Paul had literally lived and experienced this. He was raised a pharisee, under the Old Covenant and for much of his life had been blinded to the glory of the Lord in life and in the scriptures. It was only when his natural sight was taken that his spiritual eyes were opened. Having then come to Christ, Paul saw the fulness of the glory of the Lord both in his life and in the Word. It is through Christ, and through Christ alone, that the Veil is lifted and we are able to see the fulness of the glory of God. This is the message that Paul was communicating to the Corinthian believers. The Old Covenant was glorious, but the New through Christ Jesus is on another level. It exceeds in glory and should be the experience that every believer walks in.

Now the Lord is that Spirit: and where the Spirit of the Lord is, there is liberty. (2Co 3:17)

This verse continues from the previous in its reverence to the Lord Jesus Christ. For those that haven't come to cross the Veil remains, and the Word remains hidden. But for those that have come to Christ, they have the Spirit, and where the Spirit is there is liberty.

The Greek word for liberty here means freedom. Just as with Christ, the Veil is torn opening the way for believers so too with the Spirit is understanding into His incredible Word realised as he opens the scriptures to us. The truths of the Word are no longer veiled and contained; the Spirit sets them free. The Law was restrictive, but through the Spirit believers receive a freedom that isn't available to those who haven't come to Christ.

But we all, with open face beholding as in a glass the glory of the Lord, are changed into the same image from glory to glory, even as by the Spirit of the Lord. (2Co 3:18)

This is the great crescendo of Chapter 3 and within this verse are truths that should excite and challenge every believer. Paul has spent this chapter comparing the Old Covenant to the New and emphasising how the New exceeds the glory of the Old. He has then spoken about how a Veil still remains on those that haven't come to Christ and how they are unable to see the fulness of the glory of the Lord. Paul then turned his attention to believers and makes an incredibly powerful statement. Having built a foundation of truth through this chapter, Paul then takes these truths and shows how they apply to New Testament believers.

> ***But we all,***
> Not Israel who were under the Old Covenant but those who were under the New Covenant through Christ. Note the collectiveness of the language used here. It is not just for the elite, for leaders, for seasoned Christians but for **ALL** who have accepted Christ as their Lord and Saviour and live under the blessing of the New Covenant. The point that Paul is about to make is for all believers. He is using a collective tense that incorporates all believers, all those that have come to the Lord through the acceptance of the Lord Jesus Christ.
>
> ***with open face***
> Depending on your translation this reads as "with open face" or "with unveiled face".

Just like Moses, when we enter into the presence of the Lord we do so with our faces unveiled, ready to bask in the presence of the Lord. Our experience is to be the same in that respect. Just like Moses, we have been given the opportunity and access to the very presence of the Lord. How glorious a thought is that! The same countenance changing experience that Moses received time and time again is to be ours. Through Christ the Veil has been torn and as priests we are called to stand before the presence of the Lord with our faces open, ready to bask in His glory.

The difference though exists in our experiences when we step out from the presence of the Lord. When we step out of His presence, we do not veil our faces and hide His glory. As New Testament believers our faces our unveiled, not as Moses who was veiled. Our faces are always open and able to be seen. There is no hiding the glory of the New Covenant. That which was concealed and hidden under the Old is revealed and open in the New. This is the gloriousness of the New and the freedom that comes through the Spirit. Through Christ the Veil has been removed and unlike Moses when we go out into our communities, we do so with unveiled and uncovered faces.

beholding as in a glass the glory of the Lord,

The term for glass here as according to Strong's means "to mirror oneself, that is, to see reflected". In Paul's time this term would have referred to a looking glass and the thought here is that of reflection in a mirror. It was with an open face that we behold the glory of the Lord. In this respect our experience is the same as Moses'. Moses would lift the veil in the presence of the Lord, and the glory of the Lord would literally be reflected upon his face. It was these encounters that would cause the countenance of Moses to change. Moses countenance was literally enlightened by the time he spent with the Lord. Under the New Covenant this is to be the experience of every believer. But we all with open face behold the glory of the Lord. Not one man who represented God to the nation but all believers who represent Christ to the world.

The difference here is that Moses would cover his face with the veil and the glory was to be hidden from the nation for the reasons we touched on above (firstly it was not the right dispensation and secondly, the glory faded over time). The call for believers though is that we are to have unveiled faces. Under the glory of the New Covenant the Veil has been removed through Christ. The glory of the Lord is literally to reflect off our open faces unto the world around us. The world is to see and observe the glory of our countenance from our time spent in the presence of the Lord. As we press into the Lord and spend time in His presence, we literally become light bearers for the world around us, we mirror His glory to the world around us. This is yet another way where the glory of the New is greater than the glory of the Old.

We live in the dispensation where the Church, and the believers who form it, are called to be the light of the world and we shine through the reflection of the glory of the Father. It is a light we are to carry forth with open faces, declaring to the world the testimony of our faith. It is not to be a veiled, hidden light but one that is clearly displayed. We are to mirror His glory to the world around us.

are changed into the same image from glory to glory,

Paul continues that not only with an open face do we behold the glory of the Lord, but we are changed into the same image from glory to glory. Under the Old Covenant economy, the access to the glory of the Lord was limited. Moses would enter before the Lord and receive a fresh impartation, but when he left the presence of the Lord the glory would start to fade until he went in again to the presence of the Lord. It was a continual recharge if you will.

For believers under the New Covenant though, we live in the dispensation of the Holy Place and the great dividing Veil has been torn through Christ. We have continual access to the glory of the Lord and as we avail ourselves of that, we are changed from glory to glory. It is not a process of recharge but a process of transformation into the image of Christ (Rom 8:29). As we spend more and more time in the presence of the Lord we are changed from glory to glory and reflect Him brighter and brighter.

It is both a marvellous promise and a challenge to us as believers.

even as by the Spirit of the Lord.

All of this is done by the Spirit of the Lord. It is not works, it is not self-effort but it is done through the Spirit as we faithfully seek the Father. It is a spiritual transformation performed by the Spirit of the Lord in the lives of His people.

Throughout this incredible chapter of Corinthians Paul has paralleled the Old Covenant and New Covenant and through comparing and contrasting them has constantly confirmed and reaffirmed how the New is greater than the Old. In the table below we list all of the comparisons that Paul used and see the constant emphasis on how the New exceeds the Old.

OLD COVENANT	NEW COVENANT
Epistle of Law	Epistle of Christ
Written in ink	Written by the Spirit
Tables of stone	Fleshy tables of the heart
Old Testament	New Testament
Of the letter	Of the Spirit
Letter killeth	Spirit gives life
Ministration of death	Ministration of Spirit
Glorious	More glorious
Ministration of condemnation	Ministration of righteousness
Glorious	Exceeds in glory
Glory	Glory that excelleth
Done away with	Remaineth
Glorious	More glorious
Moses	Believers
Minister of the Old Testament	Ministers of the New Testament
Veiled	Unveiled
Pre Christ	After Christ
Fading glory	From glory to glory
Death	Life
Moses as Priest	Believers as Priests

The comparing and contrasting used by Paul was for the single purpose of helping the reader to understand that the New is greater than the Old. That is what he was trying to communicate to the Corinthian believers.

The crux of Paul's message was that the Old Covenant had such a glory attached to it that it physically changed the appearance of Moses. Moses' face shone in reflection from his time in the presence of the Lord. And as amazing as a thought as that is to behold in the mind, the reality is that there lies a greater experience for **every** believer under the New Covenant.

Moses got to experience the effects of the glory of the Lord as no other individual did in the Old Testament. He received the imparted glory upon his countenance, but he had to veil it and it was a glory that faded during his times absent from the Most Holy Place.

For New Testament believers though we are under a New Covenant and a new dispensation. The Veil that separated Old Testament believers from the glory of the Lord has been removed and we all, with unveiled faces are transformed into the image of God as we press into His presence more and more.

Our experience is to be greater than that of Moses'. What was temporary for Moses is meant to be permanent for us. What was veiled for Moses is unveiled for us. What Moses hid from the nation we are to display to the world around us. What was glorious upon Moses is to be even more glorious upon us.

With unveiled faces our countenance is to reflect the glory of the Lord in an ever brightening and increasing manner as the Spirit works in us. We are to be spiritual beacons of light in the places where the Lord has called us to minister.

The Old was glorious but the glory of the New is so great that the Old pales in comparison.

APPLICATION

The Old Covenant and the Dispensation of Law finished at the Cross of Calvary. As believers who have accepted the Lord Jesus Christ as our Lord and Saviour we are under the New Covenant and a new Dispensation. Through the sacrifice of Christ, the Veil has been torn and we now have continual access to the presence of the Lord. It is not a presence that is hidden away as it was under the Old, but it is a presence that is readily available for all who would seek it.

Whilst the covenant we dwell under is greater than that Moses lived under, we can still learn a number of things from how Moses interacted with the Lord's presence. There are lessons from Moses that have a clear application to believers today.

The Call To The Individual

A. Proximity

Proximity can be defined as the distance between two objects. The closer the objects are, the closer the proximity is. The countenance of Moses was not changed when he was distanced from the Lord, but when he was in close proximity. The Lord had a set spot, whether it was on Mount Sinai, or in the Tabernacle. The Lord's presence was in a designated place. It was Moses who chose how close in proximity he got to the presence of the Lord. The responsibility lay upon him, but it was only in the moments of close proximity that the countenance of Moses was changed. It was when Moses pressed into relationship with the Lord that he received the impartation of the Spirit.

For us as believers the exact same truth applies. Yes the Veil has been torn and yes the presence of the Lord has been revealed, but it is us as individuals who determine how close in proximity we get to this. The availability is there, the Lord is there but we determine the proximity.

The truth is that the Lord is reaching out in relationship to all of mankind. The Father's heart is for His children. The Lord wants to be in close proximity to us, but the amount of distance is a choice determined through our actions.

Moses chose a continual close proximity, we have the same choice.

B. Purpose

Moses was intentional in his interactions with the Lord. He never stumbled into the presence of the Lord by accident. There was purpose to his actions and that purpose was a desire to be in the presence of the Lord and grow in relationship with the Lord.

C. Continual

Moses' journey into the presence of the Lord was not a once off. One encounter with the Lord's presence was not the story of Moses life. Moses continually presented himself before the presence of the Lord. He continually entered into the Most Holy Place, removing his veil and basked in the marvellous light of the presence of the Lord.

For Moses, his continual entering into the presence of the Lord recharged the glory that was upon his countenance. Moses could continually enter into the Lord's presence, but he couldn't continually stay there. Moses had to leave the presence and during his time away from it, the glory of his countenance would fade.

As believers under the New Covenant, we can continually stay in the presence of the Lord and as we do that we are changed from glory to glory. It is an increasing reflection that occurs upon our countenance if we continue in it. We need to never be satisfied with our previous encounters of the Lord and continually want to receive a fresh impartation from Him.

D. Relationship

And the LORD spake unto Moses face to face, as a man speaketh unto his friend. (Exo 33:11)

Moses' interactions with the Lord were built upon relationship. A relationship is built and grown when both parties commit time and effort to it. The Lord always fulfils His side, but there is a responsibility upon the side of man to commit to growing the relationship. Relationship can never be a one-way street.

SUMMARY

There is a challenge, if you will, that comes from this chapter of Corinthians, and it is one the writer believes Paul was trying to stir in the hearts of the Corinthian believers. If Moses was under the Old Covenant, which is less glorious than the New, and yet his countenance was so glorious that he had to veil it, how much greater should the countenance of believers be who are under a more glorious covenant.

Moses was under the Old and yet his face shone so much from the glory he experienced that he had to veil it. We though are under the New and have a glory that does not fade, but one that goes from glory to glory. The experience of Moses is to be the experience of every believer in an even greater way. There is to be a light upon the countenance of every believer that only continues to grow as they continue to seek the presence of the Lord. Our countenance should stand out. There should be a definable difference in us that people can observe just as the nation of Israel observed the change in the countenance of Moses.

The question is, if this isn't our experience, why isn't it? The words of the Lord through the Apostle Paul are fairly clear. The New Covenant is in every way more abundantly more glorious than the Old and the experience of every believer is to be greater than that of Moses. This should not be something that condemns us, but it should be something that stirs the Spirit within us to go after the Lord in an even greater way than we ever have before. This is an experience literally waiting for the people of the Lord to grasp hold of and leap into. This is something that we will look at in the subsequent sections of this study.

Our purpose for now has been to see the call that exists for believers to shine. The call to the individual is to have a countenance that shines brighter than that of Moses. The glory that we are to experience is immeasurably greater than that which Moses did. We are called to shine! We are called to reflect His glory! We are called to reflect with a greater glory than that of Moses. His glory is to reflect off us and impact the world around us.

THE CALL TO THE CHURCH

Having in our previous section looked at the call to shine to the individual, we now turn our attention to looking at the call to shine that exists for the Church. It should be noted here that when we refer to the Church we are not referring to a building or denomination. The Church is formed when believers come together in unity, forming the many membered body of Christ. It is the gathering of believers together, with Christ in the midst, that forms His Church (Matt 18:20). The Church is a spiritual building made of believers gathered together in unity.

It is when believers come together as beacons of individual light, forming the Church, that the power of the light intensifies and increases. When the Church comes together, it is literally to be light forces joining and amalgamating to form an even brighter light in a given location. The call for believers is to not forsake gathering together (Heb 10:25), and whilst that can be hard at times, there is power that comes from unified corporate light that is much needed in the world today. So, when we talk about the Church, we are talking about believers coming together in the name of Jesus, in unity and with purpose.

In looking at the call to the Church to shine, we start by looking back to the Golden Lampstand. The Golden Lampstand is first introduced to us in the Tabernacle of Moses. There we saw that the Golden Lampstand was the only vessel of light in the Holy Place. In our look at the Tabernacle of Moses we touched very briefly on the Golden Lampstand, but for this next section we will dive a little deeper into it. Whilst the Golden Lampstand first comes into light in the Tabernacle, it is a truth that flows throughout the entirety of Scripture. Like so many truths in Scripture, we see that from the starting point there are streams that build and widen with each successive mention as the Lord continues to build the truth that He is trying to communicate to mankind. This is indeed the case with the Golden Lampstand.

For the purpose of this section, we will start by considering the design and purpose of the Golden Lampstand. As we progress, we will begin to see the application that this has in regard to the call to the Church to shine.

Design

The Golden Lampstand was an incredible piece of furniture and is a theme, which as we will see, flows throughout scripture. The Golden Lampstands design is detailed for us in Exodus 25:31-40 and Exodus 37:17-24. The reader is encouraged to read over theses passages to gain an understanding of the Golden Lampstand. For the writer, the Tabernacle and its furnishing have been keys which have helped unlock scriptural truths. It would be the writer's encouragement to not just quickly read over these passages, but for the reader to take the time to meditate on the Words of the Lord in these accounts. When we take the time to sow His Word in our spirit it allows the opportunity for a future harvest.

In looking at the Golden Lampstand, our purpose here is to consider the design of this marvellous God inspired piece in detail so that the reader will have a clear understanding of the God given pattern that Moses received. It is having this understanding that will lay the foundation for not only this section but also the proceeding sections of this study.

A. Designed By

Exo 25:40 And look that thou make them after their pattern, which was shewed thee in the mount.

It is important for the reader to remember here that the Golden Lampstand was designed by the Lord. Whilst the Golden Lampstand was made by man, it was God who authored it and laid out the instructions for it. Moses received the revelation of the Golden Lampstand through the vision that the Lord gave him. Moses recorded the pattern, but God was the designer. He revealed the pattern to Moses and Moses was to have it replicated precisely. This is true for the entire Tabernacle of Moses. It was all to be made exactly as what was shown to Moses. The pattern had to be followed. There existed no room for artistic license. The Golden Lampstand was to match the specifications that the Lord revealed to Moses precisely. It was a God designed piece.

B. Made of

*Exo 25:31 And thou shalt make a candlestick of **pure gold**:*

The Golden Lampstand was made of pure gold. Other pieces of Tabernacle furniture were made of wood overlaid with gold or other metals, but the Golden Lampstand was made of pure gold alone.

The Golden Lampstand wasn't to be made of just any gold though, it was to be made of pure gold. Pure gold speaks of that which has been passed through the fires of refinement and has had all dross and impurities removed. It speaks of that which is absolutely pure, undefiled and without contaminant. It speaks of that which has been perfected.

C. Made by

*Exo 25:31 And thou shalt make a candlestick of pure gold: of **beaten work** shall the candlestick be made:*

The Golden Lampstand was made of beaten work. The Hebrew word for beaten work means "rounded work, moulded by hammering" and is also translated beaten. The Golden Lampstand was moulded through beating the gold into shape. The thought here is of one piece of gold being worked and moulded to create a finished product. The Lampstand was not bits and pieces joined together. It was not many pieces coming together to form one, it was just one piece. It sets forth the picture of unity within the Lampstand. The Golden Lampstand had distinctions in its design, yet it was wholly and completely one.

D. Size

Exo 25:39 Of a talent of pure gold shall he make it, with all these vessels.

The Golden Lampstand is one of only two pieces of Tabernacle furniture that were not given specific measurements. Apart from the Golden Lampstand and the Brazen Laver, every other piece had exact design measurements that had to be adhered to.

The only thing that we are told regarding the Golden Lampstand is that it and its vessels were to be made from a talent of pure gold.

E. Shaft

Exo 25:31 And thou shalt make a candlestick of pure gold: ......: his shaft, ...

The shaft was the central piece of the Golden Lampstand. It was from this centre that the rest of the Golden Lampstand branched out. The shaft provided the centre and balance of the Golden Lampstand. It was the foundational strength for the Lampstand.

F. Branches

Exo 25:32 And six branches shall come out of the sides of it; three branches of the candlestick out of the one side, and three branches of the candlestick out of the other side:

The Golden Lampstand had a total of six branches, three on either side of the shaft. There were three on the left and three on the right. These branches ascended up the Lampstand in pairs. There were two at the bottom, two in the middle and two at the top. The branches formed a mirror image as they ascended up the design of the lampstand. The shaft acted like the trunk of a tree and the branches fed out from this.

It is worth remembering here that the Golden Lampstand was all of one piece. Whilst there were different branches and a distinction in the various parts, all were perfectly united and whole. There was a oneness with the shaft and branches.

G. Knop, Bud, Almonds

Exo 25:33-34 Three bowls made like unto almonds, with a knop and a flower in one branch; and three bowls made like almonds in the other branch, with a knop and a flower: so in the six branches that come out of the candlestick. (34) And in the candlestick shall be four bowls made like unto almonds, with their knops and their flowers.

Within the design of the branches and the shaft the Lord laid out a pattern that was to be worked into the design. The pattern given was a threefold one which consisted of a knop, a bud and an almond. This is a reference to the almond tree when it is blossoming and bringing forth fruit. We see this same pattern with Aaron's rod when it budded setting forth Aaron and the tribe of Levi as the ones chosen to minister before the Lord to the nation of Israel. In Numbers 17:8 we read:

> *And it came to pass, that on the morrow Moses went into the tabernacle of witness; and, behold, the rod of Aaron for the house of Levi was budded, and brought forth buds, and bloomed blossoms, and yielded almonds. (Num 17:8)*

What we see in both of these cases is the progression of fruitfulness. The Knop or bud leads to the flower which leads to the fruit i.e., the almond in this case. It is a beautiful picture.

This pattern was to be repeated three times in each of the six branches, i.e., knop, flower, fruit; knop, flower, fruit; knop, flower, fruit. In the Shaft this threefold pattern was to be repeated four times.

H. Extra Knops

Exo 25:35 And there shall be a knop under two branches of the same, and a knop under two branches of the same, and a knop under two branches of the same, according to the six branches that proceed out of the candlestick.

There are two schools of thought amongst expositors with the knops mentioned here.

The first is that these knops refer to the ones already in the pattern of the shaft. The reader will remember that the threefold pattern of knop, bud and almond is repeated four times in the shaft. Some expositors hold that the knops referred to in the above verse are those knops that are already in the shaft. That is, a pair of branches would proceed from the first knop of the pattern. Then at the next knop, the second pair of branches proceeded. At the third knop the third and final set of branches proceeded. This would leave the final part of the pattern, i.e., knop, bud and almond, as the top of the shaft.

The other school of thought is that these were extra knops. These were three knops, one stacked upon the other, that were moulded underneath the fourfold pattern of the shaft. That is, there was a knop with a pair of branches, a knop and a pair of branches, a knop and a pair of branches and then the shaft and its pattern on top of this. This view holds that the branches came out of these extra knops and that the pattern in the shaft was untouched. This is the view that the writer would lean towards.

I. Lamps

Exo 25:37 And thou shalt make the seven lamps thereof: and they shall light the lamps thereof, that they may give light over against it.

Whilst the Golden Lampstand is at times referred to as the Golden Candlestick also, the term candlestick is not an adequate reflection of how the Golden Lampstand operated. A candle is something that will eventually burn out and have to be replaced. It has a limited life and speaks of self-consumption. The Lampstand though had oil lamps. These were maintained through a continual supply of oil and never needed to be replaced. There was a continuity of light through the lamps of the Lampstand.

Within the Lampstand there were a total of seven lamps. One lamp upon each branch and a lamp on top of the main shaft making seven in total. These lamps provided a unified, collective light for the environment around them.

J. Vessel

Exo 25:38 And the tongs thereof, and the snuffdishes thereof, shall be of pure gold.

The vessels associated with the Golden Lampstand were also made of pure gold. Everything to do with the Golden Lampstand had the connotation of purity attached to it.

K. Position

Exo 26:35 And thou shalt set the table without the vail, and the candlestick over against the table on the side of the tabernacle toward the south: and thou shalt put the table on the north side.

The Golden Lampstand sat within the Holy Place of the Tabernacle of Meeting. It was within the first part of the tent structure of the Tabernacle and sat on the south side of the Tabernacle immediately opposite the Golden Table of Shewbread.

L. Purpose

As we touched on in our brief look at the Tabernacle, the purpose of the Golden Lampstand was to provide light. The Outer Court had the light of the sun. The Most Holy place had the light of the glory of God. The Holy Place though was within the closed tent cut off from the light of the sun and separated from the light of the glory of God by the Veil that stood between the Holy Place and the Most Holy Place. The only provision of light within the Holy Place was the light of the Lampstand. It existed to shine and provide light where there would have otherwise been darkness.

M. Lighting of

And Moses and Aaron went into the tabernacle of the congregation, and came out, and blessed the people: and the glory of the LORD appeared unto all the people. And there came a fire out from before the LORD, and consumed upon the altar the burnt offering and the fat: which when all the people saw, they shouted, and fell on their faces. (Lev 9:23-24)

At the dedication of the Tabernacle, as a sign of the Lord's acceptance, divine fire come out from the presence of the Lord in the Most Holy Place and consumed the offerings that had been placed upon the altar. This divine fire lit the fire of the Brazen Altar, and this fire was to never go out. This flame was provided by the Lord, but it was the duty of the priesthood to maintain.

It is thought by some expositors that it was the fire from the divinely lit Brazen Altar that was used to light the Golden Lampstand. This is a view that the writer would agree with. Everything to do with the Golden Lampstand echoes the thoughts of purity. Why would the fire used to light it be any different? It was the divinely provided fire of the Lord that ignited the Lampstand.

N. Attended to

Exo 30:7 And Aaron shall burn thereon sweet incense every morning: when he dresseth the lamps

Part of the priest's role was to attend to the Golden Lampstand, and this was referred to as dressing the lamps. This dressing involved both supplying oil to the lamps and also trimming the wicks. The continual supply of oil ensured that the lamp shone continually as mandated by the Lord. The trimming of the wicks involved removing the burnt-out part of the wicks to ensure the light that shone was pure and unshrouded by smoke. There was to be absolute clarity in the light that the Lampstand provided.

O. The Oil

Lev 24:2 Command the children of Israel, that they bring unto thee pure oil olive beaten for the light, to cause the lamps to burn continually.

The oil of for the Golden Lampstand was to come from pure olive oil. This oil was produced through the fruit of the olive tree being beaten, causing the oil to flow out. Note the similarity here to the Golden Lampstand itself. The Golden Lampstand was made of pure gold, beaten or hammered into shape. Here the oil comes from pure olives beaten for light.

It is interesting to note here that the supply of the olive oil was a responsibility that lay upon the congregation of Israel. The priest would keep the oil to the lamps continually topped up, but his ability to do this was dependent upon the faithfulness of the congregation to ensure the supply of oil was always there.

SUMMARY

The Golden Lampstand was an incredible piece of Tabernacle furniture, fashioned out of one piece of pure gold. Its design consisted of a central shaft with six branches coming off it and ascending in pairs. In worked within the branches and shaft was a repeated threefold pattern of a knop, flower and a fruit. Atop of the branches and shaft sat seven golden lamps that provided the light for the Holy Place and were attended to by the Priest.

From what we have just gleaned from our look at the Golden Lampstand, we are presented with an image of the Golden Lampstand that would resemble something like the picture on the next page:

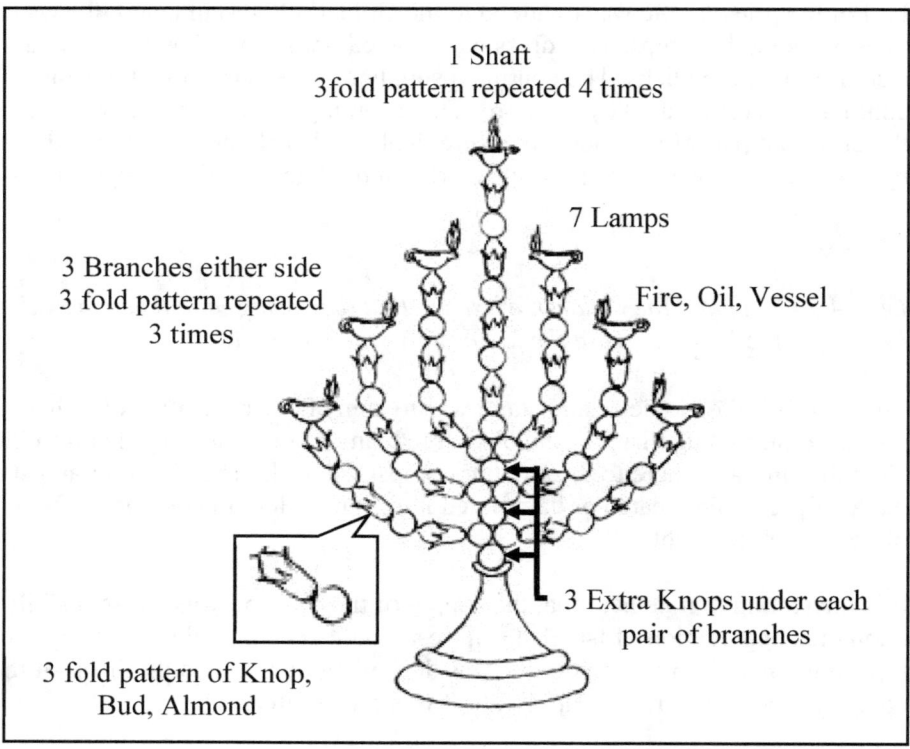

For the purpose of this section, we have done a quick overview of the Golden Lampstands design, but it is one that should give the reader a solid base for what we are about to consider. As we progress in this study, there will be numerous truths gleaned from our consideration of the Golden Lampstand in this section that we will see applied to the Church and its call to shine.

THE CHURCH AND THE GOLDEN LAMPSTAND

Having just spent time considering the revelation of the Golden Lampstand in the book of Exodus, we now turn our attention to the final book in the Bible, the book of Revelation. As we progress here the reader will soon begin to see the reason for our focus on the Golden Lampstand, its design and operation, and its application to the call of the Church to shine.

In Revelation Chapter 1, John saw an amazing vision of the Son of Man. For the purpose of this section, we are going to focus on verses 10-20 of Revelation Chapter 1. The reader is encouraged to read over this passage several times before moving forward. It is in these verses that we glean some important truths which form the focus of this section.

The Call To The Church

As we did in our consideration of the call to the individual, we will work through these verses bit by bit, noting and expanding on certain points as we go. Whilst there is a wealth of information within these verses, our focus is on that which reveals the call to shine to the Church.

Rev 1:10-11: I was in the Spirit on the Lord's day, and heard behind me a great voice, as of a trumpet, Saying, I am Alpha and Omega, the first and the last: and, What thou seest, write in a book, and send it unto the seven churches which are in Asia; unto Ephesus, and unto Smyrna, and unto Pergamos, and unto Thyatira, and unto Sardis, and unto Philadelphia, and unto Laodicea.

John was in the Spirit on the Lord's Day and as he was resting in the presence of the Lord, he heard the sound of a great voice behind him. So great was the voice it is compared to the sounding of a trumpet. As John listened, the voice spoke and said I am the Alpha and Omega, the first and last. The voice John heard is undoubtedly the voice of the Lord. The language is inapplicable to any angel, or any other being. It is a Godly title.

After informing John of who He was, the Lord told John to write down everything that he saw and send it to the seven churches that were in Asia. The revelation that John was receiving was to be written down in a book and recorded for the seven churches. What John saw was meant for more than himself, it was a message for the Church. That which the Lord would reveal to John was a revelation of truth which the Church needed to hear.

Whilst the words in Scripture are that the vision was for the seven Churches of Asia, any Word of the Lord to a Church within the context of the Bible is applicable to the whole Church. Just as the Epistles of Paul to the Corinthian and Galatian Churches have application to the whole Church so to do the words of the Lord to John here. This was a message not only for the local Church, but also the Church collectively.

Rev 1:12 And I turned to see the voice that spake with me. And being turned, I saw seven golden candlesticks;

John turned to see the voice that was speaking to him. This is a natural human response. John turned in order to try to engage with the one who was communicating with him. John heard the voice behind him and as he turned in that direction, rather than seeing an individual he saw seven Golden Candlesticks.

The Greek word for candlestick as used here literally means lampstand and for the sake of this section we are going to refer to it as such. As John turned he saw seven Lampstands. These were not ordinary lampstands though, these were seven Golden Lampstands.

The Golden Lampstand is a theme that runs through scripture and is particularly synonymous with the Tabernacle of Moses, as we discussed in our earlier section. From a scriptural context there is absolutely no mistaking the linkage that is occurring here. The mention of a Golden Lampstand is a clear reference to the Tabernacle of Moses. John, as a Jew, would have had a clear understanding of exactly what he was seeing here. The

Golden Lampstand was birthed in the Tabernacle, flows through scripture and finds its fulfilment, here, in the book of Revelation.

The voice of the Lord told John to record what he was about to see for the seven churches and as John turned to see the voice, the very first thing that he saw were seven Golden Lampstands. This was the deliberate intention of the Lord here. The Golden Lampstand is of key significance in what was being revealed to John.

Rev 1:13-15 And in the midst of the seven candlesticks one like unto the Son of man, clothed with a garment down to the foot, and girt about the paps with a golden girdle. His head and his hairs were white like wool, as white as snow; and his eyes were as a flame of fire; And his feet like unto fine brass, as if they burned in a furnace; and his voice as the sound of many waters.

As John looked closer, he saw beyond the Lampstands and saw that there was actually a figure standing in the midst of them. This was the second thing that John saw.

It would seem inferred here that the Lampstands were not all bunched together, but rather separated to some degree. There was enough separation between them that someone could stand in the middle of them. The Lampstands formed a perimeter if you will around this individual. The individual was in the middle and the Lampstands surrounded Him.

This individual looked like unto the Son of man. This individual was not like unto the son of man but was the Son of Man. There is no mistaking the individual here. The language used here is inapplicable to any other individual. It was the Lord Jesus Christ who called out to John with a trumpet like voice and as John turned to look upon Him, he saw Jesus standing in the middle of the seven Golden Lampstands. It was Jesus here, giving a revelation to John about His Church and for His Church.

As John focused in on Jesus in the midst of the Lampstands, he saw Jesus clothed in a garment down to His feet and girt with a golden girdle. John's focus was being drawn in here. His vision had moved past the Golden Lampstands and was now transfixed upon his Lord and Saviour. Christ stood here in His Priestly robes in the midst of the Lampstands. It was Jesus in His office of High Priest that John was seeing here. Part of the priest's role in the Old Testament economy was to attend to the Golden Lampstand. Here we have Jesus, adorned in his Priestley robes, overseeing the seven Golden Lampstands. Jesus is our Great High Priest forever after the order of Melchizedek (Ps 110:4, Heb 5:6). As our Great High Priest, He stands in the midst of the Lampstands observing and tending to them.

Rev 1:16 And he had in his right hand seven stars: and out of his mouth went a sharp twoedged sword: and his countenance was as the sun shineth in his strength.

As the Lord Jesus stood in the midst of the seven Lampstands, John observes that there were seven stars in His right hand.

John also saw a two-edged sword proceed from His mouth. The Two-edged sword speaks of the Sword of the Spirit, which is the Word of God (Eph 6:17, Heb 4:12). The Word proceeds from He who is the fulness of the Word as a sharp dual edged blade. This further attests to the fact that it was Jesus standing before John.

We then read that His countenance was as the sun. There was a magnificent glory radiating from Jesus. It would be the writers' thoughts that this was a brightness that increased as John focused in on Jesus. Whilst John was initially able to see Jesus in the midst of the Lampstands and observe His appearance and clothing, the more he focused in upon Jesus the brighter Jesus countenance became in the eyes of John. As John focused his attention on Jesus, it got to the point where Jesus' countenance was as bright as the sun. The Son shone as the Sun.

Rev 1:17 And when I saw him, I fell at his feet as dead. And he laid his right hand upon me, saying unto me, Fear not; I am the first and the last:

As John realised who it was, he fell to the ground in reverential awe. It was an act of reverence and Godly fear as John realised he was standing in the presence of his Lord and Saviour. Jesus though immediately reached out and comforted him. He spoke words of reassurance, comfort and peace. Jesus extended His right hand to John here to restore John to his former state.

Rev 1:18-19 I am he that liveth, and was dead; and, behold, I am alive for evermore, Amen; and have the keys of hell and of death. (19) Write the things which thou hast seen, and the things which are, and the things which shall be hereafter;

Jesus then continued and through His words confirmed to John that it was indeed his saviour that was talking with him. The language here again is inapplicable to anyone but Jesus. What an overwhelming experience this must have been for John. John the disciple whom Jesus loved. John the disciple who leaned on Jesus' breast. John who had walked and followed Jesus through His ministry on earth now saw his beloved Saviour again.

Jesus stated that He is the one that was alive, died but now lives forevermore. Jesus was the forerunner through which we get to experience eternal life. He is the one who died, rose and lives forever more. The language is again inapplicable to any other person.

Jesus continued and instructed John to again write down everything that he had seen so far and all of the things that are about to be revealed unto him. It is literally this revelation that John received through the vision he saw that would later become the Book of Revelation we read today. The Lord wanted the message He was giving to John to be communicated to the Church. He wanted the truths that John was receiving to be given to the body. There was truth, purpose and application in it. It was a message that was meant to be spread to the body of Christ.

The Call To The Church

Rev 1:20 The mystery of the seven stars which thou sawest in my right hand, and the seven golden candlesticks. The seven stars are the angels of the seven churches: and the seven candlesticks which thou sawest are the seven churches.

Most of what we have looked at so far has been establishing that it was Jesus, standing in the midst of the seven Golden Lampstands, who was talking to John. We have gone over these points fairly quickly and for a more detailed explanation the reader is encouraged to read "The Book of Revelation: An Exposition" by Kevin Conner. This is an incredibly detailed exposition that will exponentially increase the understanding of any student of the Word.

Jesus, having made His presence known to John, now set about explaining the vision to John. It is here that Jesus interpreted for John that which he had already seen. Scripture always interprets scripture, and it is here He who is the living Word, Jesus, interpreted for John the vision he had seen.

The Greek word for mystery here means 'secret, or hidden thing'. Throughout the Bible, the Lord uses symbols and/or types to communicate truth to mankind in a way that man can understand. The Word of God always interprets the symbols He uses. In this particular verse, Jesus interprets two things for John, one of which has great relevance for what we are looking at.

The first thing we see is that Jesus told John that the seven stars which he saw in Jesus' right hand were actually seven angels of the seven Churches. The Greek word for angel here means messenger. From the language of Jesus interpretation, it is evident that He is referring to the seven leaders of the seven churches of Asia and not seven angelic beings. It is the leaders of His churches that are in His right hand. Just as His right hand was upon John a verses ago, so it is upon the leaders He has placed in His Churches. His leaders are in His hands.

The second thing we can observe is that Jesus then goes on to explain to John the seven Golden Lampstands. This is the point that has particular application for us in the purposes of seeing the call to the Church to shine. Jesus told John that the seven Golden Lampstands which he saw were the seven churches of Asia. There is no mistaking the Words of Jesus here as He interprets the symbol of the Golden Lampstand, "the seven lampstands which thou saw are the seven churches". One lampstand represented one Church. There was the lampstand of Ephesus, the lampstand of Smyrna, the lampstand of Pergamos and so forth. Each Church was represented by a lampstand.

There is no mistaking the words of the Lord. The Lampstand speaks of and points to the Church. The picture in Chapter 1 of Revelation is of Jesus standing in the midst of His churches. Jesus stands as Great High Priest in the middle of His churches. These churches are revealed in symbolic form to John as Lampstands, but Jesus tells us that these are in fact representations of His Church.

The Golden Lampstand symbolises the Church. When Jesus sees His Church, He sees a Lampstand and within that one interpretation there comes forth a wealth of truth and application for the Church. All that we have looked at from the seed that was planted regarding the Golden Lampstand in Exodus flows through scripture and finds its fulfilment here in Revelation 1:20.

In this passage from Revelation, we have seen that John was in the Spirit on the Lords day and heard a voice. As he turned, he first of all saw seven Golden Lampstands. As he focused in more intently, he began to see Jesus, standing in the midst of the Lampstands clothed in Priestley garments. The essence of what John saw here was a Tabernacle scene of the Priest attending to the Golden Lampstand performing what was known as the daily ministrations. Jesus takes this truth, one that would have been familiar to John as a Jew, and bringing this Old Testament truth through to the New Testament, interprets it for John, telling him that the Lampstands are in fact the Church and that He, Jesus, tends to them as the Great High Priest. This is the Heavenly reality of that which Moses saw in vision form. This is the fulfilment of the shadow. The Golden Lampstand speaks of the Church and Jesus stands in the midst overseeing its operation. Having seen this truth from Revelation we now consider how this truth and our overview of the Golden Lampstand relate and how they highlight the call to the Church to shine.

THE APPLICATION

The Lampstand was a vessel created with the purpose of bearing light. Its seven branches were crowned with seven lamps. These lamps were to burn continually and provide light for the area surrounding it. This aspect of the Golden Lampstand has an immediate application to the Church in terms of its call to shine. The Church is to be as the Golden Lampstand. The Church is called to be a vessel of light. That is part of its purpose and part of the image that John saw in his vision from the Lord.

As we saw in our overview of the Tabernacle of Moses, the Golden Lampstand stood in the Holy Place with the express purpose of providing light. Its core role was to shine and its ability to do so was maintained as the Priest attended to it. In Revelation we see that the Church is to shine forth and continues to do so as Jesus stands in the midst attending to the Golden Lampstands. When we understand that the Church is the interpretation of the Lampstand suddenly the truths of the Lampstand take on a new and greater significance. These are truths that we will consider in further sections. For now though, our focus is on the call to shine.

The Church is literally the fulfilment of the Golden Lampstand. The Church is an instrument of light, created according to the divine pattern of the Lord with the purpose to shine and light the environment in which it is placed. The Golden Lampstand stood upon an earthen floor in the Tabernacle of Moses and brought forth light. The Church, in our days, are God's vessels upon the earth designed with the purpose to show forth His glorious light in the areas where God has placed them.

The Call To The Church

This call of the Lampstand to the Church deepens further when we understand the role of the Lampstand and how it applies to the age that we live in. We touched on this briefly in our consideration of the call to the individual, when we looked at why Moses veiled his face. Here we will expand upon these thoughts and hopefully answer any lingering questions the reader may have had.

In our brief overview of the Tabernacle, we noted that the Tabernacle had three distinct yet related areas. The segments of the Tabernacle were the Outer Court, the Holy Place and the Most Holy Place. Each of these areas were interrelated but also clearly defined as separate and each had its own distinct furniture and entry points. As we noted earlier in our study each of these three areas had their own distinct light source. There were three areas, each with its own entry and each with its own light source. Whilst there is clear distinction between the three there is also a connection between them which is highlighted through the path of progression in the Tabernacle of Moses.

As a reminder, below is a repeat of the diagram we considered in our brief look at the Tabernacle:

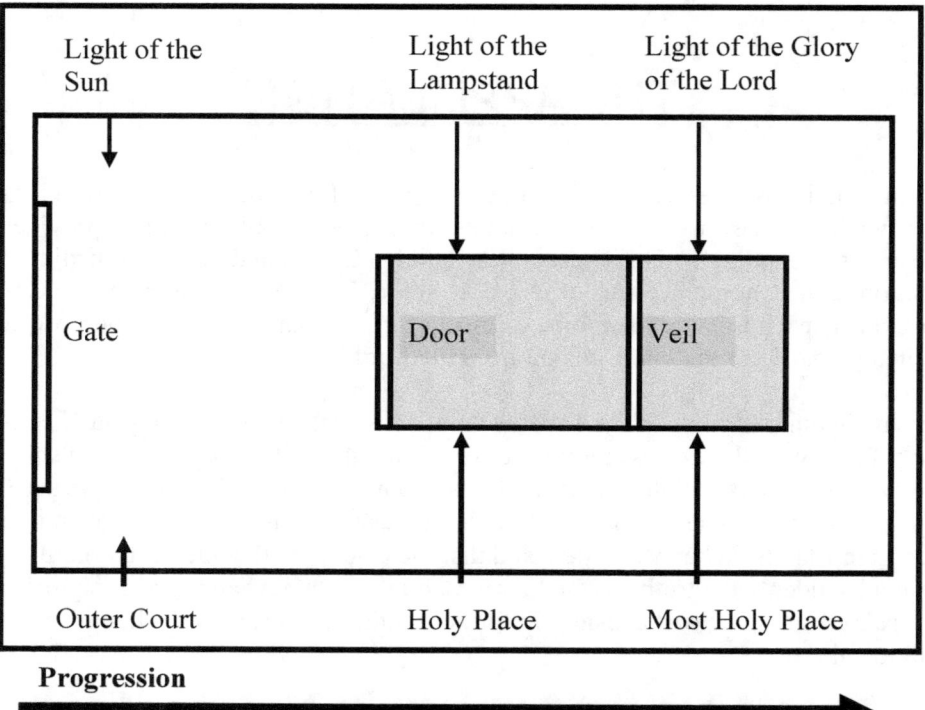

When we look at the layout of the Tabernacle of Moses in terms of its three distinct segments, it reveals a timeline in relation to God's dealing with man. The Tabernacle was not just a mere building, it sets forth prophetic truth that has application to believers and the Church of today. The three areas of the Tabernacle speak of three distinct yet related time periods that progress from Adam through to the last pages of Revelation. Just as with the Tabernacle, these time periods flow from one to the next, but each is marked by its clear entry and finishing point.

In 1 Corinthians, Paul though inspiration of the Holy Spirit says of the Old Testament writings:

> *1Co 10:11 Now all these things happened unto them for ensamples: and they are written for our admonition, upon whom the ends of the world are come.*

The truths of the Old Testament were not just for the people of that time. They carry forth prophetic truth that has application for us who live in the days of the time of the end. Gods sets forth His truth so that we might have an understanding of His call for us in the days in which we live.

As we consider the timeline that the Tabernacle reveals we will look at the Outer Court, the Most Holy Place and then finish with the Holy Place and the application to the Church. As we do this it is the writer's hope that the reader will begin to see the truth of what the Lord has set forth and the application that it has to the call to the Church to shine.

The Outer Court

The Outer Court was the first of the Tabernacle areas and it was the biggest of all Tabernacle areas. This was the first place that one would enter. It marked the beginning of the Tabernacle. It was an open area, consisting of a perimeter fence and one entry known as the door. This area was open to the elements and was illuminated by the light of the sun.

Within the outer court stood the Brazen Laver and the Brazen Altar. These two instruments were for washing and sacrifice. No one could proceed further into the Tabernacle without coming before these two items.

The Outer Court was a place of sacrifice and judgement. It was where blood was shed, and cleansing occurred. It was where Israel would come and present their offerings and sacrifices before the Lord.

The Outer Court speaks of the age of sacrifice. It is by far the biggest area and covers the largest amount of time.

When we look at the entirety of scripture, we see that sacrifice was first introduced by the Lord to man in Genesis 3:21. There we read that after the fall of man when Adam and Eve sinned by transgressing the Word of the Lord, that the Lord provided coats of skin for Adam and Eve to hide their nakedness.

> *Unto Adam also and to his wife did the LORD God make coats of skins, and clothed them.*
> *(Gen 3:21)*

The question that arises from this is where did these coats of skin come from to clothe Adam and Eve? Adam and Eve were given coats of skin by the Lord to cover their nakedness, but where did God get the skins to make the coats to cover them with? Whilst it is not absolutely stated, the answer to this, which is attested to and confirmed through the Word of God is that the coats of skin came from the death of a substitute victim. The only atonement for sin is through blood. Hebrews 9 tell us that:

> *Heb 9:22 And almost all things are by the law purged with blood; and without shedding of blood is no remission.*

Adam and Eve had sinned! They had broken the Word of God and done that which they were commanded not to. From the very beginning, at the place where sin originated in man, God set forth the truth that the only way for sin to be forgiven was through the provision of blood. In Genesis the Lord sets forth the truth to Adam and Eve of the need for sacrifice to make atonement for sin. The Lord not only presented the sacrifice for Adam and Eve, but He set forth for them the standard for how man was to interact with God. The Lord offered the sacrifice, and He took the skins from these substitute victims, those that had made atonement for Adam and Eve, and used them as a covering for them.

This need for sacrifice that was instituted at the fall of man continued right through the Old Testament until the day that Christ offered Himself as the perfect sacrifice, fulfilling all of the Old Testament types and truths and once and for all meeting the requirements of the law. The writer of Hebrews continues in Hebrews chapter 9 and says:

> *Heb 9:26 For then must he often have suffered since the foundation of the world: but now once in the end of the world hath he(Christ) appeared to put away sin by the sacrifice of himself.*

When Christ offered himself as the true Passover Lamb, He fulfilled the need for sacrifice once and for all. His sacrifice ended the need for any other sacrifice and closed off that period of God's dealing with man. Calvary completed that which was introduced in Eden. The second Adam fulfilled that which was instituted because of the first Adam.

The Outer Court speaks of the time from the fall of man where sacrifice was introduced up until the time of Christ offering Himself upon the cross of Calvary, once and for all fulfilling the requirements of the law and finishing the need for natural sacrifices to be made. This is a period of roughly four thousand years from Adam to Calvary. This was the time where sacrifice was instituted, where it was followed by the patriarchs in their worship of God, mandated under the law by God and fulfilled by Jesus. This was the Age of Sacrifice. From Adam to Christ marks the start of the Outer Court up until the entry to the Holy Place.

The Most Holy Place

The Most Holy Place is the third area of the Tabernacle, and it is the smallest of the Tabernacle areas. It was the most inner part of the Tabernacle structure and apart from Moses, the High Priest would enter this place once a year on the Great Day of Atonement. Within this area stood one piece of furniture, the Ark of the Covenant. The Ark was a wooden box overlaid with pure gold. Within the Ark were the tables of law, a jar of manna and Aaron's rod that budded. Its lid was made of pure gold and its design consisted of two cherubim's sitting atop of the lid and looking toward each other and down to the middle of the lid. This lid, whilst magnificent in design, was made of one piece of gold. Upon this lid the blood of the sacrificial victim on the Great Day of Atonement was sprinkled each year. This was a blood-stained lid.

The Ark represented the throne of God upon the earth and this lid was known as the mercy seat. It was upon this blood-stained mercy seat that the presence of the living God was enthroned when the Tabernacle was in camp. The Ark was the throne of God upon the earth.

The Most Holy Place was inhabited by the very glory of God, and it was the light of His glory that illuminated this space. The Most Holy Place was cut off from the outside light of the sun by the walls of the Tabernacle and the layers of curtains that covered its roof and sides. It was also separated from the light of the Holy Place by the curtain of the Veil. It was here that the very presence of the Lord dwelt, and it was His presence that illuminated this area.

In Revelation 19 we read of the return of our Lord Jesus Christ, known as the second coming of Jesus. It was here that John saw the Lord Jesus return riding upon His white horse. The Lord comes with the armies of Heaven, and He comes with a focus on the earth. In Revelation 20, as the vision to John continued, we go on to read that upon His return Jesus sets up His kingdom upon the earth for a set period of time.

> *Rev 20:6 Blessed and holy is he that hath part in the first resurrection: on such the second death hath no power, but they shall be priests of God and of Christ, and shall reign with him a thousand years.*

This kingdom is for those that have accepted the Lord Jesus Christ and this kingdom is set up upon the earth for a period of one thousand years. It is a kingdom age where believers will dwell in the very presence of their glorified resurrected Saviour. Believers shall be priests and they shall reign with Christ for one thousand years.

The Most Holy place points forward to this time. Just as the glory of the Lord rested upon the Ark which sat on an earthen floor in the Tabernacle of Moses so too in the coming kingdom age will the glory of God rest upon this earth for a period of time. It is here that believers will dwell in the very presence of their long awaited King. This kingdom age starts with the return of the Son of God as He ushers in His kingdom upon the earth. It is a kingdom age that will be illuminated by the presence of He who is the express image of the Lord (Heb1:3).

The Holy Place

In between the Outer Court and the Most Holy Place was the area known as the Holy Place. This was the middle part of the Tabernacle areas. The Holy Place was the first section of the Tent structure of the Tabernacle and it was double the size of the Most Holy Place. Within this area was the Golden Table of Shewbread, the Golden Lampstand and the Golden Altar of Incense. Like the Most Holy Place, the Holy Place was separated from the outside by the walls of the Tabernacle and the four curtains that formed its roof and flowed down its sides. It was further separated from the Outer Court by the curtain known as the Door and as we touched on above was separated from the Most Holy Place by the curtain known as the Veil.

The Holy Place was its own unique area. Whilst there was a clear progression in the flow of the Tabernacle, there was also clear distinction in the areas. The area of the Holy Place was clearly defined as separate to the Outer Court and the Most Holy Place. It was sheltered from the light of the sun and also concealed from the light of the glory of God. The only thing to provide light within this space was the Golden Lampstand. It was by the light of the Golden Lampstand that ministry was able to occur and without it, the area would have been bathed in darkness.

We noted above that the Outer Court represented the age of sacrifice, and this finished when Christ offered Himself at Calvary. We also noted that the Most Holy place speaks of the kingdom age and that this comes into being when Christ returns. And so we see that the Holy place is bookended by the ministry of Christ. At one end stands the ascension of Christ after His sacrifice at Calvary and at the other stands the return of Christ in His second coming. These mark the start and the end of the age that the Holy Place points to.

We also noted above that the Outer Court had the light of the sun, and the Most Holy Place had the light of the glory of God, or the light of the Son. The Holy Place though had the light of the Golden Lampstand, which as we have seen in this section is symbolic of the Church. The Holy Place speaks of the time we are in which is known as the Church age. Between the age of sacrifice and the kingdom age stands the Church age. Just like the Tabernacle, these three ages are progressive. The age of sacrifice leads to the Church age which in turn leads to the kingdom age. But just as they are progressive, they are also distinct in and of themselves. The age of sacrifice is not the Church age, and the Church age is not the kingdom age. They are three clearly distinct time frames.

This time that we as believers live in is not referred to as the Church age simply because the Church now exists. It is called the Church age because the Church as the Golden Lampstand is the only means of light in the age in which we live. The sun was for the Outer Court, while the glory of God was for the Most Holy Place. The Holy Place had the Golden Lampstand alone for light. The Church is called in this time to be the bearer of light in a world that is otherwise in darkness. Within the Holy Place there was only one means of light which stood upon the earthen floor. In this age there is only one means of light to bring clarity upon this earth, the Church. This is called the Church age because of the vital necessity for the Church to fulfil that which it has been called and predestined to do.

What we have discussed here is illustrated below:

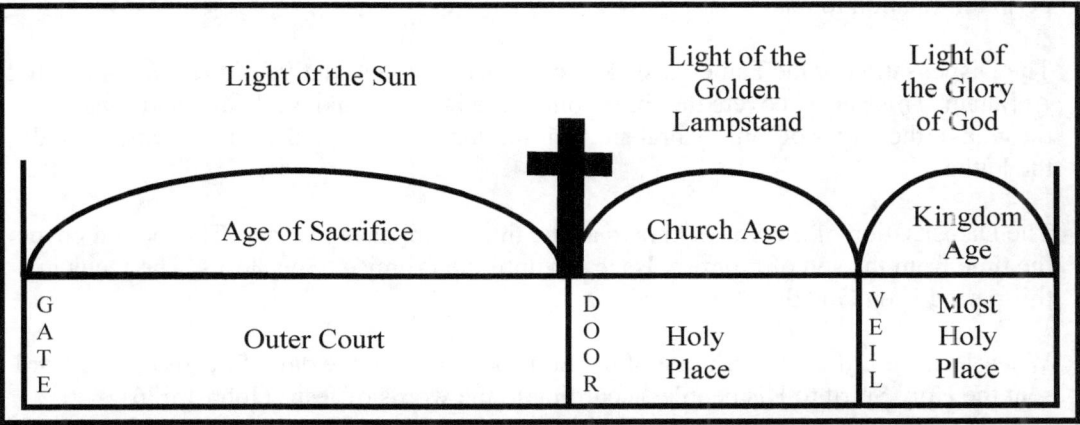

In order to further clarify our thoughts on this and again highlight to the reader the vital necessity of the Church to shine, let us consider the words of Jesus. Jesus' words here will not only further confirm the above but also add some additional thoughts for us to consider as we move forward in this study.

In John Chapter 9 Jesus says:

> *Joh 9:3-5 Jesus answered, Neither hath this man sinned, nor his parents: but that the works of God should be made manifest in him. (4) I must work the works of him that sent me, while it is day: the night cometh, when no man can work. (5)* **<u>As long as I am in the world, I am the light of the world</u>**.

The words of Jesus were that "as long as I am in the world, I am the light of the world". Jesus was indeed the light of the world. At the cross of Calvary though, we see that the Lord set forth a natural truth that had spiritual implications. As Jesus hung upon the cross the sun was darkened in the middle of the day. This not only fulfilled the truths of the Passover Lamb being killed at evening (Ex 12:6), but also set forth the truth that the light of the world was about to leave. As we have just read Jesus said, "as long as I am in the world, I am the light of the world". When Jesus died upon the cross of Calvary and shortly after ascended to Heaven the Son set. He who was the light of the world was no longer in the world.

The Call To The Church

At Calvary, when Jesus died upon the cross, not only did the light of the world set, but what is known as the period of the Dispensation of the Son ended as well. A dispensation of time is a clearly defined period with characteristics that are clearly evident. In relation to God's dealing with man, expositors of the Word put forward that there are three dispensations of time. Each of the three dispensations seen in scripture relate to a particular period of time and each dispensation is uniquely associated with one member of the God head. These distinct periods don't deny the existence or work of the other members of the Godhead, but rather they show forth the focus of each in their given time period in relation to man.

The Dispensation of the Father is spoken of as being representative of the time of Adam to Abraham. This period covers the time from the father of mankind, Adam, and runs through to the father of faith, Abraham. Within this time period there is a focus on God the Father.

The Dispensation of the Son is known as the time from Isaac to Jesus. This period covers the time from the son of promise, Isaac, up until the Promised Son, Jesus. The focus in this period is on God the Son.

When Jesus left, the Dispensation of the Son ended and on the day of Pentecost the Lord sent the Holy Spirit to His people, according to the words of Jesus (John 15:26), signifying the start of the Dispensation of the Holy Spirit. The Dispensation of the Holy Spirit runs from the cross of Calvary up until the return of Jesus. Between Christs' ascension and His return, the focus is on God the Holy Spirit. We, as New Testament believers, are in the Dispensation of the Holy Spirit. As we progress in this study, we will see how vitally connected this Church age and the Dispensation of the Holy Spirit are. The two are inseparable in terms of the call for the Church to shine. Suffice to say for now, is that the Dispensation of the Son set at Calvary as His light left this world and the Dispensation of the Holy Spirit began.

But the Son has promised to return! This happens, as we have said, at the end of the Dispensation of the Holy Spirit and Church age. When Jesus returns, we will see the Son once again rise and provide spiritual light to this world. When Christ returns the Heavens are opened and He comes forth in the fulness of His glory (Rev 19:11). The literal veil of the skies is removed as Christ proceeds from His heavenly throne room. There will be absolutely no mistaking the return of the King as the glory of the Son rises across our lands. This will be a magnificent spiritual glory that floods the earth and the universe. This will be an incredible fulfilment of the truths of the Most Holy Place as our King sits enthroned upon His earth and we bask in the glory of His presence and magnificent light.

And so we have the Son set at Calvary, the end of the Outer Court. The Son rises at the start of the Most Holy Place when our beloved Saviour returns. In between though stands the Holy Place, the Church age and the Dispensation of the Holy Spirit. The only means of light in this period is that of the Church, fulfilling the truths of the Golden Lampstand. What we see adds to our earlier discoveries and is illustrated by the diagram on the following page.

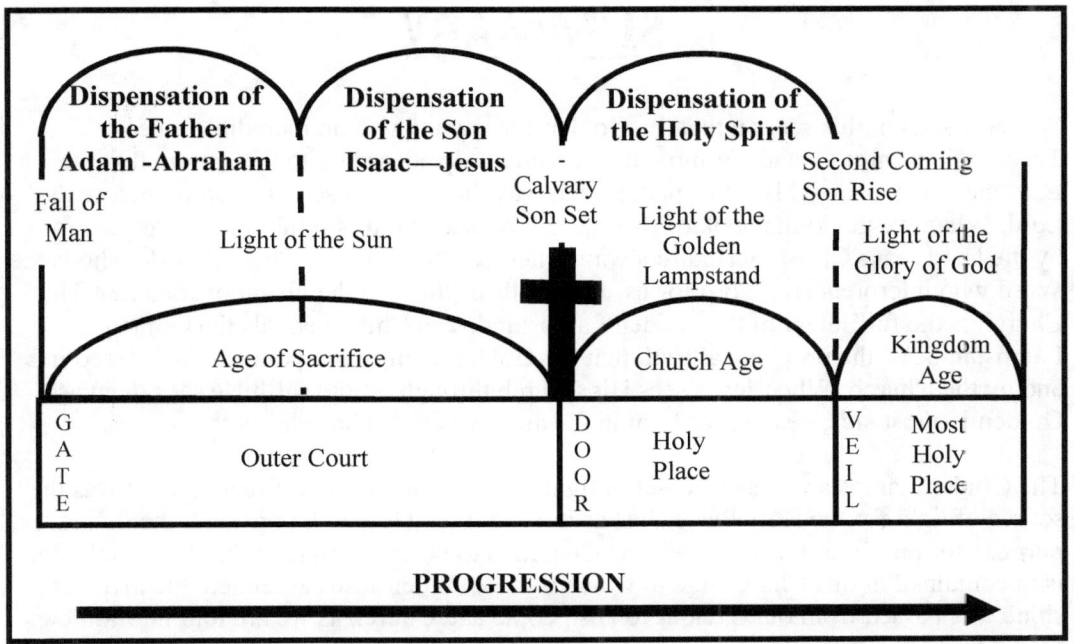

We, as New Testament believers, are living in the Church age, the Dispensation of the Holy Spirit and the time of the Golden Lampstand. It is a time where the words of Jesus In Matthew 5:14 have a pertinent application to the Church:

<u>Ye are the light of the world</u>. A city that is set on an hill cannot be hid.

The mantle of Jesus in John 9 is passed to His Church in Matthew 5. Whilst Jesus was in the world, He was the light of the world, but that role now falls to His Church. Just as the Golden Lampstand was the only means of light in the Holy Place so too is the Church the only means of light for the earth in the days in which we live. It is vital that we understand that it is not just a good thing for the Church to shine, it is a vital necessity. In this Church age in which we live, the only means of light for the world to look to is displayed through the Church. There is an onus on believers and the Church to shine forth in the days we are in. The Church was created with a far greater purpose than to just exist. It was created to shine and provide light to the environments which surround it. The Church is to bear light upon this earth. It is not to be hidden. It is not to be dimmed. The Church is to shine forth within this age with a brightness that is evident to all and fulfil the call laid upon it by our Lord and Saviour. The Church is the light of the world and if it isn't operating in this capacity then darkness is prevailing.

SUMMARY

We have seen in this section that the Golden Lampstand was an incredible piece of Tabernacle furniture, made of intricate craftsmanship according to the pattern that the Lord gave to Moses. This was a pattern that was shown to Moses as he stood before the Lord. When we get to the book of Revelation, we see that this symbol is interpreted for us by the Lord Jesus Christ. Scripture always interprets Scripture and here it is He who is the Word who interprets His Word for us. Jesus tells us through the vision of John that The Church is the fulfilment of the Golden Lampstand. The Church equals the Golden Lampstand. All the prophetical truth that the Golden Lampstand points to is fulfilled in and by the Church. When Jesus sees His Church throughout the earth He sees them as Golden Lampstands, beacons of light in the areas where He has placed them.

The Golden Lampstand was a vessel of light within its area of the Tabernacle. It was the source of light for the Holy Place. Just as it was for the Golden Lampstand, the divine purpose for the Church is to shine. The Church is to be an instrument that bears light that is uncontained in this Church age in which we live. When Jesus ascended, the mantle to shine was passed from our Saviour to His people and Church as we are told in Matthew 5:14. Until He returns the onus for the provision of light upon this earth rests with His Church.

The Call to the Church is to shine for it is that purpose unto which it was created. The Lords' design for the Church is for it to be a spiritual beacon of light for the age in which we live. It is to be that city upon the hill. If the Church is not shining forth it is not fulfilling the mandate that was laid upon it. The Church is God's vessel for light upon the earth in the days in which we live. In this Church age and this Dispensation of the Holy Spirit, the Church is called to shine. It is the only vessel of light and has been designed by the Lord to be a vessel that reflects His glory upon the earth.

Part A Summary

PART A SUMMARY

This study is based on the premise that within scripture there is a call for believers and the Church to reflect the glory of the Lord and shine in the places where God has planted them. It was in meditating upon this thought that the writer felt the Lord speak to him from 2 Kings 3. In investigating this passage, we read how the kings of Israel, Judah and Edom joined together to go out in battle against the king of Moab. Seven days into their journey, the kings found themselves in a situation where they were without water and facing the very real possibility of being defeated in battle. In desperation, they sought the Word of the Lord through the prophet Elisha. It was here that the kings received the call to dig. Within this call the Lord outlined to them the deliverance that would follow if they would be obedient unto His Word. The kings were faithful to the Word of the Lord, and they filled the valley full of ditches. On the next morning the Lord proved true to His word and miraculously filled the ditches that had been dug, as He caused water to flow from Edom. Whilst this brought immediate relief to the kings and the host, we also saw that as the sun rose and shone upon the waters of the wells, it caused a reflection which subsequently brought about the victory for the kings and their armies.

In considering all this we noted that there was a four-step process involved here. This process consisted of Digging, Infilling, Reflection and Victory. These are four consecutive steps, with each proceeding step completely dependent upon the one/ones that have preceded it.

It was from this that the Lord spoke a message to the writer, that the writer felt had application to us as believers and corporately as the Church. In considering this process we saw that the reflection is the central part or the outworking that the world saw. The digging and infilling enabled the reflection to occur. Similarly, the victory only occurred because the reflection had happened. In considering whether this passage from 2 Kings 3, and the process observed, did in fact have application to believers and the Church, we discussed that within the Word of God their must then be a call to individuals and the

Part A Summary

Church to shine. If there is a call to shine, if we are called to have the same outworking, then the process from 2 Kings 3 has application to us as believers and congregations.

The call to us as individuals is to reflect the glory of the Lord in a way that Moses never could. Because of the sacrifice of Jesus, believers now have access, as Moses did, to the Most Holy Place. The Most Holy Place is where the glory of God dwells, it is where He resides, it is His throne room. The experience for believers is to be the same as that of Moses. We have access to the very presence of God. The outworking though is different. After being in the presence of the Lord, Moses would veil his face, hiding the glory of God that had transferred upon his countenance from the world in which he lived. We though, live in the time where the Veil has been torn, as Christ died upon the cross of Calvary. Just as access has been opened for believers so too have the out workings. As believers we are to go out not as Moses did, but with unveiled faces, reflecting the glory of the Lord to the world around us. We do not cover that which God has done in us, but let it outwardly show. Through Christ the way has been made open and through Christ the Veil has been torn. As we spend time dwelling in the presence of the Lord, we receive His spiritual light. His light is literally transferred to us and rather than having it fade as did Moses, we go from glory to glory as we are transformed into the glory of God. It is with this glory that we go out into the world, shining forth as a beacon of truth. We are called to be a people who reflect His glory to the world around us. We are called to shine with a greater glory than that of Moses.

The Call to the Church is revealed to us through the Golden Lampstand. The Golden Lampstand was a vessel of light, created to shine within the Holy Place. The Golden Lampstand was the only means of light within this area and without it this part of the Tabernacle would have been in darkness. It was a vessel designed by God to fulfil a specific purpose. In the Book of Revelation we saw that the Golden Lampstand is symbolic of the Church. Like the Golden the Lampstand the Church has been created by God as a vessel of light with a purpose to fulfil. The Church is to shine forth in this Church age and Dispensation of the Holy Spirit. Within this age the Church is the only means of light and without it darkness resounds. The Church is called to stand upon this earth and shine forth. It is to be as a city on a hill, unmistakable and unmissable. The Church is to be a Lampstand upon this earth shining light in the areas where God has placed it. The Church is called to shine.

Believers are to shine forth as Moses, but with unveiled faces. The Church is to shine forth as the Golden Lampstand fulfilling that which was set forth in symbolic form. The call to shine in scripture is unmistakable and it is vital in the days in which we live. As the world gets darker and darker the need for believers and the Church to shine only grows in importance and urgency. The world needs the followers of Christ to shine. Just as natural darkness is measured by the absence of light so too is spiritual. The only way for the spiritual light to increase upon our towns, cities, states and countries is for believers and the Church to shine as brightly as they have been called to.

Both of these examples emphasise the necessity for believers to shine forth, reflecting the glory of God. These examples confirm our premise. If we stop and consider this in a little more detail though, we see that not only do these examples confirm the call to shine, all three accounts interlock and present the same truths of how shining or reflection occurs.

In 2 Kings 3, at the time of the morning sacrifice we read that as the sun was rising, the sun shone upon the waters and caused a reflection to be seen. The sun is a divinely created element and it speaks of glory, brightness, and light. It speaks of the glory of God in whose presence nothing unclean can stand. In Matthew 17 we read that on the mount of transfiguration Jesus' face did shine as the sun, such was the brightness of His glory. In the New Jerusalem there is no need of a sun because of the brightness and glory of God.

As the sun shone upon the waters that had filled the wells, the enemies of Israel saw a great shining and reflection. Here we see that the Sun was the source of the brightness and shining. The source though, shone upon the waters. The water had filled the wells that had been dug caused the glory of the sun to be reflected. Here we see that the waters acted as a vessel. The sun was the source, the waters were the vessel and as the two met, there was a reflection or shining that occurred. There was a source, there was a vessel and there was a shining forth.

With Moses we read that his face literally shone, but it had nothing to do with the man! Moses face literally reflected the glory of God. He reflected the glory of the Lord as the moon reflects the glory of the sun. As Moses spent time in the presence of the Lord, his face absorbed and reflected the glory that he stood before. In the case of Moses, the source of the glory was the Lord. It was the very presence of the Lord before whom Moses stood. Moses, and more particularly Moses' face, was the vessel used to reflect the glory of God and the vessel only. Again, there was a source, there was a vessel and there was a shining forth. It was a shining forth of the glory of God that occurred through Moses, not because of Moses.

Finally, the Golden Lampstand shone through the provision of divine fire from the Lord on the day of the dedication of the Tabernacle of Moses. Likewise, the Lampstand of the Church was lit through the provision of fire on the Great Day of Pentecost. It is the fire of the Lord that lit both the natural and spiritual Golden Lampstands. The source of the light was the divine fire of the Lord. The Golden Lampstand in the Tabernacle and its spiritual counterpart, the Church, are the vessels which carry forth the effect of the divine source. There is again a source, there is a vessel and there is a shining forth. The Lampstands role was to be a vessel to shine forth with the glory of God.

And so through these three instances we see the same truths repeated and the call confirmed. In each example considered there was a reflection or shining that occurred. Moses shone and reflected, the Golden Lampstand shone and reflected and the water of 2 Kings shone and reflected. But in each case that which reflected and shone was not the source of the light, but rather a vessel. In each instance there was a source, there was a vessel and there was an effect when these two met. The reflection and the shining occurred when the vessel and the source met. Both were required for the effect to occur.

Part A Summary

	2 KINGS 3	**MOSES**	**GOLDEN LAMPSTAND**
SOURCE	The sun Divinely created source	The Lord Divine Source	The Divine Fire of the Lord Divine Source
VESSEL	The water	Moses' Face	The Golden Lampstand
JOINT EFFECT	Reflected and shone forth with Glory of the sun	Reflected and shone forth with Glory of the Lord	Reflected and shone forth with the Glory of divine fire

In each of these three examples we see the common link of reflection. Moses' face reflected and shone the glory of God. The Golden Lampstand reflected and shone the divine fire of the Lord. The water of 2 Kings reflected and shone the glory of the sun. Each of these three examples show us what happens when the source and the vessel meet in unity. There is a reflection and shining forth of the glory of God when this occurs. It was only as the vessels connected with the source that we see the evidence of the joint effect. The vessel of itself could do nothing! They all needed the source, and it was only when the vessel and the source met that the joint effect showed forth.

And so we see through these three examples that the call to shine is not only confirmed through the Biblical standard of two or three witnesses, but all three examples also speak the one and the same truth. The outworking in each example is the same, reflecting the glory of God. The means of the outworking is also exactly the same, when the vessel and the source meet, there the reflection and shining occurs. Through these examples we see that not only is a premise confirmed, that their exists in scripture a call for believers and the Church to shine, they also highlight that the process from 2 Kings 3 has application to believers and the Church. If the outworking is the same, and the means of the outworking is the same, then the steps before and the step after that 2 Kings highlight also have application.

If we apply the full process of 2 Kings to our above examples, we see the following:

	2 KINGS 3	**MOSES**	**GOLDEN LAMPSTAND**
DIGGING	The kings and army were commanded by the Word of the Lord through Elisha to dig.	?	?
INFILLING	In the morning the Lord provided the water to fill what had been dug.	?	?

Part A Summary

REFLECTION	Reflected and Shone forth with Glory of the sun Divinely created source Vessel on earth Effect when both meet	Reflected and Shone forth with Glory of the Lord Divine Source Vessel on earth Effect when both meet	Reflected and Shone forth with the Glory of divine fire Divine Source Vessel on earth Effect when both meet
VICTORY	This brought about a great a great victory because of the previous steps being fulfilled. As the Vessels (Wells) reflected and then victory came.	?	?

The purpose of our look at 2 Kings 3 was to highlight that which the Lord put on the writer's heart. There is indeed a call for the people of God to shine and reflect the glory of God. Before we can fully do that though there are steps that we have to take in accordance with the Word of God. The three examples above show us the linkage between the source and the vessel that is needed for the shining and reflection to occur. Moses could not shine forth without the presence of God. The Lampstand couldn't shine forth without the divine fire. The water couldn't reflect without the glory of the sun. The two need to be in unison.

What we can see from above is that 2 Kings provides us with the steps that are necessary for the vessels to be ready to act as beacons of reflection. 2 Kings teaches us that before a vessel can be ready to reflect the glory of the source there must first be 1) digging and 2) an infilling that occurs. It was only upon these two steps being fulfilled prior that the sun could then reflect off the water. Just as in 2 Kings, before we as the Lord's vessels can shine, there is preparation that must be done.

Our 2 Kings passage shows us as believers how we need to prepare ourselves as individuals and churches to be ready to reflect the glory of God. The same process that we see from the account of 2 Kings applies to that of believers and the Church. For the Church to be the vessel of the Golden Lampstand it must first prepare itself. Before we as individuals can reflect the glory of God in a greater way than that of Moses, we must first prepare ourselves.

Before we can reflect His glory, we have to first be infilled. Before we can be infilled, we have to first dig. This is the process to shine, and it is only upon these things that we can then truly reflect the glory of God in the magnitude that we have been created to. In order to be ready as vessels of the Lord we must first of all dig, and then be infilled. As 2 Kings showed us, these steps are both progressive and sequential. Digging leads to infilling, infilling to reflection and so forth. One cannot be skipped for each is dependent upon the previous.

Part A Summary

It is when we do this, when we prepare ourselves to be vessels of reflection through digging and being infilled, we then experience the victory of the Lord as His light shines forth and the enemy is driven back. If we want to see spiritual victory in and around us, we have to follow the process back to the first step as revealed through the 2 Kings 3 account. We have to begin at the starting point and move forward from there. Before we are vessels ready to reflect and shine, we have to dig, and we have to be infilled.

Shining or Reflection is not something that just happens. It is a result that comes from what has been previously done by individuals and the Church. For us to shine we need not only be aware that there is a process to shining, but we must also have an understanding of what this process involves. Just as with the 2 Kings account every step was absolutely vital for the next step to occur. We cannot reflect the glory of God as we have been called to if we have not first been infilled. We cannot be infilled if we have not first dug. Our ability to fulfil the call of God to shine is directly linked to how we follow the steps that His Word outlines for us. If we are truly going to be the light bearers individually and corporately that our world so desperately needs, then we need to be following the process for how this occurs.

As we move forward in our next sections, we will continue to build upon the truths we have laid out here and as we do so we will see how we fulfil this wonderful call of the Lord to Shine. When we, as believers and churches, reflect His glory we shine as vessels of light upon this earth. Shining isn't something that just happens. In the natural we have the ability to turn lights on and off with the flick of a switch. With a click the light is on and with a click the light is off. In the spiritual though the process to turn a light on is not as simple. Rather than a simple click, there is a process involved in turning on spiritual lights individually and as a Church. This brings us to our next section. Having seen that we are indeed called to shine and reflect His glory, we now consider how we do this in light of what we learned in 2 Kings 3. It is as we gain an understanding of these four stages that we can begin the process to shine as we have been called to.

We are indeed called to shine. We are called to shine as individuals and churches to the world around us. We are called to be vessels and reflect His glory. We have seen how our premise has been confirmed by the Word of God. In the mouth of two or three witnesses this has been established. In doing that we have seen how our account from 2 Kings 3 and our two examples interlock and speak one and the same truth. We are called to shine and there is a process that enables this to happen. Having established our premise, we now move into our next section where we consider the process to shine.

PART B
THE
PROCESS

PART B INTRODUCTION

In the first section of this study, we spent time investigating and establishing that within scripture there exists a call for believers individually and corporately, as the Church, to shine. This "shining" involves believers being as spiritual light in a world that is otherwise in darkness. Believers are to stand out as beacons of light and be noticeably different in the areas where God has placed them.

Having established the call to shine, we now turn our attention to the process of how this occurs. In our looks at 2 Kings 3 we noted that there was a four-step process centred around the reflection or shining that occurred. As a reminder these stages were Digging, Infilling, Reflection and Victory.

As we considered these, and the message that the Lord placed on the writer's heart, we noted how each of these stages were sequential, with each subsequent stage utterly dependent upon the one the preceded it. Victory was based upon the reflection occurring, without the reflection there was no victory. The reflection though, could only occur because the wells had been infilled with water. The infilling could only occur because the kings and their armies where faithful to the Word of the Lord and dug the valley full of ditches. Each resultant step was completely dependent upon the one/ones before it.

Whilst we have seen how these stages related to the kings and their armies in 2 Kings 3, our purpose here is to see the application that they have to us as individuals and corporately as the Church. We have seen how reflection or shining ties all that we have looked at together, but our Kings account shows us that there are steps that precede and follow this. Having investigated our premise, we now focus in on investigating the process.

As individuals, if we are to shine with a greater glory than that of Moses, we need to understand how this occurs. Corporately, if His Church is truly going to shine forth as a Golden Lampstand, then we need to understand how this occurs. This is an understanding

Part B Introduction

that can only come through examining the Word of God and seeing the truth that is contained within it regarding this call. We can only ever truly shine forth when we have a scriptural understanding of how this occurs.

The purpose of this section is to do just that. As we go through and examine His Word, we will see that the Lord has laid out in scripture for us just how we are to fulfil this call. God is ever faithful and His Word inexhaustible. The Lord not only calls us to shine, He also equips us with the understanding and teaching to enable us to fulfil that call. As we consider this process from 2 Kings 3, we will see how it is confirmed through the Word of God, how it applies and what it means to us as individuals and corporately as the Church.

DIGGING

And he said, Thus saith the LORD, Make this valley full of ditches.(2Ki 3:16)

In this section we will consider the thought of digging as seen from the 2 Kings 3 account. We will spend some time here considering just what digging is and what we can learn from 2 Kings 3 before then moving on to see its spiritual application to individuals and the Church.

Digging is the first step of the process that we see revealed in our previous section. In their time of desperation, the kings sought the Word of the Lord through the prophet Elisha, and the Lord's hand of intervention in their situation and upcoming battle. The response that came from the Lord to them started with a responsibility of action on the part of man in the form of digging. As a reminder, at the time the kings and armies of Israel were called to dig, they were seven days into a journey, heading to battle and had run out of water. The men would have been exhausted and lacking strength and yet the call of the Lord through Elisha was for them to dig. These were armed men, probably not equipped to fill a valley full of ditches. They were more likely to be carrying swords, shields and spears rather than shovels and picks. The Lord wasn't interested in what they did or didn't have though. The focus of the Lord was not on how they were feeling. The Lord was going to provide what they needed in more ways than they could realise, but for this to occur they first of all had to dig.

As we learned from 2 Kings 3, the digging had to occur before the infilling and subsequent reflection could occur. Each step was absolutely reliant on the one before it. We cannot shine if we have not been infilled and we cannot be infilled if we haven't dug. Digging is really the foundation for the whole process. It is from this foundation that the proceeding steps build off.

Our purpose here is to look at just how we as believers and congregations need to dig so that we might be ready for the infilling of the Lord and then be able to reflect His glory.

Our call is to shine but this cannot be fulfilled if the steps prior to this have not been achieved. Digging is essential as it prepares us to be able to receive the fulness of infilling that the Lord has for us. Just as with the 2 Kings 3 account, it is the part of the process that is the responsibility of man and is one that plays a pivotal part in our ability to shine. The only way that we can truly fulfil the call to shine is by first of all digging.

The reader is encouraged to keep in mind throughout this section that digging is the first step of the process that allows us to shine. Shining is our purpose and our end goal but digging is the starting point for us to be able to fulfil this call.

WHAT IS DIGGING?

Digging can simply be defined as the act that allows infilling to occur. This is evidenced through the account of 2 Kings 3 and as we progress we will see how that same truth applies to believers.

When we consider the task that the armies of Israel undertook in 2 Kings 3 and what the task of digging in the natural actually involves, we can observe a number of things that have a spiritual application to us as believers. Throughout the Bible, the Lord will often speak spiritual truths to man through natural experiences (1 Cor 15:46). This is the case here. The actions of the armies and kings speak a number of truths that have a spiritual application to us as believers.

As we progress beyond this section on digging, these points will hopefully begin to take on a greater significance in the mind of the reader. Whilst these may seem simple and obvious, we must keep in mind that the responsibility for digging, as in 2 Kings 3, lays solely upon man.

In breaking down digging, in light of the 2 Kings 3 account, the following points can be observed.

A. Digging is a Choice

   When the prophet Elisha spoke the Word of the Lord to the united kings, the kings had a choice to make. It was a choice to act in faith and have their men dig or a choice to dismiss the words of the prophet as nonsense. We need to remember that these three kings were returning to their armies, who were in a state of desperation for water. They were not coming back with an immediate solution to the problem at hand! They were bringing back an answer from the Lord that required the armies to give more of what little strength they had left. Rather than an answer, the kings were returning with a task. The easy option would have been to dismiss the Word of the Lord through Elisha. This is especially true when we remember the fact that Jehoshaphat was the only God fearing king among the group. The other two kings had little to no relationship with the Lord. In response to the Word of the Lord the kings had the choice to dig or not to dig.

Likewise, the men of the armies had a choice to make. Would they obey the command of their kings and in obedience dig, or would they refuse, failing to see any wisdom in the edicts of their leaders? In every respect, the message the kings brought back made absolutely no sense. The problem before the kings and their armies was not a lack of holes in the ground, it was a lack of water! From a natural standpoint they didn't need wells. They didn't need a supply of water that had the capacity to sustain them for an extended period, what they needed was a supply of water to get them out of the jam they were in and rejuvenate them. Digging the valley full of ditches made no sense. It made no sense in regard to receiving water and it made no sense for them to exert themselves before an impending battle. The men of the armies had a choice. They had a choice to dig or not to dig.

Digging, as with any decision that man makes, starts with a choice. We can be asked to dig, we can be told over and over about the benefits of digging, we can even see the need to dig but in the end, we alone can make the choice to dig. It is a choice that rests with each and every individual and Church. It is the same choice that rested with the kings and their armies. We can choose to dig or we can choose not to dig. Digging is a choice and likewise not digging is also a choice. They are choices that we alone as individuals choose to make. We cannot blame anyone else or pass that decision off, it is our choice and our choice alone. The choice is the responsibility of each individual.

B. Digging is an Action

Holes don't just get dug and they certainly don't dig themselves. They require action on the part of man. In the example of 2 Kings 3 this was the only action laid upon man in the miracle that God was going to work. The armies of Israel had to dig. They didn't have to fetch the water, they didn't have to fill the holes with water, but they had to dig the wells. It was an action laid upon the people to fulfil. It required them to stop what they were doing and physically fulfil that which the Lord had called them to do.

The decision to dig starts with a choice, but the evidence of the choice is seen through the action that is taken. If no action follows a decision, then the decision is in vain. It remains as a good thought but nothing more. It is only when man responds to his decision and puts effort into seeing it fulfilled through action that we see the results of a decision.

Digging takes action. A decision is required, but action must follow. Action requires effort on the part of man to see the decision realised. Action ratifies a choice.

Digging

C. Digging takes Time

   To dig a hole requires an investment of time. It is a task that only occurs as time is dedicated to it. It is a cost that the digger has to be willing to pay. The harder the ground the more time it takes. The bigger the hole the more time it takes. Other things which may be preferential to the individual have to be put off so that the required time can be dedicated to the task of digging. For the armies of Israel, the time that they would have been resting and preparing for battle needed to be invested in the task of digging. This in the natural made no sense. They had to sacrifice 'their time' in order to fulfil that which the Lord was asking them too.

   To dig takes an investment of time that the person digging must be willing to sacrifice. It requires the giving up of other priorities and desires in order to see the goal achieved. Man has to be willing to invest his time in the process of digging. It is an investment in God's ways and not necessarily in the things that we want to be doing. It is sacrificing our time to dedicate it unto His purposes.

D. Digging takes Effort

   Digging is not an easy task. It takes effort and it requires strength. And as with time, the bigger the hole and the harder the ground the greater the expenditure of effort and energy.

   To dig requires man to expend his strength. This was the conundrum that faced the kings and the armies of Israel. Why would the Lord have them use their effort and energy on digging rather than preserving it for the coming battle? Theirs was not to question though, theirs was to trust and to focus their effort on that which had been commanded of them by the Lord.

   Digging is going to require our strength, especially in those times when we feel like we are in a weakened state, as the armies of Israel were. It is through these times that perhaps a greater effort is required to maintain that which we have set our minds to. Digging requires an effort mentally, spiritually and physically. It requires man to commit his strength to the task at hand. It is not something that will always be easy, though there may be times when it will be. It is not something that we will always feel like doing, though there will be times when it will be. Digging takes continual effort no matter the state we find ourselves in. It takes a continual application of our strength, even when we are in a weakened state, when it's not easy and when we don't feel like doing it.

E. Digging requires Endurance

   There comes a point in digging any hole where the digger needs a break or is ready to give up. At a certain point the ground becomes too hard, or the digger feels like they have expended too much energy. To continue to dig when these points are reached requires endurance. It requires pushing through the pain and exhaustion. It requires ignoring the distractions. It requires staying focused on the task at hand and continuing in it.

For the armies of Israel, their endurance was evidenced through what they dug. They did not simply dig one hole, they filled the valley full of ditches. They continued digging and digging and digging until that which the Lord had commanded had been fulfilled. Their job was to fill the valley full of ditches and they didn't stop until this was achieved.

For believers, as we will see as we progress, our call is to perpetually dig. We are to dig and dig and dig. Our lives are to be full of ditches that allow the Lord to pour the fulness of His blessing in. When we are tired, when other "priorities" come up, when other tasks seem more important, we cannot afford to neglect that which we have been called to do, to dig. We need endurance to fulfil the call.

F. Digging involves Repetition

Digging is not a complicated task. It is essentially one action repeated over and over until the hole is dug. The shovel goes in, lifts the soil out and dumps it to the side. Then the shovel goes in again and the action is repeated.

Digging for believers is also not a complicated thing. As we will see, it involves a few simple actions repeated over and over again until the hole is dug. The caution for believers though, is to not allow repetition to turn into tradition. We dig because the Lord has commanded us to so that we may fulfil the call to shine. We are to ever keep our eyes on the call of the Lord and the promise He gives regarding what happens when we are faithful in our digging. It may be repetitious but digging is life giving. If our eyes remain transfixed on why we are digging and not the act of digging, then we avoid the trap of falling into tradition.

G. Digging requires Maintenance

For the kings and armies of Israel the holes that they dug had a very short-term focus. They provided almost immediate relief and victory. There was no real follow up or maintenance required.

For any holes or wells to stand the test of time though, they need to be maintained. Overtime edges collapse and the soil that falls in starts to fill the well if they are neglected. In order for that which has been dug to stand the test of time, it needs the continual attention of the person who dug it.

For believers digging is not a once off event. That which the Lord calls us to dig, we are to maintain and ensure that the holes we have dug stand the test of time. Our call is not only to dig the wells, but also to maintain them.

H. Digging requires Faith

   The whole act of digging for the kings and the armies of Israel was a matter of faith. It was trusting the call of the Lord and trusting that He would fulfil that which He said He would. In the natural it made absolutely no sense. It always takes faith to look beyond the natural.

   For believers the call to dig takes the same faith. We need to have an unwavering trust in the Lord and in His Word that we are called to dig so that we might spiritually shine. It takes faith to believe that that which is being invested in will allow the Lord to achieve His will. It takes faith to set aside what we believe needs to be done and what we believe needs to happen and trust in the Lord, that His way is higher. It is a faith act to take the Lord at His Word. Whilst digging may seem like such a simple action, it takes faith to believe that the simple can achieve great things. Sometimes it takes more faith to believe in the small things. God has a habit of using the foolish things of the world to confound the wise, we just have to believe Him for it.

As believers, the lessons from 2 Kings 3 have an application to us on a spiritual level. We are unmistakably called to shine, and in order for us to do this we have to start with the act of digging. Digging is a choice that requires action, time, effort and endurance. It requires repetition, maintenance and faith. These are all aspects that we as believers need to apply when we dig spiritually. Digging is not a relaxing activity, and neither is it one that can be ignored. Digging carries with it a great spiritual weight and it is something we need to have a greater appreciation for and understanding of. As believers and churches, we need to understand the importance that digging has in regard to our spiritual lives and walks.

WHERE DO WE DIG?

So far from 2 Kings 3 we have seen that digging is necessary for infilling and the subsequent reflection that occurs. We have also considered a breakdown of what digging actually involves. The question that remains though, is just how or where do we spiritually dig? It is one thing to understand what digging is and what it involves, but this is all in vain and of little use if we don't know where or how to dig spiritually.

When individuals would dig for wells, their purpose was to find water so that the well would fill. The purpose was to not dig a hole, the purpose was to dig a well that would be filled. Likewise, spiritually we do not want to be digging in vain. We don't want empty holes! We want to tap into spiritual reservoirs that allow a spiritual flow that fills us beyond measure.

The purpose in this section is to take the truths of digging that we have discovered so far and highlight to the reader where these are to be applied. God's desire is to see us filled to overflowing, but for that to happen we have to dig in the places where He has called us to dig.

If we remember from the 2 Kings 3 account, the Lord was very specific to the kings in regard to where they were to dig.

*And he said, Thus saith the LORD, Make **this valley** full of ditches. (2Ki 3:16)*

The Lord clearly instructed the kings where to dig! It was not a case of dig some holes anywhere you like! The Word of the Lord was to make **this valley** full of ditches. The Lord instructed them exactly where they were to dig. It was this designated place of the Lord that would not only allow for the infilling of the people but would also see the defeat of the enemy. The place the Lord told them to dig was strategic and it was for the ultimate benefit of the people of Israel. The Lord was telling them where to dig so that the infilling could and would occur. He didn't want them digging in vain, He wanted them to dig strategically. The promise of infilling required them to dig where the Lord had told them to.

Likewise, the Lord, through His Word, has given us, spiritual Israel, very specific places to dig. The Lord does not want us digging in vain. Through His Word the Lord reveals to man where he is to dig if he wants to receive the fulness of infilling that the Lord has for him. Just as the kings were told where to dig, so too are we. In the coming pages we are going to investigate just where these are so that we likewise may dig in the strategic places of the Lord and receive His infilling and the subsequent victory for our lands. To discover where these are, we are going to turn to the book of Zechariah and examine a vision given to Zechariah by the Lord. It is a vision that reveals much truth that is applicable to New Testament believers and the Church today. We will start by looking at the vision itself and then break it down to consider its interpretation and the application that it has to us.

The Vision

The book of Zechariah covers a period of approximately forty years, between roughly 520BC and 480BC. It was written to the Kingdom of Judah after their Babylonian captivity and according to some expositors, has more Messianic predictions than any other of the minor prophetical books.

Our particular focus in this section is on Zechariah Chapter 4. In this chapter Zechariah received a prophetic vision from the Lord and also a prophetic word for an individual. These are two distinctions that the reader must keep in mind as they read over Zechariah 4. Confusion can sometimes come as the prophetic word comes in the midst of the vision. As we read over Zechariah Chapter 4, we start with the vision, we then move into a prophetic word for an individual, before returning again to the vision. It is important that we grasp this distinction.

Zechariah 4:1-5	Prophetic Vision
Zechariah 4:6-10	Prophetic Word for an Individual
Zechariah 4:11-14	Prophetic Vison

Zechariah 4 starts with the vision of the Golden Lampstand. Symbolically within this chapter, there was truth that Zechariah would understand. The Golden Lampstand is undeniably linked to the Temple, and Zechariah would have had an understanding of not only the Lampstand but also its function within the Tabernacle/Temple system. From this vision of Zechariah there came a word of encouragement to Zerubbabel to continue in the work he was undertaking despite the opposition he was facing. Zerubbabel was in the midst of overseeing the rebuild of the temple. At the time of the prophetic word there was no Temple, and the Golden Lampstand was not in operation. The prophetic word Zerubbabel received from the Lord was encouraging him to continue in this endeavour. The Lampstand in operation, as seen in the vision of Zechariah, was a word of confirmation to Zerubbabel. This was a truth to Zerubbabel, but it wasn't the fulness of truth that the vision spoke of. The Lord used the image of the Golden Lampstand to speak a word to Zerubbabel, but within the vision itself is truth that goes beyond Zerubbabel.

A similar thing is seen in Jeremiah Chapter 1, where Jeremiah is debating with the Lord about being chosen as His vessel. In response to this the Lord gave Jeremiah a vision and asked him what he saw. Jeremiah responded that he saw the rod of an almond tree. Other translations interpret this as a branch of an almond tree. The question to ask here is how did Jeremiah know the branch was from an almond tree? What made it so distinct that Jeremiah could immediately recognise what sort of tree that the branch came from? There must have been an evidence of fruit and/or flower to show this truth and allow Jeremiah to distinguish it from branches that came from other trees. The image Jeremiah saw was of an almond branch that had blossomed and brought forth fruit. This image was a reference back to the rod of Aaron which the Lord used to signify the choice of Aaron as His representative from amongst all Israel. The reader is encouraged to read Numbers 17 for fuller details on this. Being an Israelite, Jeremiah would have understood the significance of this rod, what it had meant to Aaron and what the Lord was saying to him. The Lord used that rod to speak a truth to Jeremiah, but it wasn't the fulness of truth concerning the rod. The revelation given to Jeremiah didn't contain the fulness of truth that the Word reveals about Aarons rod that budded. The Lord used the rod to highlight to Jeremiah that he had been chosen by the Lord to be His representative to and for the people, just as He had previously chosen Aaron. But the Word to Jeremiah was not the fulness of truth that the rod of Aaron reveals.

Such is the case in the vision given to Zechariah that we are considering. The vision of Zechariah contains more truth than that which is applied to Zerubbabel. The vision showed the Golden Lampstand in operation which the Lord used to give a Word of confirmation to Zerubbabel that he should continue in the work he was doing to rebuild the temple. The vision showed a Golden Lampstand functioning which only occurs when the temple is functioning. This was the encouragement to Zerubbabel. That which he was undertaking would be achieved, despite the opposition he was facing.

The vision though speaks of more than just a Golden Lampstand in operation, it showed how the Golden Lampstand operated. It is when we consider this vision of Zechariah in the light of the entirety of scripture that we begin to see the fulness contained within the vision. As we let scripture interpret scripture, we start to understand just what the Lord was showing Zechariah. The vision was of a Golden Lampstand in operation, that was confirmation. The fulness of the vision though and how the Golden Lampstand operated contains truth relevant to the believers and the Church today.

Our focus for this section is going to be specifically on that which applies to the Church from Zechariah 4. This is covered in verses 1-5 and 11-14, as detailed in the table above. The reader is encouraged to read over these passages several times before moving forward here. For our purposes here, we will break down each verse to clarify exactly what the Lord was showing to Zechariah, so that we have a clear understanding of the vision before considering its interpretation and application. In doing this, we will seek to lay out all the pieces of the puzzle for the readers' consideration. As we look at the interpretation and application, we will bring the pieces together and let them naturally fit as the Word of God shows us. We will not force or manipulate the pieces to fit. As we do this, we will see the fulness of the picture as revealed to Zechariah.

For now, though, let us consider just what Zechariah saw.

And the angel that talked with me came again, and waked me, as a man that is wakened out of his sleep, (Zec 4:1)

Chapter 4 starts with Zechariah stating that an angel came and woke him. The indication from scripture here is that this was not the first visit this angel had paid to Zechariah. Zechariahs' words here are that the angel came again. This was an angel that we read originally appeared to Zechariah in Chapter 1.

It should be noted here that the Hebrew word for angel, as used here, means a messenger, specifically of God. This word can mean angel, prophet, priest or teacher. It is the context of scripture that indicates the interpretation for us. From the context of Zechariah, it appears that this angel, was a messenger of God that repeatedly appeared to Zechariah and was linked to the giving and interpreting of what the Lord was showing and speaking to Zechariah.

Here the angel came and stirred Zechariah as a man is wakened out of his sleep. Notice the language used here. Zechariah is trying to explain what he experienced by using comparative language. Zechariah wasn't actually woken but was stirred by the angel to see the vision that God was revealing to him. Paul experienced something similar as detailed in second Corinthians:

> *I knew a man in Christ above fourteen years ago, (whether in the body, I cannot tell; or whether out of the body, I cannot tell: God knoweth;) such an one caught up to the third heaven. And I knew such a man, (whether in the body, or out of the body, I cannot tell: God knoweth;) How that he was caught up into paradise, and heard unspeakable words, which it is not lawful for a man to utter. (2Co 12:2-4)*

There is such a realness to what some individuals experience that it is hard to quantify as to whether they are in a dream or in reality. This is what Paul experienced and it is the writer's belief that this is what Zechariah experienced. He received a revelation from the

Lord in the Spirit that was so tangible it was hard to qualify whether he was awake or seeing a vision.

And said unto me, What seest thou? And I said, I have looked, and behold a candlestick all of gold, with a bowl upon the top of it, and his seven lamps thereon, and seven pipes to the seven lamps, which are upon the top thereof: (Zec 4:2)

As Zechariah was stirred by the angel, he was posed with a question, what do you see? This was the same question posed to both Jeremiah and Amos when the Lord was showing them things in the spiritual (Jer 1:11, Jer 1:13, Jer 24:3, Amos 8:2).

From Zechariah's response it is clear that he was seeing a vision from the Lord. Zechariah stated that he saw a Candlestick (Lampstand) all of gold with it seven branches and seven lamps. Sitting above the Golden Lampstand was a Bowl. Connecting the Bowl to the Lampstand were seven Pipes. The seven pipes were connected to the Bowl and each pipe ran from the Bowl to one of the seven lamps upon the Golden Lampstand.

What we see here is a vision of gold. Gold speaks of kingship, God, the divine nature. Here we see the Golden Lampstand. We see here a Holy Place scene. All pieces of furniture and all utensils within the Holy Place were made of gold. Though it is not explicitly stated the Bowl and the seven pipes mentioned here are undoubtedly gold as well. There could not be an inferior substance used for the Bowl or used for the Pipes which connect the Bowl to the Golden Lampstand. This is something that we will consider more fully later on.

It should also be noted that in verse 12 we read of two more pipes where it is explicitly mentioned that they are gold. The information given there confirms our thought that the pipes in verse 2 are undoubtedly gold as well.

As we progress this point should become clearer to the reader. For now though, what we see is a Golden Lampstand with a Bowl above it and seven pipes connecting the Bowl to the seven lamps of the Golden Lampstand.

And two olive trees by it, one upon the right side of the bowl, and the other upon the left side thereof. (Zec 4:3)

Zechariah continues describing what he saw. Beside the Golden Bowl there were two olive trees, one on the right side of the Bowl and one upon the left side of the Bowl. Again, it may be asked how did Zechariah know that they were olive trees? They must have had the shape of an olive tree and possibly the fruit for Zechariah to be so sure that they were olive trees. There must have been distinctive qualities for Zechariah to readily identify these two trees as olive trees.

So I answered and spake to the angel that talked with me, saying, What are these, my lord? Then the angel that talked with me answered and said unto me, Knowest thou not what these be? And I said, No, my lord. (Zec 4:4-5)

Zechariah was being shown something by the Lord, but he didn't have a full understanding of what he was seeing. He responded to the angel who had asked him what do you see, but now turns the question back. This is what I have seen, but what does it mean? The angel though doesn't answer. The angel turns the question back to Zechariah essentially asking, don't you know what this means?

One has to admire the honesty of Zechariah here. Rather than being caught in pride and feigning that he had some idea, he answers honestly, "no I don't know what these are". How often do we get afraid of not knowing the right answer or being found out? How often do we try and make out we have an understanding of something, when the reality is we don't? Zechariah here openly and honestly admits his lack of understanding and his need of an explanation. Such shows the humility of the man and his genuine desire to grow in understanding.

It was here that the angel revealed his word of encouragement to Zerubbabel which we have discussed in our opening comments. We will jump from here down to verse 11 of Zechariah 4 to continue our consideration of the vision.

Then answered I, and said unto him, What are these two olive trees upon the right side of the candlestick and upon the left side thereof? (Zec 4:11)

Zechariah picks straight up where he had left off. He was not letting go of this question and he was not satisfied with the answer he was given in verse 5. Zechariah spoke up and again prompted the angel as to the meaning of the two olive trees upon the right side and left side of the Golden Lampstand. Zechariah was as Jacob when he wrestled for a blessing from the angel and wouldn't let go. Zechariah, as the persistent widow, keeps asking until he got an answer.

In verse 3 we are told that the two olive trees stand upon the right and left of the Golden Bowl. Here we are told that the olive trees stand upon the right and left of the Golden Lampstand. Such is not a contradiction, but highlights the fact that the Golden Bowl and the Golden Lampstand are connected. The Golden Bowl sits immediately above the Golden Lampstand and is connected to it by seven Golden Pipes. The Golden Bowl and the Golden Lampstand are as one part of the vision. The two olive trees stand upon the right and left of this. When Zechariah said that they are standing on the right and left of the Golden Bowl, and the right and left of the Golden Lampstand, he was saying one and the same thing.

And I answered again, and said unto him, What be these two olive branches which through the two Golden Pipes empty the Golden Oil out of themselves? (Zec 4:12)

It would seem from reading this verse that Zechariah was possibly still considering the vision, or even looking at it closer, as within this verse we are provided with some new information.

Zechariah again asked the angel what the meaning of the two olive trees was. This was a part of the vision that Zechariah didn't fully comprehend. He could see that these two olive branches or olive trees emptied Golden Oil out of themselves, but that didn't make sense. Whilst not making sense to Zechariah, the description he gives us here provides us with more insight into the vision that he saw.

In verse 3 we are simply told that Zechariah saw two olive trees, one standing upon the right side of the bowl and the other on the left. In our current verse we are given more detail regarding this. Here Zechariah tells us that these two olive trees are connected to two Golden Pipes. It is through these Golden Pipes that the olive oil pours out. But where does this oil pour out into? To answer that let us recap what we have discovered so far.

What we have seen that in the vision is there is a Golden Lampstand with seven Golden Pipes. This is undeniably the same Golden Lampstand that was featured in the Tabernacle of Moses and the same Golden Lampstand that flows through the Word of God. Above the Golden Lampstand is a Golden Bowl. Connecting the Golden Bowl to the Golden Lampstand are seven Golden Pipes. The first question we have to ask is what purpose do the Golden Bowl and pipes play? In order for the Golden Lampstand to continually shine it needed a continual supply of oil. As we have already discovered, the priest would supply this pure olive oil daily so that it would continually shine. In this vision of Zechariah we see the means of that occurring. Gold always speaks of the divine, God, that which is completely pure. Gold was used exclusively for all vessels of the Holy Place, including those of the Golden Lampstand. The Golden Bowl speaks of the source of oil, and it provides this to the Golden Lampstand through each of the seven pipes. It is an image of flow. There is one source supplying each of the seven lamps of the Lampstand. Seven channels, but always one source. Each channel received the same oil from the same Golden Bowl and each channel was absolutely necessary for the Golden Lampstand to receive the fulness of oil it needed to operate as it was designed to.

The second question that follows on from this is where does this oil come from that flows from the bowl to the Golden Lampstand? The answer to this also answers our earlier question of where does the oil from the olive trees pour into? It is this verse of Zechariah that provides us with our answer.

The two olive trees are the source of oil. The two olive trees stand upon the right and left of the Golden Bowl and the Golden Lampstand, and they pour their oil out through the two Golden Pipes. These Golden Pipes pour the Golden Oil into the Golden Bowl. As we have already seen, the lamps of the Golden Lampstand which require the oil to shine are already supplied by the seven Golden Pipes from the Golden Bowl. The two pipes in question here would be superfluous if they were also to supply to the Golden Lampstand. The Golden Lampstand already has a pipe going to each lamp, it does not need any more. Further to this there is no way that the two pipes in this verse could equally supply each of the seven lamps. Seven is not divisible by two!

The supply of oil to the Golden Lampstand has already been established. The two olive trees, through the two Golden Pipes pour their oil into the Golden Bowl. The olive tree on the left pours oil out through its pipe into the Golden Bowl. Likewise, the olive tree on the right pours out its oil into the Golden Bowl through its pipe. What we see here is the complete picture of flow. The oil flows from the trees to the bowl, from the bowl to the pipes and from the pipes to the lamps of the Golden Lampstand. Such answers our question of where does the oil pour out?

The two olives trees are connected to the Golden Bowl by two Golden Pipes. The olive trees do not merely stand either side they are connected to the Golden Bowl. Further to this there is a transference that occurs! From the two olive trees flows a Golden Oil. The words of Zechariah are that the two olive trees empty the Golden Oil out of themselves through the Golden Pipes. The two olive trees are connected to the Golden Bowl by Golden Pipes and through these pipes they supply oil to the Golden Bowl.

And he answered me and said, Knowest thou not what these be? And I said, No, my lord. (Zec 4:13)

One has to again admire the honesty of Zechariah here. He is not bound in religious pride, and answers honestly, desiring to know the answer. These two olive trees were something that he did not comprehend. Even though more was revealed to Zechariah as he focused in on the vision, he still lacked an understanding of the two olive trees.

Then said he, These are the two anointed ones, that stand by the Lord of the whole earth. (Zec 4:14)

The angel answers Zechariah and explained that the two olive trees are the two anointed ones that stand by the Lord of the whole earth. Notice the definitive language used here, these are the two anointed ones, and they stand by the Lord of the whole earth. It is short and to the point as the angel interprets and gives understanding to Zechariah.

In this short chapter of Zechariah we have seen that Zechariah was stirred and received a vision from the Lord. In the vision, Zechariah saw a Golden Lampstand with seven lamps upon it. This is the Golden Lampstand of the Temple, the Golden Lampstand that was first introduced in the Tabernacle of Moses. Above the Golden Lampstand is a Golden Bowl. It is above the Golden Lampstand. From the Golden Bowl extend seven Golden Pipes, one to each lamp of the Lampstand. There is the Golden Bowl, then the Golden Pipes and then the Golden Lampstand.

On either side of the Golden Bowl and the Golden Lampstand, on the right and the left, was an olive tree. One on each side. From the olive trees extended two Golden Pipes and it was through these that they poured out their Golden Oil. The olive trees connected to the Golden Bowl through two Golden Pipes, and it is from these that they emptied themselves of oil into the Golden Bowl. It is a vision of flow that Zechariah received. From the trees to the Golden Bowl and from the Golden Bowl to the Golden Lampstand. Whilst there was a word of the Lord to Zerubbabel contained in this vision, this vision has far more prophetic truth which we will discover shortly.

A representation of what Zechariah saw can be seen below:

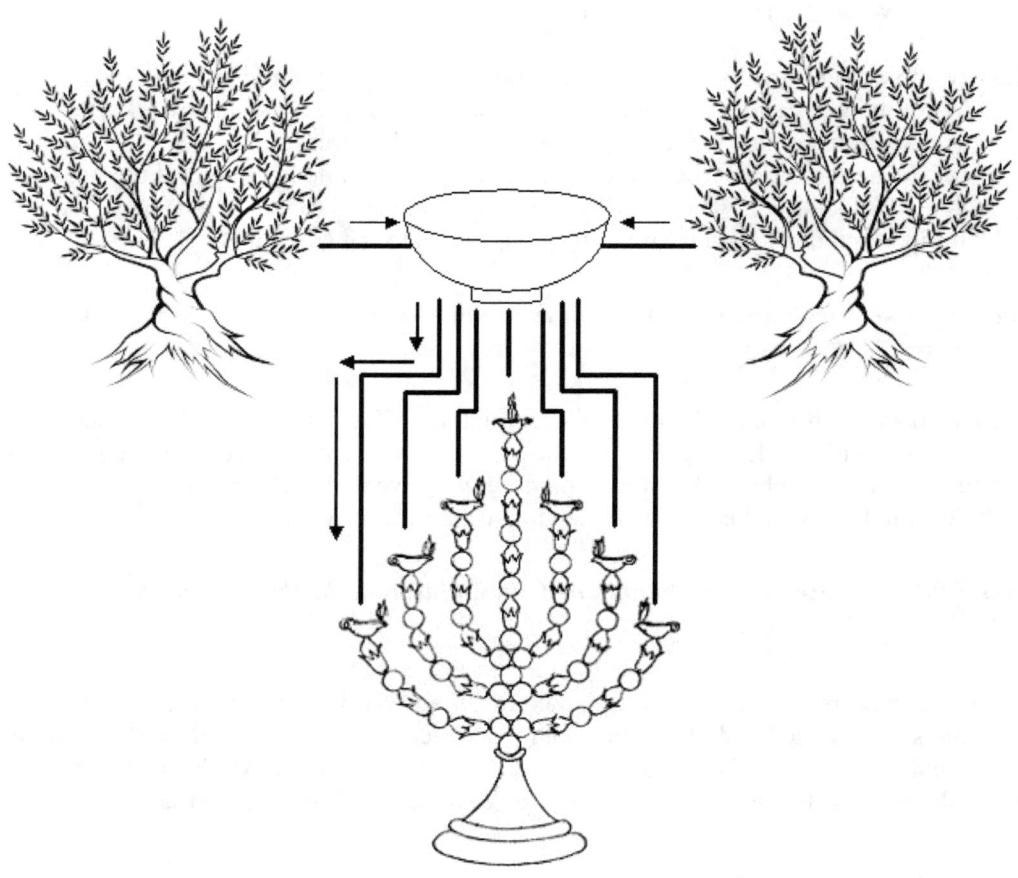

Interpretation

Having considered the vision of Zechariah, we will now spend some time considering the interpretation of it. As we have done throughout this study, we will let scripture interpret scripture and as we do that, we will unfold the truth of what the Lord was communicating to the prophet. Having done this, we will then move on to consider the application that all of this has to us and our call to dig. For now though let us consider what the Lord was speaking through this vision.

Within this vision there are five major points for us to consider, these being the Golden Lampstand with its lamps, the Golden Pipes, the Golden Bowl, the Olive trees and the

Golden Oil. Here we will consider each aspect individually initially before bringing them together to consider the fulness of truth that the vision presents.

The Lampstand and its lamps

The Lampstand and the lamps are really one and the same thing. The Golden Lampstand is designed to hold the lamps and the lamps cannot fulfil their job without the Lampstand. They are interconnected pieces of one and the same thing. In our earlier look at the design of the Golden Lampstand we saw that it was made of one piece of beaten work. There were no addons or additions. The Golden Lampstand with its lamps was one. It is one piece, completely united.

As we have seen earlier in our study, in our consideration of the Golden Lampstand, the Golden Lampstand represents the Church. The reader is referred back to our section on 'The Call to the Church' for a fuller discussion on this topic. For the sake of this section, we will just recap the relevant points.

In Revelation Chapter 1, the apostle John was on the island of Patmos and received a vision from the Lord. He saw seven Golden Lampstands and in the midst of the lampstands he saw the Son of Man. John saw Jesus here, clothed in his Priestly robes holding seven stars in His right hand. As the vision continued Jesus spoke to John and gave him the interpretation of what he saw. Jesus said:

> *The mystery of the seven stars which thou sawest in my right hand, and the seven golden candlesticks. The seven stars are the angels of the seven churches: and **the seven candlesticks** which thou sawest **are the seven churches**. (Rev 1:20)*

It was here that He who is the Word interprets the Word for us. Jesus tells John that the Lampstand represents the Church. Thus, in the very last book of the Bible we have the interpretation of a truth that was given way back in the book of Exodus. All of the symbolism surrounding the Lampstand, that progresses through the Old Testament, finds its fulfillment in the Church. The Church is the Golden Lampstand of the New Testament. The Church exists to be a beacon of light upon the earth in the various places where God has called it to be.

The first part of Zechariahs' vision with the Lampstand speaks of the Church. The Golden Lampstand is the Church.

The Golden Pipes

Whilst the seven pipes are not specifically mentioned as being of gold, it is the writers' view that this preposition is a balanced interpretation of the vision, as previously discussed. This will become clearer in the readers mind as we move forward and consider the other elements of the vision.

In total there are nine pipes mentioned in the vision of Zechariah. There are the seven pipes connecting the seven lamps of the Golden Lampstand to the Golden Bowl and then there are the two Golden Pipes connecting the two Olive trees to the Golden Bowl.
In scripture:
>Two is the number of witness.
>Seven is the number of fulness or completion.
>Nine is the number of the Holy Spirit.

These pipes speak of witness, fulness and of the Holy Spirit. These truths will again become more evident as we consider the other elements of the vision.

The pipes themselves serve a twofold purpose:

A. They connect the two Olives trees to the Golden Bowl, and they connect the Golden Bowl to the lamps of the Golden Lampstand. The pipes serve as points of connection. It shows the interrelatedness of the vision. Nothing stands alone, connection is seen throughout. From the top to the bottom there is connection.

B. They allow for flow. It is through the two Golden Pipes that the two olive trees empty their Golden Oil into the Golden Bowl, and it is through the seven pipes that this same Golden Oil flows to the seven lamps of the Golden Lampstand. The Golden Pipes not only serve as connection points, but they also exist to facilitate a flow.

It should be noted that whilst the connection of the Golden Pipes has a two-way effect, i.e. up and down, connecting the Golden Lampstand to the Golden Bowl above it and vice versa, the flow is only ever one directional, i.e. down. The pipes provide connection, that allows for the flow of the Golden Oil from the Golden Bowl down to the lamps of the Golden Lampstand. Whilst the connection is dual, the flow is singular.

The nine Golden Pipes speak of connection and that which allows flow to occur. The fact that they are gold shows that these are divine connections, ones instituted by the Lord. They are His ways and His means for connection and flow.

The Golden Oil

The oil flows from the Olive trees to the Golden Bowl and down to the lamps of the Golden Lampstand. This oil is referred to as the Golden Oil. The fact that this oil flows from the two Olive trees tells us that this is olive oil. The reference to it as Golden Oil speaks of its purity.

There is no mistaking the interpretation of this symbol. Oil throughout the Word of God is symbolic of the Holy Spirit. The two are used to show the anointing on an individual for the purposes of the Lord.

In the consecration of Aaron to the role of High priest we see that Moses was instructed to take the anointing oil and pour it upon the head of Aaron in order to anoint him (Ex 29:7).

The oil was used to anoint Aaron to his office unto the Lord. This was a process that was repeated with his sons as they were likewise anointed for service as part of the Aaronic priesthood.

When we come to the book of Samuel, we see that both the oil and Spirit are linked with the anointing of David. As Samuel rose to anoint David with the horn of oil, the Spirit of the Lord came upon David:

> *Then Samuel took the horn of **oil**, and **anointed** him in the midst of his brethren: and the **Spirit** of the LORD came upon David from that day forward. So Samuel rose up, and went to Ramah. (1Sa 16:13)*

As David was anointed with oil, the Holy Spirit came upon him. In other words, as David was anointed with oil, he was at the very same time anointed with the Spirit. The Spirit worked with that which symbolised itself. As man anointed with the natural so the Lord anointed with the spiritual. The oil and the Spirit work together. First the natural and then the spiritual. This anointing was the calling, setting apart and equipping of David for his service unto the Lord as a King/Priest.

When we come to the New Testament, we read that after Jesus was raised from the waters of baptism that the Holy Spirit came and descended upon him like a dove. Jesus was not anointed with oil! He was anointed with the Spirit. It was at this point that the ministry of Jesus really began.

And so, we see the progression of truth through the scriptures, ultimately showing the truth that the Lord was communicating. What was once a natural anointing with oil finds its fulfilment in the spiritual anointing of believers when they receive the Holy Spirit. When we accept Jesus and are baptised in the Holy Spirit, we receive the anointing of the Spirit as priests unto our God after the order of Melchizedek. The Holy Spirit anoints us for service unto the Lord. The natural of the Old Testament points to the spiritual of the New. The Oil points to the Holy Spirit.

In the natural, oil is brought forth through crushing or pressing of the olive. In the book of Leviticus, we read that the oil was produced through the beating of the olives (Lev 24:2). In the spiritual sense we understand that Jesus said that when He departed from this earth He would send the Holy Spirit as our comforter (John 16:7). Just before the cross Jesus was at the garden of Gethsemane where he poured out His heart to the Father. Gethsemane in Greek literally means oil press. As Jesus proceeded from here to the cross, He literally endured the crushing so that the oil of the Spirit could be sent forth. Jesus was crushed so that the Spirit would flow.

In the Tabernacle system olive oil was required as the fuel to keep the Golden Lampstand burning. No other fuel was allowed. But even with the olive oil that was to be used, there were additional requirements. It couldn't be just any olive oil, it had to be pure olive oil. It could not be defiled in any way, it had to be absolutely pure. There was an absolute divine standard of what had to be used for the Lampstand to function. This oil was required so that the Golden Lampstand would continually shine before the Lord in the Holy Place. Oil as a fuel source is consumed by the fire it enables, and so in order for there to be continual light, there must be a continual supply or resupply of oil. If the supply runs out, the light goes out. It is only as the oil is readily and continually provided that the lampstand can continue to burn and provide light.

We see an example of this with the parable of the ten virgins in Matthew 25:1-13. Here Jesus talks about five wise virgins and five foolish virgins. All of the virgins had a lamp but only the wise had vessels with extra oil in them. While the virgins waited for the groom to come, they slumbered and slept. In this time, their lamps were unattended and consumed what oil had been supplied. Suddenly they were awoken by the announcement of the groom's arrival. All of the virgins arose to trim their lamps and as they did this, the foolish virgins realised that they needed more oil. The problem though was they didn't have any. They appealed to the wise, but the wise virgins replied that they did not have enough to share. The oil that the wise had was needed for their lamps. The foolish virgins set off to buy oil and while they were away the groom arrived, the doors were shut, and the foolish virgins missed the wedding banquet. The lamps of the foolish virgins extinguished because there was no resupply of oil. They failed to maintain the needed supply of oil to enable the lamp to keep burning. In order for the lamp to burn, there not only needed to be an initial supply of oil, but also a continual resupply of oil.

This parable of the wise and foolish virgin teaches us several things in regard to the need of the Holy Spirit (Oil) to keep burning.

A. No oil means no light. The oil of the Holy Spirit is absolutely necessary for the lamp to burn. Oil is the fuel that makes the light possible. Without oil we are left in the same state as that of the foolish virgins.

B. Failure to take heed to the needs of the lampstand can result in the light burning out. We can never become complacent and neglect the need for the resupply of oil. Notice how in the parable all of the 10 virgins fell asleep! If we don't take heed, we lose our light.

C. You can't live on someone else's oil. The foolish couldn't survive from the oil of the wise. There was simply not enough to be shared. We need our own supply of oil to be able to keep burning.

In this vision of Zechariah, the oil is one of the central parts. It literally flows from the top to the bottom. The oil speaks to the work of the Holy Spirit and its vital necessity for the Church to be able to shine. The Church is a divinely created vessel and it can only function properly through a divinely provided source. This source is the Holy Spirit, given by the Father through the sacrifice of the Son.

As believers and the Church, we need the oil of the Holy Spirit flowing into us. Oil is not an optional extra it is a necessity. We need the pure oil of the Holy Spirit.

The Bowl

The writer would put forth that this was in fact a Golden Bowl that Zechariah saw. Whilst a Golden Bowl is not mentioned in conjunction with the Golden Lampstand in Zechariahs' vision, throughout the revelation of the Tabernacle, gold is associated with the vessels of the Lampstand and the Holy Place (1 Kings 7:49-50). Other material was not deemed by the Lord to be used in this place because of the truths He was communicating to mankind. Gold speaks of divinity and kingship; it speaks of God. The vision of Zechariah is one that shows God's perfect design. It shows how the Church, as God's designed vessel, is to fully function in this world. It is a vision filled with the truth of gold. There is the Golden Lampstand, the Golden Pipes, the Golden Oil and as the writer has put forward, the Golden Bowl. All of these speak to the fact of Gods' divine design.

The Golden Bowl is an interesting part of the vision. From our understanding of the vision, we see that the Bowl sits above the Golden Lampstand and is connected to the seven lamps of the Golden Lampstand by seven pipes. On either side of the Golden Bowl stand the two Olive trees. These are connected to the Bowl by two Golden Pipes and through these the Olive trees pour out their Golden Oil to the Bowl. From this it is safe to assume that the Bowl then supplies this same Golden Oil to the lamps of the Golden Lampstand through the seven pipes. There is a flow that occurs with the Bowl at the centre. The Bowl receives the Golden Oil and pours it out to the seven lamps. The Bowl is a vessel for the oil that sees the oil flow to the Golden Lampstand.

In the Tabernacle system the supply of oil to the Golden Lampstand was a priestly ministration. The High Priest would attend to the Lampstand morning and evening and supply the oil required to ensure that the Holy Place was provided with light. Without this ministration the Holy Place would reside in darkness. This was possibly something that Zechariah understood and is why he didn't have any questions regarding the Bowl. He understood that the Bowl was necessary to supply oil to the Golden Lampstand.

The Golden Bowl points to our Lord Jesus Christ. It is Jesus who as our Great High Priest supplies the oil of the Holy Spirit to His Church. The Bowl points to Jesus. Jesus is our divine High Priest who was given the Spirit without measure (John 3:34) and through His death that same Spirit has been given to His people. Just as the oils flows through the Golden Bowl to the Golden Lampstand so does the Spirit, sent by the Father flow through His son Jesus to the Church and the people of God.

Just as the Bowl sits above the Lampstand and provides what is required for the Lampstand to shine, so too does Christ as the head of the Church sit above the Church in the Heavenly realm and supply through Himself the blessed Holy Spirit for the purpose of equipping the Church to shine. It is through Jesus, our Golden Bowl, that the Holy Spirit flows to the Church and to the individual.

The Two Olive trees

The two olive trees are quite possibly the area of the vision that is the least clear. This was no doubt the case for Zechariah and why he repeatedly asked the angel what the two olive trees were. Three times in chapter 4 we read that Zechariah asked what the meaning of these were. He must have had a comprehension of the other parts of the vision, but the two olive trees were something he did not understand.

As a reminder, so far we have seen that the Golden Bowl speaks of Jesus as the head of the Church, sitting above the Golden Lampstand which is the Church. Connecting the two are seven Golden Pipes and it is through these pipes that the oil of the Holy Spirit flows to the Church from Christ. Beside the Golden Bowl are two olive trees, connected by two Golden Pipes and through these they pour out their Golden Oil into the Golden Bowl.

The question we have yet to answer is what are the two olive trees? As we have done throughout this study, we will let scripture interpret scripture and by doing this arrive at a clear interpretation.

The only information provided in Zechariah is that the two olive trees are the two anointed ones that stand by the Lord of all the earth. One's mind might immediately jump to the thought that these two olive trees represent the Father and the Holy Spirit who work with the Son. Thoughts and verses can be pulled from scripture that show how these three are connected with the work of God towards mankind, the Church and believers. The writer would not argue with the premise of this point but in this particular case under consideration, would lean away from this view.

We need to remember that Jesus and the Holy Spirit are already represented in this vision by the Golden Bowl and the oil. Why would there be a double reference to the Holy Spirit in this vision? Why would the tree and the oil both point to the Holy Spirit? Further to this, the term anointed ones is made of two different Hebrew words, bane and yitshar.

- Yitshar literally mean oil or anointing and there is no mistaking this interpretation of anointed from this word.

- The word bane forms the second part of this term, 'ones'. This word is used nearly five thousand times in the Old Testament and the overwhelming use is in reference to sons or children. This Word has an unmistakeable link to that which has been created.

These two olive trees would seem to have more of an earthly connection than a heavenly one. There are two individuals that have been anointed.

The specific term "two olive trees" is used three times in scripture. Twice it is used in the book of Zechariah in the vision under consideration. The only other time it is used, is in the book of Revelation. Having already looked at the examples from Zechariah let us turn our attention to their mention in Revelation and see if this aides our understanding in any way.

In Revelation 11 we read of the two witnesses who minister before the return of our Lord Jesus Christ.
There we read the following:

> *And I will give power unto my two witnesses, and they shall prophesy a thousand two hundred and threescore days, clothed in sackcloth.* **_These are the two olive trees_**, *and the two candlesticks standing before the God of the earth. (Rev 11:3-4)*

Immediately what pops out in this verse is the reference to the two olive trees. It is almost as if John is given here the answer to Zechariah's many questions. Given that this is the only other place in scripture that mentions two olive trees, we must needs ask ourselves why was this specific detail given to John? If it wasn't included this verse of Revelation, the overall flow of the verse would generally still make sense. But if the reader, as the writer, believes that every word of the Bible was given through complete inspiration of the Holy Spirit and that the Word of God is infallible, then God must have had a reason for including this detail. Was this detail included to aid our understanding of Zechariah's vision? The writer would lean to that opinion.

What is also interesting is the connection made between the olive trees and the lampstand. The verse above says that the two olive trees are also two lampstands or candlesticks. This linkage is not by chance either! The thought itself though seems a little paradoxical. That is, they are olive trees, i.e. they produce oil, and yet they are also lampstands i.e. vessels in need of oil. How can they be both? This is a question we will answer shortly.

In this verse we see that John is told about the two witnesses who are the two olive trees, and who also are represented by two lampstands that stand before the Lord of all the earth. Apart from this, there is not much information from these verses to help us interpret the two olive trees further. As we read on in Revelation 11 though, we see that some more details are provided. In verse 5 and 6 of Revelation 11 we are given some more details which shed some light on the two witnesses. Here we read:

> *And if any man will hurt them (the two witnesses), fire proceedeth out of their mouth, and devoureth their enemies: and if any man will hurt them, he must in this manner be killed. These have power to shut heaven, that it rain not in the days of their prophecy: and have power over waters to turn them to blood, and to smite the earth with all plagues, as often as they will. (Rev 11:5-6)*

When we consider the language of these verses, we can quickly determine that the description of these individuals is a clear reference to Elijah and Moses. Our purpose here is not to do an exposition on Revelation 11, but we will provide enough information for the reader to consider the truth of what is being presented.

Digging

A. Elijah

The reference to Elijah can be seen in the description of "fire proceedeth out of their mouth, and devoureth their enemies" and where it says "These have power to shut heaven, that it rain not during the days of their prophecy".

In 2 Kings 1 we read that Elijah prophesied an unfavourable word over king Ahaziah. In response to this king Ahaziah sent out a band of soldiers consisting of a captain with his fifty soldiers under his command, to go and capture Elijah. As Elijah sat upon a hill, the captain came to him and demanded that the prophet come down to be taken to the king. We need to remember here that if this was a friendly request of the king, the king would simply have sent a messenger! This was no friendly request. This was an act of aggression in response to the Word of the Lord that Elijah had spoken to the king. As the captain addressed Elijah, calling on the man of God to come down, Elijah sat upon the hill and replied:

> *… …., If I be a man of God, then let fire come down from heaven, and consume thee and thy fifty. … …… (2Ki 1:10)*

Immediately fire fell from heaven and consumed the captain and his fifty men. In response to this the king sent a second captain with his fifty men and the exact same thing occured. It wasn't until the third captain came and fear of the Lord had fallen upon the soldiers that their approach and attitude unto Elijah changed. In response to this the Lord spoke to Elijah and he went with the soldiers unto the king.

What we can note from this is that this miracle occurred at the **words** of Elijah. It was as the words were spoken out of his mouth, that the enemies of Elijah were consumed. This confirms our first point. Fire proceeds out of their mouth. As they speak fire falls.

In regard to shutting the heavens, we are told that it would not rain during the days of their prophesy. This time period is given to us at the start of Revelation 11 as being 1260 days. Again, in the days of Elijah we see a similar miracle occur. In 1 Kings 17 Elijah pronounced a drought over the land according to the Word of the Lord because of the sins of the people. This drought continued until Elijah had his stand-off with the prophets of Baal and the people returned unto the Lord (1 Kings 18). In James 5:17 we are told that this drought lasted for three and a half years.

> *Elijah was a man subject to like passions as we are, and he prayed earnestly that it might not rain: and it rained not on the earth by the space of three years and six months. And he prayed again, and the heaven gave rain, and the earth brought forth her fruit. (James 5:17-18)*

The three and a half years and 1260 days speak of one and the same period. The miracles that John is told about in Revelation are attributed to no other individual in the Bible. It is a clear and direct reference to Elijah.

B. Moses

The reference to Moses can be seen in the statement "and have power over waters to turn them to blood, and to smite the earth with all plagues, as often as they will". This is a clear reference to Moses and his time in proclaiming the judgement of the Lord against Pharaoh and the people of Egypt. There can be no mistaking the reference here. It was Moses under the direction of God who turned the water of Egypt to blood. This is seen in Exodus 7 and was the first plague of judgement suffered by the Egyptians.

After this Moses, under the Lord's direction, pronounced nine other plagues over the land of Egypt. This is referenced when the angel states:

and to smite the earth with all plagues, as often as they will.

The reference to the water turning to blood is singular. The reference to other plagues, plural, is a link and confirmation of the ministry of Moses. As was stated earlier, the purpose of this text is not to dive into an extended exhortation on the two witnesses. What we can see though, is that the language of Revelation is inapplicable to any other individuals in the Bible.

And so, we see in Revelation that the two olive trees that Zechariah puzzled over are in fact Moses and Elijah. The language of Revelation clearly points to this interpretation. It is not a truth stretched to fit but is a truth clearly and obviously seen from a plain reading of the scriptures. The plain reading of Revelation 11 reveals this to us and links this interpretation to Zechariah's vision through the reference to the two olive trees. As the writer was once taught, "When the plain sense of scripture makes sense, we don't need to seek any other sense, otherwise we end up in nonsense!" The plain sense of Revelation 11 is that the two witnesses speak of Moses and Elijah.

With Moses and Elijah being the two witnesses of Revelation 11 then they are also the two anointed ones that Zechariah 4:14 talks about. Moses and Elijah are the two Olive trees, and they stand on the left and right hand side of the Lord Jesus:

And two olive trees by it, one upon the right side of the bowl, and the other upon the left side thereof. (Zec 4:3)

This is their position given by God unto them. These are the two anointed ones that stand by the Lord. It is possibly because of this that the mother's request in Matthew 20 was denied! (Matt 20:20-23). Moses and Elijah as the two olive trees, two lampstands, two anointed ones, two witnesses, are connected to the ministry of Christ. The language of Zechariah and Revelation attests to this truth.

If the reader will cast their minds back though, we noted the paradoxical language of Revelation. The two witnesses, Moses and Elijah, are both two olive trees and two Golden Lampstands. There we noted that this seemed ambiguous. Why the dual symbolism and why the double mention? Why does the Lord point out that the two witnesses are two olive trees and yet they are also two lampstands?

In the vision of Zechariah, we have seen that the Olive trees link to the Golden Bowl which then supplies oil to the Golden Lampstand through seven pipes. The Olive trees stand beside the Golden Bowl at the top of the vision and the Golden Lampstand is seen at the bottom of the vision. There is a flow that occurs from top to bottom. With that being the case how can the lampstand and the olive trees be linked here in Revelation? How can they be both the source and the vessel? How can that which receives the oil also be that which supplies it? Surely there must be a distinction? The writer believes that there is, and would put forth that the dual symbolism of Revelation exists to communicate two distinct yet related truths. The following is put forward for the reader's consideration.

Moses and Elijah are the two anointed lampstands in terms of their humanity. They are the two witnesses of Christ and have an unmistakable link to His ministry. They are connected to Him, and their place is at His right- and left-hand side. Whilst they hold this position though, like any believer, they sit under Him and receive their infilling from Him. To put these two, in their humanity, on the same level as Jesus as the two olive trees, is unscriptural and unbalanced. In their humanity, Zech 4:12 cannot apply to them:

> *And I answered again, and said unto him, What be these two olive branches which through the two Golden Pipes empty the Golden Oil out of themselves? (Zec 4:12)*

In their humanity Moses and Elijah cannot supply oil to the Golden Bowl. In their humanity, just like us, they are lampstands, shining for the Lord in dark and perverse generations as equipped by and through Him to do so. In their humanity they are the same as you and I! Christ is their head, and they receive from Him, they do not supply to Him! Whilst they hold a high position at the right and left hand of Christ, Christ is still their head, and they sit under Him. Whilst they stand at His left- and right-hand side, they are not on the same level. The lampstands point to the humanity of Moses and Elijah.

In terms of Moses and Elijah as the two Olive trees, the writer would hold that this points to the two ministries that they held. As individuals Moses and Elijah stand forth as examples of the law and the prophets. Moses was the original law giver. He received revelation from the Lord and passed it on to Israel. It was from Moses, who wrote the first five books of the Bible, the Pentateuch, that the nation of Israel developed its laws from. These were the books of law, written by Moses.

In terms of Elijah, he unmistakably stands as a representative of the prophets. Elijah was one of the great prophets of the Old Testament and is one that never tasted of death! He was spared from this as a chariot of fire ushered him straight from earth into heaven.

As representatives of the law and the prophets, Moses and Elijah, symbolically stand as the Word of God. They stand forth as God's Word. They represent the law and the prophets. Throughout the New Testament, and particularly the ministry of Jesus, the law and the prophets was a term interchangeable with the Word of God.

> *Think not that I am come to **destroy the law, or the prophets**: I am not come to destroy, but to fulfil. (Mat 5:17)*

> *Therefore all things whatsoever ye would that men should do to you, do ye even so to them: for this **is the law and the prophets**. Mat 7:12)*

> *For all **the prophets and the law** prophesied until John. (Mat 11:13)*

> *On these two commandments hang all **the law and the prophets**. (Mat 22:40)*

> ***The law and the prophets*** *were until John: since that time the kingdom of God is preached, and every man presseth into it. (Luk 16:16)*

> *Philip findeth Nathanael, and saith unto him, We have found him, of **whom Moses in the law, and the prophets**, did write, Jesus of Nazareth, the son of Joseph. (Joh 1:45)*

> *And after the reading **of the law and the prophets** the rulers of the synagogue sent unto them, saying, Ye men and brethren, if ye have any word of exhortation for the people, say on. (Act 13:15)*

> *And when they had appointed him a day, there came many to him into his lodging; to whom he expounded and testified the kingdom of God, persuading them concerning Jesus, both out **of the law of Moses, and out of the prophets**, from morning till evening. (Act 28:23)*

> *But now the righteousness of God without the law is manifested, being witnessed by **the law and the prophets**; (Rom 3:21)*

The law and the prophets were the Word of God in Jesus' time. The law and the prophets were what Israel referred to. The law and the prophets were what was read in the synagogues. The law and the prophets were and are the Word of God. They are the fulness of the Word.

Between the books of Zechariah and Revelation, we are given the information that helps us understand the two olive trees and the two witnesses. There is no doubt that the individuals referred to are Moses and Elijah. There is no doubt as to their position, they stand at the right-hand and left-hand side of Jesus and are vitally connected to His ministry. In the application of the olive trees and the lampstands though, we see that there is a distinction in the ministries referred to of these two individuals. The two olive trees are not symbolic of the individuals, but what they stand for. They stand for the law and the prophets which is the Word of God. This was the Word of God in Jesus' time, and it is on this Word that the New Testaments is built. The two olive trees are the Word of God.

When we see the olive trees as the Word of God, it further confirms the truth of the Golden Bowl. On either side of the Golden Bowl are the two Olive trees, connected by two Golden Pipes, through which the Golden Oil flows. As we have seen the olive trees are the Word of God and the oil is the Holy Spirit. So flowing into Jesus is the Word and the Spirit. The Golden Bowl is literally full of the Word and the Spirit. This is inapplicable to any other individual other than Jesus. Jesus was given the Spirit without measure (John 3:34). He is full of the Spirit! Jesus was also the Word made flesh (John 1:14). Jesus is the embodiment of the Word. He is literally the fulness of the Word. In Jesus is the fulness of the Word and the Spirit. The Golden Bowl of Zechariah's vision attests to these truths of Jesus being the fulness of the Word and the fulness of the Sprit. The vision shows the bowl filled by the Word and by the Spirit.

RECAP

To recap what we have just looked at in this section, Zechariah saw a vision as given to him by the Lord. He saw a Golden Lampstand with its seven lamps. Above it sat a Golden Bowl. Connecting the Golden Bowl to the Golden Lampstand were seven Golden Pipes. Beside the Golden Bowl were two Olive trees, one on the right-hand side and one on the left. These were connected to the Golden Bowl by two Golden Pipes, through which the Golden Oil flowed. From here we can almost separate the vision into two parts: the top part of the vision and the bottom part of the vision.

The Top part of the vision speaks of Christ. Christ is the Golden Bowl. He is the head of the Church and stands as our Great High Priest. It is Christ in His Priestly office that we see in the vision of John in Revelation Chapter 2.

The two olive trees point to the law and the prophets which speak of the Word of God. These flow into Him who is the Word. Jesus is literally the personification of the Word, He is the Word made flesh and these Olive trees point to this fact.

The Golden Pipes pouring the Golden Oil into the Bowl speak of Christ as one who is full of the Spirit. The Word says the Christ was given the Spirit without measure (John 3:34).

Jesus is full of the Word and full of the Spirit and stands as our Great High Priest and head of the Church. This top part of the vision speaks of Christ. The symbolism is unmistakeable and inapplicable to anyone or anything else. Christ alone fits this scriptural description.

The bottom part of the vision shows the Golden Lampstand. This, as we have seen throughout this study, speaks of the Church and the believer as an individual. The book of Revelation clearly interprets this for us.

So, we have the top part of the vision and the bottom part of the vision. What connects them both is the seven Golden Pipes that flow from the Golden Bowl to the Golden Lampstand. These pipes are the connection points that allow the Holy Spirit to flow from Christ to the Church and the individual. These are the vessels that carry the oil from Jesus to His people. Without these there can be no flow and with no flow there can be no flame. It is the flow of oil that allows the Lampstand to burn continually. Each lamp needs its individual flow or else the Golden Lampstand is not shining as it has been created to. The seven lamps on the Lampstand speak of the fulness of the Spirit. There are seven pipes to supply oil to these seven lamps. Each lamp has its own pipe. God's purpose is for His Church and His people to receive the fulness of His Spirit. The Church and we as individuals need the fulness of the Spirit flowing from the Son into our lives if we are to shine as we have been called to. Anything less is below God's divine standard.

This vision of Zechariah reveals God's blueprint for how His Spirit flows to His Church and His people. His intention is for the Lampstand to shine, but He has also laid out the process for how this occurs. The question that naturally follows from this investigation is what application does this have to the Church and the New Testament believer? The message seems clear but what is the application?

THE SEVEN PIPES ARE SEVEN WELLS

When considering the vision of Zechariah and looking at what we have discovered, we can tend to assume that there is an implied flow that occurs without much responsibility on the part of man. The oil flows to the Bowl and through the pipes to the Golden Lampstand. One might say isn't it Jesus' responsibility to supply oil to the Lampstand as the Great High Priest? Upon just a superficial read of Zechariah, that would seem the indication from the vision! With this sort of diagrammatic imagery a question in the reader's mind may well be how does this relate to digging? In answering this we are going to again jump back to the Tabernacle of Moses and consider the operation and working of the Golden Lampstand.

In Leviticus 24 the Lord speaks to Moses and gives direction regarding the operation of the lampstand. There we read:

> And the LORD spake unto Moses, saying, Command the children of Israel, **<u>that they bring unto thee pure oil olive beaten for the light</u>**, to cause the lamps to burn continually. Without the vail of the testimony, in the tabernacle of the congregation, shall Aaron order it from the evening unto the morning before the LORD continually: it shall be a statute for ever in your generations. He shall

order the lamps upon the pure candlestick before the LORD continually. (Lev 24:1-4)

There are several things for us to note from this passage:

A. This was a clear and direct command of the Lord. This was not a man-made tradition but was an edict from the Lord in regard to how the Golden Lampstand was to function. This is one of the foundational truths of the Golden Lampstand and it is a truth that flows through scripture, including the vision of Zechariah. It is a truth that is tied to the Golden Lampstand and its operation.

B. We see that it was the role of Aaron, as the High Priest, to attend to the Golden Lampstand and keep the lamps in order. This is a truth we see flow to our Lord Jesus in the vision of Zechariah and also in the vision of John in Revelation 2. Jesus as our Great High Priest is the one who tends to and administers the oil to the Golden Lampstand. He is our Great High Priest, and He is the Golden Bowl.

C. The lamps on the Lampstand were to burn continually. They weren't ever to go out. All seven of them were to continually burn. The light was always to shine forth.

D. Finally, and most importantly for this section, we see that it was the responsibility of the **children of Israel** to bring the olive oil for the lamps to the burn. Note verse 2:

> *Command **the children of Israel**, that **they bring unto thee pure oil olive beaten for the light,** to **cause the lamps to burn** continually.(Lev 24:2)*

The Lord laid the command upon the children of Israel to bring the oil for the Golden Lampstand to the priests. The people had to supply the oil so that the priest could then administer it. The priest could only administer the oil **IF** the people were faithful in bringing the oil. Again, in this verse there is an emphasis on the pure beaten olive oil. The people of Israel had to work to produce this, and it had to be of a certain standard. There was both effort and a Godly standard laid upon the people. They couldn't bring just anything!

So, what we see from this look back to Leviticus is that there is a linkage between the people and the High Priest in regard to the flow of oil. There is an interrelation and dependence, one upon the other. The High Priest is standing ready, daily to attend to His duties, but there is a requirement upon the people that determines the ability of the High Priest to do this and the degree of fulness to which he can fulfil this. The people's faithfulness to the task, and their faithfulness to meet the quality standard, determined how much oil the High Priest could administer. The ability of the Golden Lampstand to continually burn was determined as much by the people as it was by the Priest.

If we apply this truth to the vision of Zechariah, we see that there is a responsibility upward that allows and determines the flow downward. A pipe has an opening on both ends. It can only work if both ends are open and clear. We know that our great High priest is faithful and true and that His desire is for the Church and for us to be burning with the fulness of supply of His Spirit. If we are not seeing this, then we need look no further than the mirror. If there is a lack of supply of His Oil, then we need to check the connection point on our end. Just as responsibility lay upon the Israelites in regard to the flow of oil, so too does it lay upon us.

At the start of this study, we noted from the 2 Kings 3 account that the digging had to happen so that the wells could be filled. The kings and their armies had to put in the effort and dig the wells before the infilling could occur. There was a responsibility that lay upon them before the Lord could infill. This is a truth applicable to what we are considering.

In considering the vision of Zechariah, we established that there are seven pipes that provide for the infilling of the Church. Before the infilling can occur though these pipes need to be open and clear. They need to be dug, just as the wells from the 2 Kings 3 account that we looked at. These seven pipes are connection points. They connect us to the source and allow the infilling to occur. The infilling happens through these connection points.

The pipes have to be open so that the oil can flow. The digging and the opening or clearing of pipes are what allow the infilling to occur. They are one and the same thing. The wells had to be dug for the water to infill. The pipes have to be clear to allow the oil to infill the lamps. They both require a responsibility on the part of man before the Lord can do His part. The wells could only be filled after they had been dug. The Golden Lampstand can only receive oil to its seven lamps if all of the pipes are clear and operational. There is a responsibility upon as us churches and individuals to make sure that each of the connection points are operational in our lives so that the fulness of the Holy Spirit can flow. Just as with the nation of Israel, there is a responsibility the lays upon us for the provision of oil.

So what we see is that the wells and the pipes both serve the same function. The wells are the vehicle that allow the infilling so that reflections can occur. The same is true of the pipes. The pipes allow the infilling so that the lamps can shine. Both the wells and the pipes are the vessels that allow the next stage to occur. The wells have to be dug for the infilling to occur, and likewise the pipes have to be open for the infilling to occur. If neither the pipes or the wells are attended to, then the infilling doesn't occur. They are one and the same thing. They serve the same function and speak the same truth.

Digging

	LAMPSTAND	WELLS	PIPES
DIGGING	The Israelites had to bring the beaten pure olive oil.	Wells had to be dug by the kings and armies.	Pipes have to be open on the end of man.
INFILLING	The High Priest attended to the lamp with what the people of Israel brought. The infilling depended on the efforts of man.	The water could only fill that which had been dug by the people. The infilling depended on man digging the wells.	The oil can only flow when the pipes are open by the people. The infilling is dependent on man opening the pipes.

These examples speak one and the same truth. There is a responsibility on the part of man before the infilling of the Lord occurs.

What remains is for us to discover what these seven wells/pipes/connection points are. This is something that is not interpreted for us specifically in the vision of Zechariah.

What is presented for the reader's consideration is that which was once taught to the writer and something that the writer has studied and also come to the same conclusion about. What we are looking at here are the connection points, those things that allow the Spirit of God to flow to and infill His people and His Church. Having established the connection of the pipes and wells, for the sake of consistency, moving forward here we will refer to these connection points as wells.

Amongst expositors there may be differences of opinion to that which the writer puts forward, but there should be no argument in regard to the existence of the connection points put forward. The seven wells which we will consider are:

A. The well of prayer.
B. The well of reading and meditating on the Word.
C. The well of sensitivity to the Holy Spirit.
D. The well of faith.
E. The well of obedience.
F. The well of speaking in tongues.
G. The well of worship and praise.

As we move forward here, we will spend time considering these in more detail explaining to the reader how these wells help us to receive from the Lord. Whilst the reader may have an initial reaction or questions to what has been listed above, the encouragement of the writer would be to keep reading and with an open mind consider what is being presented. If that which is presented doesn't sit, then put it on the shelf, but don't continue reading with a mind that is already closed off. We always need to be open to that which the Holy Spirit would want to reveal to us through the Word.

The seven wells outlined above are what the writer feels the Lord has confirmed to his heart and have particular need and application to believers and the Church of today. As we progress and consider these, we must remember that there is an onus and responsibility upon us to make sure that these connection points are fully open and operational. There may be work that is required on our end to clear these pipes and reopen them so that they can fully flow. God's command is that we play a part in the supply of oil and in the following sections that we look at, the emphasis is ever on the people of God to dig. It is the faithfulness with which we dig that will determine the magnitude of flow that we receive.

The wells we will look at are really studies in and of themselves. Our purpose here is not to do a full exposition on each, but the writer will endeavour to provide enough scriptural information to explain to the reader what these points are and how they facilitate the flow of the Holy Spirit to us as individuals and corporately as the Church. The reader is encouraged to remember that what we are looking at here are those areas that the Lord encourages us to dig into, that we might receive from Him. They are avenues that allow us to receive His infilling. These seven wells are needed for believers and the Church today. These wells require effort on the part of man, before the Lord can do His part. They are where our effort is to be put. Just as the kings had a specific place where they were to dig their wells, so to do we. As we act in obedience to the Word of God, digging where He has told us to, we then open ourselves to receive the fulness of infilling that He has for us.

THE WELL OF PRAYER

Behold, I stand at the door, and knock: if any man hear my voice, and open the door, I will come in to him, and will sup with him, and he with me. (Rev 3:20)

The first well for us to consider is the well of prayer. Prayer is an absolute necessity in the life of any believer and Church. In this section we will do a quick overview of prayer and see how it connects us so vitally to the Lord.

A. What is prayer?

Prayer in its simplest form can be described as a conversation between man and God and between God and man. Conversation is something that we are all well versed in. We have numerous conversations each and every day, whether it be in person, over the phone, via email etc.

A conversation is something that involves communication going back and forth between the parties involved. It is this back-and-forth aspect of conversation that we need to fully grasp hold of in our understanding of prayer. We often focus on the speaking part of prayer, but the reality is the listening part of prayer is just as important, if not slightly more so. When a conversation doesn't involve the speaker taking the time to listen, they are in reality simply making a speech!

Conversation is a cornerstone of any relationship and absolutely necessary for a relationship to grow and mature. Conversation is how we communicate our thoughts, feelings, frustrations, questions and fears. It is the mechanism through which a relationship develops as each party opens up and the other takes the time to listen and respond.

Throughout the Word of God, we see that the Lord has always wanted a relationship with His people, and He does this through prayerful conversation. Prayer is a spiritual conversation exchanged between man and God.

B. What prayer is not!

Having outlined an overview of what prayer is, let us look at the other side of that coin and consider what prayer is not.

1. Prayer is not presenting a list of wants to God.

    God is not a magic genie that we go to with our three wishes. Prayer is communicating with a focus of developing a relationship, it is not a petulant child nagging their parent. There is absolutely no doubt that our Heavenly Father longs to give us the desires of our heart, but this cannot and should not be our sole focus in prayer. The purpose of prayer is not for us to present our wish list, it is to present ourselves and grow our relationship with the Lord.

2. Prayer is not reciting the same words over and over.

    When speaking to the disciples in regard to prayer Jesus states:

    And when you pray do not use vain repetitions. (Matt 6:7)

    God doesn't want us repeating the same words day in and day out with our lips. He wants a conversation that stems from our hearts, and desires intimacy with Him. Imagine having a friend, who every time that you encountered them you had the exact same conversation. How conducive would that be to developing a strong, deep relationship?

    God wants more than our lip service! He wants a deep relationship with His people.

3. Prayer is not something we do only when we are in trouble.

    Prayer is to be a daily habit, not just something we cling to in times of need. In our times of need we do press in more, as our desperation levels increase, but this should be seen as a rise in our prayer rather than a starting point for it. Prayer is not our get out of jail card that we play only when we need to, prayer is to be a daily characteristic of the way we live.

4. Prayer is not only for Church leaders.

   Prayer is the call for each and every single believer. It is not reserved for the Pastor or the leaders of the Church. It is not reserved for adults or the mature. It is for every single person, from youngest to oldest. Scripture says that the Lord's ear is attentive to the cry of the righteous (Ps 34:15). When Peter quotes this Psalm, he says "that His (The Lord's) ears are open unto <u>their</u> prayers" (1 Pet 3:12). Gods' ears are open to all who would pray unto Him, and the truth is, He is ready, willing and waiting to engage with us.

5. Prayer is not a one-sided conversation.

   In Isaiah 29:13 the Lord declares:

   > ……, *Forasmuch as this people draw near me with their mouth, and with their lips do honour me, but have removed their heart far from me,* ……

   As we have said repeatedly already, prayer is a conversation, and a conversation goes two ways. The old adage goes that we were given two ears and one mouth for a reason; we should spend twice as much time listening as we do talking! This is a truth that would serve us all well in our prayer lives. As we take the time to sit and listen for the Father's voice, our spiritual ears become more finely tuned to hear the words He has for us.

C. Prayer in Scripture

For the purposes of this section, we will spend some time considering some examples of prayer in scripture to highlight its progression from creation through to New Testament believers. As we consider each example, we will highlight the various characteristics of prayer that are revealed to us. The reader is encouraged to take note that the examples we use flow from the Old to the New. God's desire for relationship with His people has never changed!

1. Adam and Eve

   In the book of Genesis, we see that in the beginning the Lord had an intimate relationship with Adam and Eve. Genesis tells us that Lord came to converse with Adam and Eve in the cool of the day (Gen 3). The original intention of the creation of man was for relationship. The Lord didn't create man and then stay hidden in His Heavenly realm. He created man with the intent of having relationship with him. In Genesis 3:9-13 we read of a conversation between God and Adam. This is a conversation based around the Lord asking Adam to explain why he had been disobedient, but within it we see some core truths necessary to build our relationship with the Lord.

> *And the LORD God called unto Adam, and said unto him, Where art thou? And he said, I heard thy voice in the garden, and I was afraid, because I was naked; and I hid myself. And he said, Who told thee that thou wast naked? Hast thou eaten of the tree, whereof I commanded thee that thou shouldest not eat? And the man said, The woman whom thou gavest to be with me, she gave me of the tree, and I did eat. (Gen 3:9-12)*

Within the conversation we see God speaking and calling to man and likewise we see man listening and responding to God. As man responds to the Lord, God in turn listens and then responds. It is a relational conversation that goes back and forth. One talks while the other listens and vice versa. This is exactly what prayer is. God, in the beginning, demonstrates the relationship He desires with man through prayer.

2. Moses

In the book of Exodus, we are introduced to Moses. Moses' first conversational encounter with the Lord is seen when he comes across the burning bush. Here the Lord spoke to Moses and Moses responded and spoke to the Lord (Ex 3). As we read these verses, we see that a conversation transpired between Moses and the Lord that continued for the whole chapter. What is interesting is that this whole conversation transpired because Moses turned aside in response to the burning bush. As Moses stepped out of his daily routine, away from the responsibilities of shepherding and the cares of life and, and approached the burning bush without distraction, it was then that the Lord spoke to Him. God was there waiting to engage with Moses, but the intent was needed on the behalf of Moses before God spoke. Intent is such a key with prayer. We never engage with God by chance. It happens when we intentionally approach Him.

The account above was Moses' first recorded conversation with the Lord, but it certainly wasn't his last. Overtime this relationship continued to grow as it was nurtured and attended to by Moses. We go on to read further on in the book of Exodus that:

> *And the LORD spake unto Moses face to face, as a man speaketh unto his friend. And he turned again into the camp: but his servant Joshua, the son of Nun, a young man, departed not out of the tabernacle. (Exo 33:11)*

This is something that we have looked at in our consideration of Moses and the call to the individual. As a quick recap, we see that Moses would communicate with the Lord as a man speaks with his friend, face to face. These were intimate conversations between the Creator and His creation. This was similar to what Adam and Eve experienced. Again, here we see that it was Moses that would approach the Lord with intent. Moses would go into the Tabernacle, communicate with the Lord and then return to the camp. The intimate relationship Moses had with the Lord existed because Moses was intentional with it and continually tended to it.

Moses' life was littered with conversations between he and God. Moses' relationship with the Lord was built through intentional conversation. This is a pattern we see repeated with men and women of God throughout the Old Testament. The individuals of the Bible who had an intimate relationship with the Lord did so because prayer was an absolute priority in their lives.

3. Elijah

In 1 Kings we read that Elijah was at a spiritual low and was seeking solace from the Lord. In search of this, Elijah headed off to what scripture calls the Mount of God in Horeb. Horeb was the same place that the Lord spoke to Moses from in the account of the burning bush. Elijah went with the intent to hear from the Lord there. What is interesting though is that although Elijah went with a complaint unto the Lord, the Lord responded with a mission for Elijah and finished it off with an encouragement that rekindled Elijah's faith. What we can observe from this is that Elijah was open to hear what the Lord had to say. His mind wasn't closed to hear only that which he wanted to hear or that which he thought he would. Elijah was open and listening to that which the Lord was wanting to communicate unto him, despite his circumstances.

With Elijah we again see the intentionality of connection with the Lord, but we also see the need to be fully open to hear what the Lord would say. We need an ear to hear what the Lord would say.

4. Jesus

When we come to the New Testament, we see the value that Jesus placed on prayer. Jesus was able to say that He and the Father were one (John 10:30). As we read the gospels, we see constantly that Jesus would often retreat to a quiet place and pray to the Father (Matt 14:23, Matt 26:26, Luke 9:28). Jesus constantly highlighted the need He had to connect with His father in prayer. It was a cornerstone of His life here on earth.

In Matthew 14, immediately after Jesus had ministered to a multitude and fed the five thousand, He sent the crowds and His disciples away so that He might retreat and pray to His Father. Jesus had just spent the day giving out to all and yet His priority was not rest and relaxation, but on connecting with His Father in prayer. Jesus prioritised that connection because He understood the need for that well in His life and the infilling that prayer provides.

5. The Early Church
In Acts 2 we read of the Great Day of Pentecost, where the Church was born and three thousand were added to it as the Spirit moved upon the hearts of the people. Following this we are told in Acts 2:42 that:

> *And they continued stedfastly in the apostles' doctrine and fellowship, and in breaking of bread, and in **prayers**. (Act 2:42)*

The word for continued stedfastly as used here means: to *be earnest towards*, that is, (to a thing) to *persevere, be constantly* diligent, or (in a place) to *attend* assiduously all the exercises, or (to a person) to *adhere* closely *to* (as a servitor).

The early Church was deliberate and constant in prayer. They continued steadfastly in it. Prayer was not a passing fad but was a constant staple of their spiritual diets. Prayer is something that was held close to by the early Church fathers.

Through these few examples we see prayer flow from Genesis through the Old Testament and into the New. Prayer has been, is, and continues to be how the people of God communicate with their Heavenly Father during their time on earth.

D. What Prayer does

In Revelation we read that Jesus in speaking to the Church of Laodicea, said:

> *Behold, I stand at the door, and knock: if any man hear my voice, and open the door, I will come in to him, and will sup with him, and he with me. (Rev 3:20)*

When we break down this verse, we see that Jesus is standing at the door wanting to come in and have relationship with us. He is at the door, not just knocking, but also calling out. This is why He said, 'if any man hears my voice". How can we hear His voice if He is not speaking? Jesus is at the door letting us know that He is there. He is knocking and calling out to us, but the onus is on us to respond. He won't just barge His way in, He waits for us to open the door of relationship unto Him.

Jesus' desire is to be in an intimate relationship with us, but the onus is on us to respond to Him and let Him in. Prayer is not an outward showing of religiosity. The pharisees were rebuked for this (Mar 12:40). Prayer is a conversation that focuses our attention on the Lord. It stems from an inner desire to grow our relationship with the Lord. We see here that Jesus' desire is to come into our house and have a meal with us. In the natural, when we have people over for a meal, we do it because we value that relationship and want to invest into it. Jesus sees us the same way! He wants to engage with us and invest in the relationship. Prayer is how this occurs. Prayer engages us with the Lord in an intimate setting where our relationship can grow and prosper.

Digging

From Genesis to Revelation, God's desire is for intimate relationship with His creation. The way that we build and maintain this is through conversation, otherwise known as prayer. Prayer is the language of spiritual conversation that builds and grows relationship. God is willing and waiting, His end of the pipe is open! The onus is on us as individuals and Churches to give prayer the focus that it needs. We don't rush conversations with people we want to hang out with. We don't cut those conversation short because something has come along and distracted us. We prioritise those conversations and we need to do so much more so with our Heavenly Father.

The important aspect here is to remember that prayer is a conversation that involves speaking and listening. Speaking may engage us with God, but it is taking that time to listen that allows us to hear and receive from Him. It is when we listen that we allow God to engage with us. The cry of the Lord to the churches in the book of Revelation is "he who has an ear let him hear." How often do we tune our ears to the voice of the Father? Are we hearing all that the Spirit would say to the Church? It is when we have a balance between speaking and listening that we find that the connection is open. Intimate prayer connects us to the Lord by causing us to focus in on Him and opens us to receive from Him. Prayer is a door for communication, which in and of itself is a two-way street. It is a pipe that allows the Holy Spirit to flow into our lives. We engage with Him, and He engages with us. When we don't engage in prayer, we leave the door shut, the pipe closed, and we rob ourselves of an avenue that allows the Holy Spirit to flow into our lives.

Prayer is a well, that when dug, allows the Lord to pour Himself into our lives.

E. Application

In Luke 19:46 and Mar 11;17, Jesus quotes from the Old Testament, and stated that His House was to be a House of prayer.

> *And he taught, saying unto them, Is it not written, My house shall be called of all nations the **house of prayer**? but ye have made it a den of thieves. (Mar 11:17)*

At this point Jesus was referring to the Temple, as this was the House of God at that time. It was a House though that had been neglected and abused and it was because of this neglect and abuse that Jesus cleansed the temple, driving out all who bought and sold.

In time though we see that this designation of the House of God moved from the natural temple to God's Spiritual building, the Church.

> *But if I tarry long, that thou mayest know how thou oughtest to behave thyself in the **house of God, which is the church of the living God**, the pillar and ground of the truth. (1Ti 3:15)*

The Church is now the House of God! The Church was born on the great day of Pentecost when God showed His divine choice of it through the fire that fell in the form of tongues of upon those that were gathered there. The Church is not a natural building, but a spiritual building made up of two or three gathered together in the name of Jesus. It is this gathering of believers in His name that makes the Church, and it is this that makes the House of God. This House, this gathering we do in the name of Jesus is the New Testament House of God and this House is to be a House of prayer. Prayer is to be as perfume in our churches. It should permeate and be evident and obvious to all who attend. Prayer should not come as a surprise but should be considered the norm.

The prayer that occurs in the House of God, the Church, builds off the prayer of the people through the week. We cannot expect the House to be one of prayer if prayer is non-existent in our lives. The two are not mutually exclusive, but rather mutually dependant. Our prayer through the week is to fuel the fire for 'prayer in the house' and the 'prayer of the house' is to send us out revitalised to pray through the week. The two work together. It is prayer in the individual's life that fuels the prayer of the Church corporately, and it is the prayer in the Church that fans the flames of prayer in the individual. Prayer has to be a priority in both. The well needs to be open and dug both individually and corporately.

As individuals and as Churches we need to have an intentionality with prayer, that sees us seek out the Lord daily with a purpose of hearing from Him and growing our relationship with Him. His desire is there! May our desire start to match His. We need to dig the well of prayer.

THE WELL OF READING AND MEDITATING ON THE WORD

For all flesh is as grass, and all the glory of man as the flower of grass. The grass withereth, and the flower thereof falleth away: But the <u>word</u> of the Lord endureth for ever. And this is the word which by the gospel is preached unto you. (1Pe 1:24-25)

My people are destroyed for lack of knowledge: (Hos 4:6)

The second well for us to look at is that of reading and mediating on the Word of God, the Bible. The Bible is to be a staple in the Christian life and not just a book we pull out on a Sunday to take to Church. In this section we will start by looking at what the Bible is, before looking at the importance of reading and meditating on the Word.

Digging

A. The Word

The Bible is the Word of God. The Bible is one book, divided into two testaments. It is made up of thirty-nine Old Testament and twenty-seven New Testament books respectively. There are a total of sixty six individual books, yet there is but one book. Whilst the Bible has parts, verses, chapters and books, the oneness of the Word cannot be overemphasised. The Bible is one united book. It is the Book of books. It is the book that God in His grace has given to mankind.

The Bible was written by various men of God, living in different centuries, in different times and with different styles. Yet throughout the Word there is a supernatural harmony of revelation, where truth flows from start to finish.

The Bible is the communication of God to man which reveals God to man. It is God's revelation of truth to all mankind. The Bible is infallible, inexhaustible and absolutely necessary in the life of each and every believer for our continued growth and development.

In the book of 1 Peter we read:

> *As newborn babes, desire the sincere **milk** of the **word**, that ye may grow thereby: (1Pe 2:2)*

Peter likens new believers unto babies and the Word is likened unto milk. Just as an infant in the natural doesn't start on solids, neither do spiritual children. The Word is something that nourishes and causes us to develop spiritually. When we first come to Christ we start on the milk of the Word. As we grow and develop spiritually though this diet begins to change. Paul echoes this thought in 1 Corinthians where we read:

> *I have fed you with **milk**, and not with **meat**: for hitherto ye were not able to bear it, neither yet now are ye able. (1Co 3:2)*

Whilst we start on milk we are meant to progress to meat. Just as in the natural there is progression in our diet, so too is there to be progression spiritually. Whilst we start on the milk of the Word, we see with this verse from Paul that as we grow, we are to progress from milk to meat. The constant thought between Peter and Corinthians is the Word of God. It is the Word of God that is part of our staple diet for our spiritual development. The Word is something that we grow and develop on. As we grow spiritually, we go from milk to meat as our spiritual diet changes to match our growth and development. The Word provides the spiritual nourishment that we need. The Word is the Lord's provision for our spiritual appetites from when we come to Christ, through to growing in Him. It is His provision for our spiritual nourishment.

In the Old Testament we read that after the supernatural deliverance of the people of Israel from Egypt by the hand of God, the nation was sustained by the Lord during their wilderness wanderings. The Lord provided for the natural appetites of the nation of Israel, morning and evening through supernatural provision. In the morning the Lord provided by manna and at night he provided quail. The Lord provided nourishment for His people. For believers, those who are spiritual Israel, the Word is our spiritual food that the Lord has given us for our spiritual sustenance. Just as the Israelites had the choice as to whether they would avail themselves of the Lord's provision of nourishment, so to do we. The Lord has provided, but it is ours to accept and avail ourselves of it. The Word supplies nourishment to our spirit and strengthens us for what lays ahead. The Word is something that we are to spiritually have an intake of on a daily basis. It provides spiritual nourishment that allows us to live and operate from a place of spiritual strength.

> *It is the spirit that quickeneth; the flesh profiteth nothing: the <u>words</u> that I speak unto you, they are spirit, and they are life. (Joh 6:63)*

His Word blesses us with life. His Word grows and develops our spiritual being. Our spiritual lives advance as we receive life from His Word.

B. Reading the Word

In every Church and for every believer there is an absolute necessity to be reading the Word of God. Often individuals will say I'm not much of a reader, so I don't read the Word. The Bible is not a book that we read for the sake of reading, it is a book we read because we want to grow in our relationship with and knowledge of the Lord. It is not a matter of being a reader, but a heart attitude of wanting to know God more. The Bible is God's revelation to us, and within it He has included absolutely everything that He believes we need to hear and know. There are no wasted spaces and no chapter fillers. The Lord, through His Word, has communicated to man everything that He wants man to know. At its very core the Word reveals God to us and His plan of salvation for mankind. It shows us His love, His purpose, His character and His truth. We may not always understand what we read, but in time God will speak to us through and about His Word if we are faithful in reading it. It is as we are consistent with His Word that we move from the milk of the Word to the meat of the Word, as discussed above.

In the book of Romans, Paul tells us:

> *So then faith cometh by hearing, and hearing by the word of God. (Rom 10:17).*

There are several things that we can observe from this. Firstly, faith comes or is grown through hearing. Our faith develops through hearing. In order for us to hear though, someone needs to be speaking or reading and we need to be attuned to the one who is speaking. There is a responsibility on someone to speak, but there is an equal responsibility upon an individual to listen. This is the first criteria for faith, there must be someone speaking, and the individual must be attentive and listening unto what is being said.

Digging

The second thing we see is that we can't be just hearing any old conversation. For faith to come and be built up, we need to be hearing the Word of God. This is the qualifier. Faith comes from hearing the Word of God. That is why it is so important that within our Church services and within our private lives we are hearing the Word of God. Simply attending Church, watching a message or listening to a podcast doesn't mean that your faith is going to grow. The Word of God has to be being spoken, and we have to have an attitude of heart that is ready, open and listening to that which is being spoken. How can faith be lit in non-believers if the Word of God isn't being spoken? How can the faith of believers grow if they are not hearing the Word? It can't! The Word of God is absolutely vital for our faith to build.

The reader may well be thinking this idea is fine for a Sunday, but how do I hear the Word when I am reading it at home? The answer may sound a little strange, but it is a simple one. Read the Word aloud. In your own quiet times with Jesus, speak the words of the Word out. Faith comes by hearing the Word! Reading aloud is something that will actually help your times with God. When we read aloud, we are using our eyes, our mouth and our ears. The majority of our senses are now engaged, helping us to focus more and be less distracted. Reading the Word aloud will absolutely help build your faith!

C. Meditating on the Word

By the term meditating on the Word, we mean to read and think over the Words of the Lord as recorded in His Bible.

In Psalm 119:148 the psalmist says he will meditate on the statutes, that is Words, of the Lord.

> *My hands also will I lift up unto thy commandments, which I have loved; and I will **meditate** in thy statutes. (Psa 119:48)*

The Hebrew word for meditate as used here, means to ponder, to converse or to utter. Meditation in a worldly sense is to repeat a chant. From a Christian perspective to meditate on the Word means to repeat what we have read, either aloud or in our mind, with the purpose of keeping the Word of the Lord at the forefront of our mind. The emphasis is on the time we give to God to seek to understand His Word by keeping it at the forefront of our minds. As we meditate, we sow His Word into our mind and spirit, which in time allows us to reap a harvest.

A great example of this is seen with Daniel in Daniel Chapter 9:1-3. In this chapter we see that Daniel had been studying the book of Jeremiah. As he had been reading over it and thinking upon it he began to understand by revelation of the Lord that the time frame regarding Jerusalem's desolation was almost completed. It was Daniel's focus on the Word that allowed the Lord to open his understanding. This was a revelation that Daniel would not have received had he not been studying the Word of God. It was

Daniel's focus upon the Word that allowed the Lord to speak to Him. As Daniel dug into the Word, the Lord infilled him with revelation.
Meditation on the Word is seeking God to understand His Word. In Proverbs we read:

It is the glory of God to conceal a thing: but the honour of kings is to search out a matter. (Pro 25:2)

The Word of God is the truth of God communicated to man. But God is Spirit, and His Word is written in spiritual language that natural man cannot always immediately make sense of. It takes time on man's part in seeking the Spirit to reveal the truth of His Word to us. This happens when we give Him the opportunity by keeping His Word at the forefront of our thoughts.

Meditating on His Word is something that requires our time and our focus. As we give time to considering and thinking upon the Word of God, we allow the Spirit time to enlighten to us exactly what is being said in the Word. As we focus in on the Word, we allow the Spirit the opportunity to speak to us through the Word. We allow the Spirit to speak by keeping His Word at the forefront of our minds. At its very core the Word is the revelation of Jesus. He was the Word made flesh, the living embodiment of the Word of God. As we give time to consider His Word, we allow the Spirit time to reveal more about Jesus to us.

D. Application

In our personal lives and in our Church gatherings, the Word of God needs to be at the forefront. The Word is part of our spiritual nourishment that helps us grow and develop as believers. Just as our natural bodies require nutrition to function so to do our spiritual bodies. We need the Word Monday, Tuesday, Wednesday, Thursday, Friday, Saturday and Sunday. One meal a week is not enough! Poor nutrition has an effect on growth and development. If we want to be growing and also raising disciples that are growing, then we need a proper diet of the Word on a daily basis. We need to be reading the Word, hearing the Word and meditating on His Word.

As we read and mediate upon His Word, we allow ourselves to be spiritually nourished, receiving from our Heavenly Father that which He has provided for our spiritual growth. As we read and meditate, we open and allow ourselves to receive from Him. Reading and Meditating upon His Word is a well that allows us to be infilled.

Digging

THE WELL OF SENSITIVITY TO THE HOLY SPIRIT

And grieve not the holy Spirit of God, whereby ye are sealed unto the day of redemption. (Eph 4:30)

The third well for us to look at is that of being sensitive to the Holy Spirit. The Holy Spirit is the third person of the trinity and, as we have considered earlier, there is a particular focus on the Holy Spirit in this current dispensation of time known as the Church age. In the book of John, Jesus outlined on four occasions that after His sacrifice He would send a comforter to His people:

> *And I will pray the Father, and he shall give you another **Comforter**, that he may abide with you for ever; (Joh 14:16)*
>
> *But the **Comforter**, which is the **Holy Ghost**, whom the Father will send in my name, he shall teach you all things, and bring all things to your remembrance, whatsoever I have said unto you. (Joh 14:26)*
>
> *But when the **Comforter** is come, whom I will send unto you from the Father, even the Spirit of truth, which proceedeth from the Father, he shall testify of me: (Joh 15:26)*
>
> *Nevertheless I tell you the truth; It is expedient for you that I go away: for if I go not away, the **Comforter** will not come unto you; but if I depart, I will send him unto you. (Joh 16:7)*

The Greek word for comforter used in these verses means: an *intercessor, consoler*. The Holy Spirit has been sent by the Father and Son for the benefit of their people in this age. The Holy Spirit is here to lead and guide us into a greater understanding of and relationship with the Lord. The Holy Spirit is here, in this age, with the Lord's people as their Comforter. He is here to help us grow and connect more intimately with the Father.

A. Why do we need to be sensitive?

The question that may come to the readers mind is that if the Holy Spirit has been sent by Jesus unto His people, why do we need to be sensitive to Him? What we need to remember is that the Holy Spirit is the third person of the God head, the trinity. The truth of the Father, Son and Spirit is that they are reaching out to us, but the level of relationship and response is determined by us. It is we, His people, that need to be aware and sensitive to the presence of the Lord and His voice. In particular reference to the Holy Spirit, the New Testament gives us two verses that highlight our need to be sensitive to the Spirit.

Paul in his discourse and final remarks to the Thessalonians stated:

> *Rejoice evermore. Pray without ceasing. In every thing give thanks: for this is the will of God in Christ Jesus concerning you.* **_Quench not the Spirit_**. *Despise not prophesyings. (1Th 5:16-20)*

The Greek word for quench as used here means to extinguish. What Paul was saying here is that within the Church and within our personal lives we have the capacity to extinguish the Spirit. Just as a fire in the natural can be extinguished so to is it with the Spirit. A fire will go out when it is extinguished deliberately or because it runs out of fuel when it hasn't been attended to and maintained. It is this second instance that the writer believes that Paul is referring to here. When we are sensitive to a fire, we are aware of its condition and maintain or increase the fuel load as necessary. When we are not sensitive to it, the fire will eventually go out, leaving some smouldering coals which will in turn eventually go cold. This is true of the Spirit! If we are not sensitive to the Spirit and ignore Him, we will quench Him and extinguish Him. The Lord is always there to help mankind, but He will never force Himself on mankind. The same is true of the Spirit with the Church and believers. He is there, but we need to be sensitive to Him.

The other verse we find in regard to being sensitive to the Holy Spirit is found in Paul's letter to the Ephesians.

> *And **_grieve not the holy Spirit_** of God, whereby ye are sealed unto the day of redemption.*
> *(Eph 4:30)*

The Greek word for grieve as used here means to distress, be sad and is translated, cause grief, grieve, be in heaviness, sorrow, be sorry.

Paul here tells us that within our churches and within our lives we have the capacity to grieve the Spirit. Such is quite a sobering thought! We, as the people of God, have the capacity to either grieve or bless the Holy Spirit.

We refer to people as insensitive when they are either unaware or unremorseful for how their actions or words have impacted another individual. Sometimes this can be deliberate, sometimes this can be unintentional and sometimes this can be through a lack of knowledge or life experience. As the people of the Lord, we need to be aware of the Holy Spirit and also be aware of what actions and words bless Him as well as what grieves Him. This is what being sensitive to the Spirit means. To be aware of His presence and how we honour His presence. We don't brush Him aside, we don't ignore him, we give Him time and embrace Him, waiting patiently upon Him.

If we are to not grieve the Spirit or quench the Spirit, then we need to be sensitive to the Spirit. This leads us to our next question.

Digging

B. How do you become sensitive?

Sensitivity in any relationship comes through time and getting to know the other individual. We see a great example of how sensitivity can be developed in the book of Samuel. In 1 Samuel 3 we read of the encounter of Samuel with the voice of the Lord. Whilst the interaction here is between Samuel and the Lord, the principles we discover are applicable to us becoming more sensitive to the Holy Spirit. The sensitivity evident between Samuel and the Lord is the same sensitivity that believers are to have with the Holy Spirit.

The reader is encouraged to read 1 Samuel Chapter 3 in its entirety before moving forward here. For our purposes we will provide a brief overview of the chapter.

In 1 Samuel 3 we read that Samuel ministered unto the Lord before Eli. Samuel was being trained up by Eli in the service of the priesthood. In these days we are told that the Word of the Lord was rare and there was no widespread revelation from God to the people. The voice of God was silent. One night as Samuel lay down to sleep at the end of a day's service, the Lord called unto him. Samuel not yet knowing the voice of the Lord ran to Eli to see what was required of him. When Samuel reached Eli, he asked him why he had called out. Eli possibly puzzled as to why Samuel was there, told Samuel that he hadn't called him, and that Samuel should go back to bed. This situation happened three times. On the third occasion Eli triggered as to what was happening. Eli told Samuel to go and lay down again, but the next time when he heard the voice, that he should respond, "Speak Lord for your servant is listening". Samuel took his master's advice and waited for the Lord to speak. When Samuel heard the call of the Lord, he responded and said, "speak Lord for your servant hears". As Samuel lay there listening, the Lord spoke to Samuel and gave him a prophetic word regarding the house of his master Eli. This was the first time that Samuel heard the voice of the Lord.

From this encounter there are several things that we can learn and can apply to being sensitive to the Holy Spirit:

1. Be in God's presence

    Samuel was one that served constantly before the Lord in the House of the Lord. Under Eli, Samuel was being trained as a priest in the House of God. Samuel's life was centred around serving God's House and about ministering before the presence of the Lord. Verse 3 tells us that the Ark of God was still in the temple at this time. This was where the presence of God dwelt. It dwelt upon the Ark, atop of the blood-stained mercy seat, in the Most Holy place. Samuel was constantly in and around the presence of the Lord. It was this lifestyle that preceded Samuel hearing the voice of the Lord. Samuel's priority of being in God's presence enabled and opened him to be able to hear the voice of the Lord.

2. Have a right heart

As we read this account of Samuel it is interesting to note that there are two men mentioned in this chapter. We have the priest of God Eli, and we have the young man Samuel who was Eli's attendant. These men were in close enough proximity that Samuel mistakenly believed he had heard Eli cry out when the Lord first spoke. Whilst the two were in close proximity the Lord did not speak to Eli. The Lord didn't speak to the established priest, but rather unto the young man Samuel. Why? The answer is quite possibly given to us in the word that Samuel received from the Lord:

> *In that day I will perform against Eli all things which I have spoken concerning his house: when I begin, I will also make an end. For I have told him that I will judge his house for ever **for the iniquity which he knoweth**; because his sons made themselves vile, and he restrained them not. (1Sa 3:12-13)*

Eli knew of the iniquity of his sons, in the way that they acted as priests unto the Lord, yet he never corrected them. To put it simply, to not address sin is to accept it. To not condemn sin is to condone it. When we accept sin, it affects our hearts. Acceptance of sin places the person who commits it above God and this in turn hardens our heart towards God. Eli placed family before God. His heart was not right!

Samuel on the other hand was of pure heart. He had childlike faith and served God out of sincerity and truth. It is the writer's belief that it was the condition of Samuel's heart that allowed Samuel to hear from God, while Eli lay ignorant and unaware of the fact that the Lord was speaking.

3. Learn to identify His voice

Learning the sound of someone's voice takes time. Samuel was initially unaware of the difference between the voice of Eli and the voice of the Lord. This was due to the fact that Samuel had never heard the voice of the Lord before. It is possible that Samuel knew the voice of Eli didn't sound quite right, but he had no prior experience to properly identify the voice of the Lord.

As we spend time listening and being attentive to someone's voice, we develop a finely tuned ear to be able to hear it and distinguish it. This truth can be seen with any parent. A parent can be surrounded by a mass of other children at a park, making noise, crying, screaming, playing. The second that the parent hears the cry of their child though, their ear is immediately tuned in. It is a voice that they know. They have spent time tuning into it, learning its sound and being readily able to identify it.

The same is true with the voice of the Lord. The more time we spend learning to hear His voice in the quiet the more finely attuned our ear becomes. After a while, like the parent in the park, we are easily able to block out other distractions and tune in to what the Lord is saying.

4. Be teachable

Samuel learned to hear the voice of the Lord as he submitted to the teaching of Eli. Samuel was able to hear the Lord's voice, but it was the teaching of Eli that helped him engage with the Lord. Without a teachable spirit Samuel would have missed this call.

For us as believers and churches, there are many things that we can still learn from fathers in the faith and those that have gone before us. We need to have that teachable spirit that allows our spiritual Eli's to be able to teach us how to be sensitive to the Holy Spirit.

5. Take time to Listen

Learning to hear His voice takes time, but if we want to continually hear His voice, we have to continually make time. Samuel was in a place of rest! He was lying in bed, recuperating from the days duties and regaining the strength needed for the day ahead. Samuel though took time out of his time, to stop and listen to the Lord. Samuel didn't have to respond to the voice of the Lord! That choice lay with him and whether he was willing to be obedient and give up his time to listen. The choice was whether Samuel was willing to sacrifice some of his rest time in order to engage with the Lord.

The same is true for us, being sensitive to the Spirit involves giving up our time in order to give Him time.

6. Dismiss distractions.

Samuel's initial focus in this chapter was on serving Eli. His mindset was on what do I have to get done right now. He was transfixed on the busyness of life and the responsibilities that lay upon him. It was this focus that initially stopped Samuel from hearing the voice of the Lord. It wasn't until Samuel stepped out of those responsibilities, that he could then put himself in a place to be able to hear God. God would always rather have us at His feet than being distracted with the cares and busyness of life (Luke 10:38-42).

Our sensitivity can get dulled at times by those things that we deem are important. Our focus and what we believe we need to achieve can desensitise us to the Holy Spirit.

Whilst being simple, these six things will help us in our lives and in our Church services to have a greater sensitivity to the Holy Spirit. Like with Samuel, these are things that need to be practiced and grown in. For Samuel, his first experience of

Digging

hearing the Lord's voice was one that set him up for a lifetime of being sensitive to the Lord.

C. Application

We are living in the dispensation of the Holy Spirit. During this time, it is imperative that we as believers and churches have a sensitivity to the Holy Spirit. The Holy Spirit has been sent by the Father, through the Son as the Comforter and Helper of the people of God in this age. He is here for our benefit and growth. It is through Him that we have the gifts and the fruits of the Spirit. These are things that are so needed in the Church today. In order for these to be able to be evidenced in our lives and churches, we need to be sensitive to the Spirit.

As seen above, sensitivity is developed through a number of different ways, but the overriding theme and the most important aspect is that of time. Developing a sensitivity takes time. The question we need to ask ourselves is do we give, allow, allocate enough time in our lives, in our meetings, in our services to be sensitive to the Holy Spirit? We cannot expect the Spirit to move if we aren't being sensitive to Him! We cannot expect the Spirit to pour out if we don't allow Him to. We can declare our need of the Spirit to move, but are we actually being sensitive to Him and giving Him the room to move?

We need to dig deep in the well of sensitivity to the Holy Spirit. We need to commit the time to tune our sensitivity and become attuned unto Him. When we are attuned to Him, He can then flow. It was through Samuel's sensitivity that the Lord was able to pour into him. The same is true for us. As we become sensitive to the Spirit, we stop doing those things that quench and grieve Him, and we allow Him to pour into our lives and services. As we dig the well of sensitivity, we allow Him the opportunity to infill.

THE WELL OF FAITH

But without faith it is impossible to please him: for he that cometh to God must believe that he is, and that he is a rewarder of them that diligently seek him. (Heb 11:6)

The fourth well for us to look at is the well of faith. Faith is an absolutely vital part of every believer's relationship with the Lord. It is through faith that we come to the Lord. If we are to grow in our relationship with Him, then our faith is a muscle that needs to be exercised and grown. As we trust the Lord more and more, we are to go from faith to faith. That is, our level of faith is to increase more and more as we grow and develop our relationship with the Lord.

A. What is Faith

Faith is a belief and trust in who God is and what His Word says, in spite of our knowledge, circumstances and doubts. The writer of Hebrews starts the great chapter of faith by saying:

> *Now faith is the substance of things hoped for, the evidence of things not seen. (Heb 11:1)*

Faith is that which we hope for and is the belief of things we haven't yet seen or can't yet see. Faith is not having knowledge, but rather it is believing in God in the absence of knowledge or proof. Knowledge is something that is based on experience and what has been learned. Knowledge is built from that which is demonstratable. Faith operates on a level higher than knowledge. Faith is a belief in the Lord that cannot be proved by knowledge or experience. Faith is belief in that which we cannot see and that which we hope for.

Faith is a response to the Lord. It is a belief in Him, a belief in His Word and a belief in what He calls us to do. Throughout Hebrews Chapter 11, we see constant examples of this, but for the sake of time let us just consider the example of Noah that the writer of Hebrews refers too.

In Hebrews 11:7 we read:

> *By faith Noah, being warned of God of things not seen as yet, moved with fear, prepared an ark to the saving of his house; by the which he condemned the world, and became heir of the righteousness which is by faith. (Heb 11:7)*

Within this there is a wealth of information for us to consider. Let's break this verse down a little to see what truth is being communicated to us.

By faith Noah,

Noah was a man of faith. Noah had faith and acted on that faith. The account that follows is because of the faith of Noah.

being warned of God of things not seen as yet,

Noah was warned by God of things not yet seen. There are two thoughts for us to consider in this statement. The Lord warned Noah long in advance that He was going to destroy the world through a flood. This was a prophetic warning to Noah. The Lord was letting Noah know what was going to happen long before it ever would. The warning Noah received came some one hundred years before the fulfilment of the Word of the Lord.

Whilst Noah was warned of things that had not yet happened, scripture would seem to infer that there is more involved here. The following is given for the reader's consideration.

In Genesis 2:5 we read of the first mention of rain in the Bible:

> *And every plant of the field before it was in the earth, and every herb of the field before it grew: **for the LORD God had not caused it to rain upon the earth**, and there was not a man to till the ground. But there went up a mist from the earth, and watered the whole face of the ground. (Gen 2:5-6)*

Initially the earth was not watered by rain! Such seems removed from our understanding of how the world works. Nevertheless, we read here that before the Lord introduced rain, He caused a mist to come up which watered the face of the earth. The inference of scripture would seem to indicate a greenhouse like effect initially existed. It was through this that the earth was watered, and plant life was supported.

The next mention we have of rain doesn't occur until we get to Genesis 7:4. There we read of the Lord talking to Noah and the Lord says:

> *For yet seven days, and **I will cause it to rain upon the earth forty days and forty nights**; and every living substance that I have made will I destroy from off the face of the earth. (Gen 7:4)*

This is the second mention in scripture of rain upon the earth. In our times we take rain for granted as it is a common place occurrence. But for Noah this may not have been the case. It would seem inferred from scripture that up until the time of Noah, the Lord had watered the earth through the mist He caused to come upon it. It is not until Genesis 7:11, when the Lord opened the windows of heaven, that rain poured out upon the land.

For Noah it is possible this was his first experience of rain. This is the meaning in Hebrews of "things not yet seen". God revealed a prophetic word to Noah that Noah couldn't fully envisage. The concept was foreign to him. Noah needed faith to believe in this thing not yet seen. It is this thought that adds another dimension to the faith of Noah. Noah responded to the warning of a flood. Something he had never seen and something he had no idea about how it could possibly occur.

moved with fear,

Noah's faith prompted him to respond. This was not a fear of God, but a reverential fear for the Word of the Lord. Noah revered the Lord and His Word and responded to it accordingly. Noah's faith resulted in action.

prepared an ark to the saving of his house;

Noah's reverence for the Word of the Lord prompted him to action. Noah's faith in what God had said, saw him take on that which God had called him to. It was a ridiculous task. It was a massive ship, not near an ocean and designed to carry masses of animals. How would Noah even round the animals up, let alone float the ship?

by the which he condemned the world,

His faith stood in contrast to the unbelief of the world. The actions of Noah and his belief in the Lord and His Word stood in stark contrast to the world.

and became heir of the righteousness which is by faith. (Heb 11:7)

Noah's faith in the saving power of God saw him become an heir of righteousness.

Noah had an unwavering faith in what God had said. He didn't need to be able to explain it. He didn't need to know the details of it. He didn't need it to make sense. He didn't need to have all of the answers. He trusted God's Word and aligned his actions to it. Noah believed what the Lord said would happen and he believed in the Lord's ability to preserve him through it.

Faith is looking beyond the natural and believing in a God who is supernatural. Faith is the unwavering belief in God and His Word. Faith is the substance of things hoped for and the evidence of things not yet seen.

B. How do we enact faith?

Having had a look at what faith is, the question becomes how do we enact faith and how do we grow in faith in our walks with the Lord? To answer this, let's look at an example from scripture.

In Matthew 14 we read the account of Jesus walking on the water. Scripture tells us that after a time of ministry, Jesus had sent the disciples off in a boat while He retreated to a solitary place and prayed. As the boat was on the sea it encountered contrary winds and was being tossed to and fro by the waves of the sea. At about the fourth watch of the night Jesus set out, walking on the sea. As the disciples sat in the boat being tossed to and fro, they saw a figure on the water. They didn't immediately recognise that it was Jesus. They cried out in fear thinking that they were seeing a spirit. Immediately Jesus called to reassure and calm them, "it is me, be not afraid". At hearing the voice of Jesus, Peter responded that if it was really Jesus, He should call him to come out on the water. Jesus simply responded "come". Peter upon hearing this, stepped out of the boat and headed to Jesus upon the water. For a while Peter was fine, but as the wind and its effects caught his eyes, he became afraid, and started to sink in the sea. In fear, Peter called out to Jesus to save him. Jesus immediately stretched forth His hand and lifted Peter up and took him back to the boat.

From this account there are several things that we can observe about enacting and walking in faith.

Digging

1. Word
   And he said <u>Come</u> Matt 14:29

   Faith is always a response to the Word of the Lord. Any action without the Word is presumption based on an assumption. The Word of the Lord always comes first, and faith responds to that. Here Peter poses a question, but he waits for a Word from the Lord. Jesus, who is the Word, says "come".

   A Word can come through an individual, through reading the Bible or we may hear the voice of the Lord ourselves. Faith starts with a response to the voice of the Lord. The writer is not saying that we always need to have a Word from God before stepping out, but rather that our Faith must always be aligned to the Word of God, whether hearing from God directly or through His Word. Faith is based on the Word.

2. Response
   And when Peter was come Matt 14:29

   Faith requires a response. That is the essence of faith. Faith is not just hearing the voice of God, it is responding to it. Peter heard and Peter responded. Response to the Word demonstrates our faith in what God has said.

   Just like in our example from 2 Kings 3, faith was not evidenced when the kings heard the Word of the Lord through Elisha, their faith was evidenced when they responded to it and dug the wells! Faith is shown through action.

3. Step
   Peter was come down out of the ship Matt 14:29

   The ship represented security and trust for Peter. The ship was a safe place. The ship was where his friends were. The ship had kept him safe thus far from the storm. The ship was in the natural the smartest place for Peter to be. The call though, was to come out of the ship.

   Peter had to separate himself from everything that was comfortable and a source of security. He had to literally step out into the unknown, and the only thing he had to hold onto was the Word of God. They say the first step is sometimes the hardest, and such is often the case with faith related matters. Faith requires us to step out of our comfort zone, trusting in the Word of the Lord.

4. Walk
   He walked on the water Matt 14:29

   The first step is just one of many that will follow. Whilst the first step is often the hardest as we leave our places of security, the truth is that every proceeding step takes us further and further from these places of safety and closer to the place where God is calling us to. Faith is a walk that starts with a step.

There is a song that goes 'every step I take, is a step of faith'. That is so true. Our walk of faith is made up of individual steps of faith. Peter's walk was just like ours. One foot in front of the other holding on to the Word of faith.

5. Focus
   To go to Jesus Matt 14:29

   Peter's focus was on Jesus. The reader is encouraged to read the entire account in Matthew 14, where it can be seen that as long as Peter's focus was on Jesus, he was fine. It was not until his focus was distracted that problems arose.

   Faith requires us to keep our focus on Him who is the author of our faith. Faith is a walk that leads us to Jesus as we focus in on Him. A walk of faith is one that leads us to Jesus.

From this account we see the steps of faith. We see the evidence of these steps not only with Peter but also with Noah and the other heroes of faith mentioned in Hebrews 11. In order to show to the reader how these steps occur in the life of every believer we will consider the examples of Noah and Abraham from Hebrews 11 here to highlight how these steps apply to each of us in our response to God.

	PETER	**ABRAHAM**	**NOAH**
WORD	Come.	Promised Land.	Build an Ark.
RESPONSE	Went to the edge of the boat.	Packed up his things.	Moved with Godly fear.
STEP	Stepped out.	Stepped away from his home and homeland.	Started building.
WALK	Walked on the water.	Journeyed to the land of promise.	Continued for 100 years.
FOCUS	Went to Jesus.	Waited for the city whose builder was God.	Salvation of the Lord.

Faith is something that only we can enact. God can't enact it for us. Others can't enact our faith. Our faith is only enacted when **we** respond in belief to God through the above steps. As we respond to the Word of God and walk with a focus on Jesus, we enact our faith.

C. Application

In order for us to accept Jesus and believe in God we need faith. Faith is an essential for us to be born into the Kingdom of Heaven, but it doesn't stop there. In order for us to continue growing we need to not only continue to operate in faith, but also continue to grow in it.

Faith connects us to God. Faith allows us to come to God, to hear from God, to respond to Him and to step into the things He has for us. Faith is an absolute essential in our lives and in our Churches. It is a pipe that allows us to receive from the Lord and advance in the things He has called us to, as He continually supplies through the pipe of faith.

Digging the well of faith draws us closer to Jesus. Just as Peter's walk of faith brought him closer to Jesus, so too does ours.

> *But without faith it is impossible to please him: for he that cometh to God must believe that he is, and that he is a rewarder of them that diligently seek him. (Heb 11:6)*

Our faith pleases God, and as we approach Him in our walk of faith, He rewards us. Our walk of faith allows us to receive from the Lord. Faith opens us up to receive from the Lord.

THE WELL OF OBEDIENCE

But he said, Yea rather, blessed are they that hear the word of God, and keep it. (Luk 11:28)

The fifth well for us to consider is the well of obedience. Obedience may sound a little strange, but what we need to remember here is that we are talking about those things that connect us to God. If we flip this thought for a second, we would all have no doubt that disobedience is something that causes a disconnect between us and the Lord.

We see a clear example of this with Adam and Eve. When living in obedience to the Word of God, Adam and Eve had an intimate connection with the Lord. The Lord would come and walk and talk with them in the garden. When they disobeyed though, we see that disobedience caused a disconnect between them and God. The relationship that they had once enjoyed was forever changed when they were disobedient to the Word of the Lord. If disobedience causes a disconnect with the Lord, as evidenced by this example of Adam and Eve, then the converse is also true, i.e. that obedience causes us to connect with the Lord. It is this point that the writer will elaborate on, highlighting to the reader the importance of obedience in our relationship with the Lord.

In the verse quoted at the top of this page Jesus stated that blessed **are not** the people who simply hear the Word. What He said was, that blessed are the people who **hear** the Word and **keep** it! In order to keep the Word, we need to be obedient to it. The meaning of keeping the Word is to obey the Word. This is what Adam and Eve didn't do. They heard the Word but they didn't keep it. They heard God say don't eat of the tree, but they didn't obey that Word. As believers, we are to hear the Word and we are to keep it. We are not to pick and choose that which we want to keep. We are to hear the Words of the Lord and we are to keep them. The Lord is after our **FULL** obedience.

We see a great example of this in 1 Samuel 15. There Saul had received instruction from the Lord that he was to go out and destroy Amalek and everything that was found, carrying out the judgement of the Lord. Saul set out in response to this call, but he was not fully obedient to it. Saul responded to the Word but was only obedient to a measure. Saul elected to keep the king of Amalek and all the best of the herds and flocks alive under the guise of having them to worship the Lord with. The Lord then sent the prophet Samuel to challenge Saul on his disobedience in this matter. When confronted by the prophet Samuel over his sin, Saul tried to explain his error away righteously, claiming that he had only been disobedient so that he could honour the Lord in sacrifice. Samuel's response to this excuse was short yet sharp:

> *And Samuel said, "Has the LORD as great delight in burnt offerings and sacrifices, as in **obeying the voice** of the LORD? Behold, to obey is better than sacrifice, and to listen than the fat of rams. (1Sa 15:22)*

The Lord wasn't interested in the "righteousness" of Saul's actions! He was after obedience to the Word that He had given Saul. The Lord has spoken His Word to Saul through Samuel. Saul had received the Word, yet he didn't obey. He heard the Word, but he didn't keep the Word. We cannot keep the Word by disobeying it, even if we try to righteously justify our actions!

Throughout the Word of the Lord, obedience is highlighted again and again as something that connects the people of God to their Maker. Obedience to the Word of God aligns us with the Lord and His will. Let us consider some examples from scripture which clearly point to this truth.

A. Cain and Abel

> The account of Cain and Abel can be found in Genesis 4. Cain and Abel were brothers, the sons of Adam and Eve. Cain was a tiller of the ground and Abel kept sheep. In the process of time both of the brothers brought offerings unto the Lord. Cain brought the fruit of the ground whilst Abel brought one of his flock. Genesis tells us that:
>
>> *...... And the LORD had respect unto Abel and to his offering: But unto Cain and to his offering he had not respect. And Cain was very wroth, and his countenance fell. (Gen 4:4-5)*
>
> The question from this is why was God pleased with Abel, but had no respect for Cain's? Didn't they both bring offerings unto Hi?. In answering this, the book of Hebrews tells us that:

> *By faith Abel offered unto God a more excellent sacrifice than Cain, by which he obtained witness that he was righteous, God testifying of his gifts: and by it he being dead yet speaketh. (Heb 11:4)*

By **faith** Abel offered his sacrifice! The direct implication of this is that Cain did not offer his offering with faith. We have considered the connection of faith in an earlier point. There we saw that part of faith is the belief in what God has said. Here we see Abel enact his faith through obedience to the Word!

God had demonstrated back in the Garden of Eden, after Adam and Eve had sinned, how He was to be approached in offering and sacrifice. The truth of the need for a sacrifice involving the shedding of blood had been demonstrated. It was the skins from these sacrificial offerings that were used by the Lord to clothe Adam and Eve. The Lord there demonstrated to Adam and Eve how sacrifice and offering were to be done.

For Adam and Eve that which their sin exposed was covered by the sacrifice of another. The Lord there demonstrated to man how He was to be approached in sacrifice. This was no doubt a truth that Adam and Eve had passed down to their children and possibly demonstrated to them as well (how else would Abel know to do this!) Abel acted in obedience to the Word of God that had been demonstrated, and it is for this reason that God looked with respect and favour upon his offering. The obedience of Abel to the truths God had laid out, brought about a connection.

Conversely the disobedience of Cain brought a disconnection, that then spiralled into further disobedience. Obedience leads to a path of blessing whilst disobedience leads to a path of cursing. Cain and Abel demonstrate this to us. Abel chose obedience while Cain believed he knew better and made his own rules. It was the obedience of Abel that aligned Him with the Lord and allowed Him to receive the blessing of favour.

Aligning ourselves to the Word and being obedient to it, establishes a connection between us and God that allows Him to flow into our lives.

B. Deuteronomy

In Deuteronomy Chapters 28-30 we read that Moses laid out for the people of Israel the path of blessing or cursing that lay before them as they prepared to finally enter the promised land. The reader is encouraged to read these chapters fully before moving on here. It is here that Moses in a sense was starting to give a closing exhortation to his ministry. Moses would not enter the promised land, and in these chapters he laid everything out for the people of Israel to continue to walk with the Lord.

At the end of these chapters Moses closed by saying:

> *I call heaven and earth to record this day against you, that I have set before you life and death, blessing and cursing: therefore choose life, that both thou and thy seed may live: That thou mayest love the LORD thy God, and that thou **mayest obey his voice**, and that thou mayest cleave unto him: for he is thy life, and the length of thy days: that thou mayest dwell in the land which the LORD sware unto thy fathers, to Abraham, to Isaac, and to Jacob, to give them. (Deu 30:19-20)*

Moses had laid out everything for the people of Israel. He had told them the two options that stood before them, but there was a choice that lay before the people of Israel. Life or Death. Blessing or Cursing. This choice centred around their obedience or disobedience unto the Lord. Moses' encouragement was for them to love the Lord, obey His voice and cleave unto Him. The path of life involved being obedient unto the Lord. In other words, obedience was a key!

If we look back to Chapter 28 where Moses discussed the blessings and curses that stood before the people, we see how the Lord defined what obedience and disobedience looked like.

> *And it shall come to pass, if thou shalt hearken **diligently unto the voice** of the LORD thy God, to observe and to **do all his commandments** which I command thee this day, that the LORD thy God will set thee on high above all nations of the earth: And all these blessings shall come on thee, and overtake thee, if thou shalt hearken unto the voice of the LORD thy God. (Deu 28:1-2)*

> *But it shall come to pass, if thou **wilt not hearken unto the voice of the LORD** thy God, to observe to do **all his commandments and his statutes** which I command thee this day; that all these curses shall come upon thee, and overtake thee: (Deu 28:15)*

Obedience and disobedience were defined as whether or not Israel would adhere to the voice of the Lord and the commandments and statutes that He had given. That is, their obedience or disobedience was defined by whether they followed the Word of the Lord or not. As with Adam and Eve, we see that obedience was determined upon adherence to the Word of God. And just like with Adam and Eve, obedience would lead to life and disobedience to death.

Moses was trying to emphasise to the people of Israel the vital importance of their obedience unto the Lord. Their obedience built their relationship with the Lord and kept them connected to Him and protected by Him. It was this connection through obedience between Israel and the Lord that allowed Him to enter into their lives and bless them.

Obedience is a choice, and one that has ramifications. Obedience facilitates the connection that allows God to flow into the lives of His people.

C. Old Testament Israel

It we stop for a minute and consider an overview of Israel in the Old Testament, we see time and time again what happened through obedience and disobedience unto the Lord. Obedience unto the Lord always brought connection between the people and God. Likewise, disobedience always brought about a disconnection. As the people began to disobey God, they began to wander from Him. The more they disobeyed, the further they wandered. The disconnection grew through disobedience. When they came to their senses though and returned to the Lord, in obedience, we see that the connection was reformed, and the connection continued to grow through their obedience.

When we look at the history of Old Testament Israel we see a cycle of obedience, complacency, disobedience and repentance. Israel was obedient unto the Lord, but they then became complacent in His blessings. This led to disobedience, which brought the judgement of God upon the people. When they finally realised their situation, they would repent and return to the path of obedience. This was a pattern that repeated over and over again. As the New Testament Church and believers, we need to be ever on guard against complacency and make sure we are walking in obedience. We can never let the blessings of obedience distract us from the need for it.

The exact same truths of Old Testament Israel apply to Spiritual Israel, the Church and the believers who form it. Our obedience will connect us to God, or our disobedience will disconnect us from Him.

D. Jesus on Obedience

In Matthew 7:21-27 Jesus gave an interesting discourse to his followers. There He said:

> *"Not everyone who says to me, 'Lord, Lord,' will enter the kingdom of heaven, but the one who does the will of my Father who is in heaven. On that day many will say to me, 'Lord, Lord, did we not prophesy in your name, and cast out demons in your name, and do many mighty works in your name?' And then will I declare to them, 'I never knew you; depart from me, you workers of lawlessness.'* (Mat 7:21-23)

In this passage Jesus iterated the necessity of obedience in our relationship with the Lord. He stated that not everyone who cries Lord, Lord will enter the Kingdom of Heaven, but he **who does** the Father's will. In other words, it is the ones who are being obedient that enter! We then go on to read of the exploits of those Jesus says He doesn't know. Upon first reading this, it can seem a little confronting and surprising. The truth of what is being said though is that it is not the things that we do in His name, but the obedience that we demonstrate unto His Word by which He will know us. That is what God is looking for. It is often said that actions speak louder than words but here we see that obedience to His Word speaks louder than any religious actions in His name! The Lord is looking for those who are obedient.

Following this Jesus then goes on to illustrate the importance of obedience through the parable of the wise and foolish builders. This parable can sometimes be misinterpreted as we assume the rock being referred to here is Jesus. In scripture this is often the case, but for this parable the key is given in the first verse where Jesus said:

> *"Everyone then who hears these words of mine and does them will be like a wise man who built his house on the rock. (Mat 7:24)*

Jesus started by saying that he who hears these words and does them. In other words, he who is obedient to the Word of God. The key here is obedience to the Word. It is obedience to the Word that Jesus likens to a man who builds his house on a rock. Similarly, it is disobedience to the Word, i.e. he who hears and does not do, that is compared to the man who built upon the sand. The rock in this parable represents obedience unto the Words of Jesus.

Jesus in this passage is further iterating the necessity of obedience unto His Words. It is obedience to the Word that is an absolute necessity for the people of God. It connects us to Him, through relationship. It is through obedience that Jesus says I know you. It also provides us with a strength in the storms of life to be able to stand, because our connection is not rooted in the temporary but in Him who is eternal.

E. Application

Hopefully through these few examples we have considered, the reader has seen that the need for obedience to the Lord and His Word is something that has existed since the beginning of creation. When we are obedient to the Lord and His Word, it aligns us with God and allows Him to fill us with His spiritual life.

God is the same yesterday, today and forever. Whilst God is love, God is also just. It is not one at the expense of the other. It is the justness of God that means that He can't bless a people who are disobedient. That is a violation of His nature. The blessing of God comes through the obedience of His people. We are called to be obedient.

As we dig the well of obedience, by keeping all of His Word, we allow ourselves to receive from Him. As with natural Israel, when spiritual Israel walks in obedience to the Words of the Lord, we open ourselves to the blessings of the Lord. Obedience connects us unto the Lord and opens us up to receive from Him.

Digging

THE WELL OF SPEAKING IN TONGUES

The sixth well for us to look at is the well of speaking in tongues. Speaking in tongues is something often associated with Pentecostal Churches, and at times possibly seen by those outside as something that is a little strange. Nothing though, could be further from the truth. We serve a God who created language, who speaks and understands every language. Speaking in tongues is simply a God given unction to be able to speak in a language, heavenly or earthly, not known to the person speaking it. It is an empowerment that occurs through the anointing of the Holy Spirit.

Within the Word of God, we see speaking in tongues is revealed in two different ways in the lives of believers. There is speaking in tongues and there is also the gift of tongues. Speaking in tongues is available for all believers who have been baptised with the Holy Spirit, whereas the gift of tongues also involves interpretation and is given by the Lord to some believers according to His will.

For our purposes here, we are focusing on speaking in tongues as this is something available for each and every believer and it is this that forms a vital connection between the Lord and His people. We will start this section by considering when the Lord introduced tongues to His people, before going on to see what it does in the lives of believers.

A. Tongues and the Church

We are first introduced to speaking in tongues with the birth of the Church in Acts chapter 2. Here we read that on the great day of Pentecost, the disciples of the Lord were gathered together in one place. They were being obedient to the words of Jesus, waiting for the Helper that He had promised them. As they were there gathered together in the upper room, there was the sound of a mighty rushing wind, which filled the house. After this sound there appeared tongues of fire, which descended and came to rest upon each and every one of them. As this happened we read:

> *And they were all filled with the Holy Spirit and began to speak in other tongues as the Spirit gave them utterance. (Act 2:4)*

As they were filled with the Holy Spirit, they then began to speak in other tongues as the Spirit gave them utterance. They were first **filled** with the Spirit and then they spoke in tongues. Tongues was an external manifestation of an internal event. As they were filled with the Spirit, the Spirit then enabled them to speak in tongues.

The Greek word for tongue, as used in this verse, can mean either the tongue as a natural member of the body or it can mean a language used by a particular nation. It is this second sense that is being referred to here. When the disciples spoke in other tongues, they were not sprouting off mindless gibberish. On the contrary as the Spirit filled them, they were enabled to speak in languages not known to them. Tongues are a spirit enabled language.

The filling of the Holy Spirit and speaking in tongues are intrinsically linked. Note Peter's address to the crowd that was observing what was unfolding on the great fay of Pentecost. To explain what was happening Peter quoted from the prophet Joel and said:

> *But this is that which was spoken by the prophet Joel; And it shall come to pass in the last days, saith God, I will pour out of my Spirit upon all flesh: and your sons and your daughters shall prophesy, and your young men shall see visions, and your old men shall dream dreams: And on my servants and on my handmaidens I will pour out in those days of my Spirit; and they shall prophesy: (Act 2:16-18)*

If we examine this address, there are several things that we can glean from the prophet Joel in regard to the last days:

1. The Lord would pour out His Spirit on all flesh.
2. There would be prophesy.
3. There would be visions.
4. There would be dreams.

If we consider these four things and what happened with the disciples, we see that not everything immediately aligns. Those that were in Jerusalem, stopped to watch the disciples speaking in other tongues. It was not prophesy, it was not a vision and nor was it a dream. In order to explain the situation to the onlookers, Peter under inspiration from the Holy Spirit, quoted from Joel and said that what was happening was evidence of the Lord pouring His Spirit out upon all flesh. The truth that the Lord was establishing through Peter was that speaking in tongues aligns with the Lord pouring out His Spirit. The Holy Spirit is the gift of God to His Church and His people. We see in Acts 2 that when the disciples received and were filled with the Spirit, they then spoke in other languages. The birth of the Church saw the gifts of the Holy Spirit and the gifts of tongues for His people.

Peter's message to those who were witnessing the various languages being spoken, as given by the Spirit, was that this was the outpouring of the Spirit prophesised through Joel. Tongues or spiritual language is the ability given by the Spirit when we receive and are filled by Him.

The early Church gave us this example and as we move through the New Testament, we see this pattern repeat. As believers came to Jesus, were baptised in water and baptised in the Holy Spirit that they then were able to speak in tongues as the Spirit gave them utterance.

Tongues is something for every believer. It is not something that was just reserved for the early Church, it is for each and every believer in Christ. We come to and receive Jesus, receive our baptism in water and our baptism in the Holy Spirit. It is as we receive and are filled with the Spirit, that the Spirit enables us to utter a language not known to us. It is not a head thing but a heart thing. It is an enabling of the Spirit, but it takes us to exercise our faith and trust God to speak out what He has enabled us to. It will not make sense to us, because tongues is a language unknown to us. It is not an unknown language just an unknown language to us.

It is the writer's belief that scripture shows that in tongues there is both an application of spiritual language and natural language.

If the reader looks back to Acts 2:7-11, they will see the truth of this in regard to natural languages. The feast of Pentecost brought Jews from all nations back to Jerusalem. The disciples were all Galileans and yet as the Spirit enabled them to speak languages unknown to them, those visiting heard them declare the glories of God in their own native languages.

> *And they were all amazed and marvelled, saying one to another, Behold, **are not all these which speak Galilaeans**? And how **hear we every man in our own tongue**, wherein we were born? Parthians, and Medes, and Elamites, and the dwellers in Mesopotamia, and in Judaea, and Cappadocia, in Pontus, and Asia, Phrygia, and Pamphylia, in Egypt, and in the parts of Libya about Cyrene, and strangers of Rome, Jews and proselytes, Cretes and Arabians, **we do hear them speak in our tongues the wonderful works of God**. (Act 2:7-11)*

The disciples may not have understood what they were saying, but there were those in the crowd that could. Speaking in tongues overcame a natural language barrier. It allowed the disciples to speak in a tongue unknown to them, but known to others. In doing so, they testified of the glories of God in a way that their audience could fully understand.

As we have said already, tongues is not incohesive mutterings. It is a language unknown to us, be it spiritual language or natural language, but it is not a language that is unknown to God. God is the creator of language. He created angels and man with their own languages. At the tower of Babel He separated man into different languages that caused division. On the day of Pentecost, as God gave His people the ability to speak in tongues He brought unity, overcoming the language barrier, bringing people together in His name. God speaks all and understands all. When His Spirit moves within us, we are literally just the mouthpiece for what He is trying to say. In the natural manifestation tongues allows His people to declare the glories of God in language unknown to them.

As we said above, there is also a spiritual application of speaking in tongues, and this is something that we will consider in our next point.

B. What it does

We have seen the effect of tongues with natural language in the above example from Acts 2. There it created a unification that crossed the language barrier as the disciples glorified God as the Spirit gave them utterance in various languages. There we saw an outward working, as speaking in tongues helped others hear of the glories of God.

In this point we want to look at the personal importance of tongues with our connection to the Lord. Our focus here is on the internal working. In the book of Romans Paul stated:

> *Likewise the Spirit helps us in our weakness. For we do not know what to pray for as we ought, but the **Spirit himself intercedes** for us **with groanings too deep for words**. (Rom 8:26)*

Here Paul stated that when we speak in tongues, the Spirit helps us in our weakness. When we don't know what to pray, or can't seem to find the right words, it is the Spirit who intercedes on our behalf. In the writer's opinion, Paul here is speaking of the spiritual language that we mentioned above. When our words are simply not adequate, the Spirit helps us by presenting what is on our hearts to the Lord in a language that can effectively communicate the fulness of our burden. The Spirit helps us voice the fulness of what at times our native languages cannot.

For anyone who speaks another language, they will be aware, that at times, there are no direct translations of a word from one language to another. Sometimes the words are just not adequate. It is the writer's opinion that this is what Paul is alluding to in this verse. There is a heavenly language that can fully express every thought, inkling and feeling that we have. Our natural languages simply do not possess at times the ability to fully communicate everything that is upon our hearts. It is the Spirit who intercedes on our behalf by helping us communicate these things in a heavenly language that fully conveys what we are wanting to say. This is the thought of:

> *the Spirit himself intercedes for us **with groanings too deep for words**. (Rom 8:26)*

Tongues helps us to connect with God by helping us communicate with Him more fully. It is a gift for all who believe. Paul in 1 Corinthians 14 goes on to tell us a few further things that speaking in tongues does for the believer. From this epistle we learn that when we speak in tongues:

1. We speak to God

   > ***For he that speaketh in an unknown tongue** speaketh not unto men, **but unto God**: for no man understandeth him; howbeit in the spirit he speaketh mysteries. (1Co 14:2)*

Our native languages are used to communicate with anyone and everyone. There is no real distinction in who we speak to. But tongues is a language that we speak solely unto God. When we speak in tongues, we are speaking exclusively unto the Lord. It creates an immediate connection with our Heavenly Father. In this regard tongues can be likened unto the old phone operators who would put the connection jacks into the desired recipients phone line. Tongues connects us immediately unto the Lord. It is a language that we can utter to no one else but Him. Tongues is a conversation that we have solely with our Lord.

2. We build ourselves up

*He that speaketh in an unknown tongue **edifieth himself**; but he that prophesieth edifieth the church.(1Co 14:4)*

In this verse Paul compares tongues to prophesy in terms of a Church setting. In describing the difference Paul sets forth that tongues, unless there is an interpretation, is for personal edification whereas prophesy is for the edification of the Church.

The Greek word for edify in this verse means "to *be* a *house builder*, that is, *construct* or (figuratively) *confirm"* and is translated as build(-er, -ing, up), edify or embolden.

Paul here tells us that when we speak in tongues, we are actually building ourselves up. We embolden ourselves. We edify ourselves. Speaking in tongues builds our spiritual man. As we through faith give voice to the words that the Spirit speaks through us, we build our spiritual selves up. We are literally constructing and reinforcing our Spirit man.

Speaking in tongues connects us to the Lord and allows His spirit to build us up from the inside out. It is an internal strengthening.

3. We pray in the Spirit

*For if I pray in an unknown tongue, **my spirit prayeth**, but my understanding is unfruitful.*
(1Co 14:14)

The third thing that we see is that when we pray in tongues, we are not aware of what we are praying. Our understanding is unfruitful because it is not our minds praying but His Spirit through us. It is a spiritual act where we communicate to the Lord without agenda or distraction. It takes our communication with the Lord to the next level. When we pray in tongues, we are engaging His Spirit within us.

C. Application

But you, beloved, building yourselves up in your most holy faith and praying in the Holy Spirit, (Jud 1:20)

Tongues is a gift for each, and every believer and it is definitely, most assuredly, something that connects us to the Lord in a deeper way. It is a gift from God set forth in the early Church and it is something that as Jude said, we are to continue in. As churches and believers, we need to be praying in the Holy Spirit. Yes, things need to be done decently and in order, as the Word of God attests to, but we must not overlook the things of God for fear that people will be put off. Tongues is given by the Lord to help us pray the things that we can't put words to and for our building up. Spiritual prayer builds our spiritual man. It is a gift from God that enhances our relationship through helping us to communicate better with the Lord.

Speaking in tongues opens us up to the Lord, engages His Spirit within us and builds our spiritual man. Speaking in tongues is a connection that allows the Lord to minister to us.

THE WELL OF WORSHIP AND PRAISE

The seventh and final well for us to consider is the well of worship and praise. Worship and praise are scriptural truths that can be seen from Genesis to Revelation. Throughout the Word of God, the people of God have always connected to the Lord through worship. At just a quick glance of the scriptures we see that:

- Abraham worshipped Gen 22:5
- Jacob worshipped Heb 11:21
- David worshipped 2 Sa 12:20, 2 Sam 15:32
- Paul worshipped Acts 24:14

More examples could be given, but such is suffice for now to highlight the truth that worship and praise are scriptural truths to be lived out in the lives of believers. Whilst the method has possibly changed over time and through the Testaments, the truth has not. As we move from the Old Testament through to the New, we see the natural examples take on a spiritual application, yet the foundational truths remain unchanged.

Worship is an act that man offers to God out of a humble and thankful heart. It is approaching God according to His Word in humility and reverence. Worship is not a Sunday event but a lifestyle that is lived throughout the week in each of our lives. Worship is something that should permeate from our lives.

Again, our purpose here is not to do a full exposition on worship for that would be a study in itself. Our purpose here is provide an understanding of praise and worship and how it connects us to the Lord.

A. What Worship Is.

Praise and worship are sometimes joined together or are at other times terms that are used interchangeably. Whilst it is true that the two are linked, there are differences between them that we as believers should be aware of. The writer would put forth that worship is the banner that encompasses Praise. Praise is a part of how we worship, but it is in and of itself not the fulness of worship. In order to try and explain this more fully, let us consider each of these individually.

1. Praise.

Praise is generally a starting point that leads us into worship. Praise is generally louder, more upbeat and it stirs us to start worshipping God. Praise is a declaration of the goodness of God and His faithfulness to His Word. In praise, we declare the truths of God in spite of our circumstances. Praise causes us to look beyond what is happening around us and the things that are going on in our lives. It causes us to lift our gaze to our Heavenly Father and start declaring the truths that He is greater than every situation. Praise helps to fan the fire in our spiritual man and like Samson, causes us to rise, breaking the bonds that the enemy has tried to bind us with. We will quickly look at two examples that affirm this truth.

I) Joshua

In Joshua we read how the nation of Israel finally entered the promised land. In Joshua 6 we read that the people came to their first real test within the land, Jericho. Jericho was a walled city, that seemed impenetrable. Scripture tells us at this time that the city was tightly shut, with no one coming or going. In response to this the Lord told Joshua that for six days the Israelites were to march around the city, led by the ark of God and remain completely silent. On the seventh day, the nation was to march around the city seven times, and on the seventh time around, when the priests sounded the trumpets the people were to raise their voices and shout. In verse 5 of Joshua 6 we read that they were to "shout with a great shout". The second word for shout here in the Hebrew means "an acclamation of joy or a battle cry". As the priests blew the trumpets and the people shouted unto the Lord in joy, the walls of Jericho fell and Israel had the victory.

In hinds sight it is easy to just roll through this account, but if we stop to pause for a moment, we can gain a better understanding of the reality here. Israel was walking in the will and promises of God. Before them stood an obstacle that was preventing them from moving into the fulness of what the Lord had for them. It seemed impossible and the Word of God for the victory seemed illogical. But as the people trusted the Word of God and as they lifted their voices in praise, the obstacles in the natural came tumbling down. As they fixed their eyes on Him who is above and lifted their voices to Him, that which seemed insurmountable in the natural, became immediately possible. Praise lifts us above the natural, as we declare the truths of the supernatural God that we serve!

II) Paul

In Acts 16 we read that Paul and Silas had gone to Macedonia to preach the gospel according to the Word of the Lord. In doing this, they encountered some spiritual resistance and found themselves locked up in prison. Acts tells us that they had been put in the most secure part of the prison to make sure that they couldn't escape.

Paul and Silas had been completely obedient to the Word of the Lord and His calling and yet they were bound and locked in prison. They had every right to be upset and confused regarding their circumstances. Where they were did not make sense with the call that God had for them.

Rather than mope and complain though, or sit and be frustrated at God, Acts tells us that Paul and Silas prayed and sang praises to God. According to Strong's, the implication of the Greek word for praise here is to celebrate God in song. Paul and Silas were praising God in spite of their circumstances. We then go onto read of the power of praise.

> *And at midnight Paul and Silas prayed, and **sang praises unto God**: and the prisoners heard them. And suddenly there was a great earthquake, so that the foundations of the prison were shaken: and **immediately all the doors were opened, and every one's bands were loosed**. (Act 16:25-26)*

As Paul and Silas praised, their bonds were loosed, and the prison doors were opened. In other words, as Paul and Silas began declaring and celebrating the goodness of God, the things of the world that had tried to keep them boxed in, tied down and oppressed were loosed. Praise brought freedom. As they pressed in in praise, despite their circumstances, praise saw their circumstances change. The truth is our praise will always transform our circumstances. We should never let circumstances dictate our praise, because praise has the power to transform our circumstances. Praise is the declaration that God is greater than the circumstances that we are facing.

Praise lifts our eyes off our circumstances, as we focus in and declare the truths of who God is and what He has done. As we do that, we find that the spiritual changes the natural. It is an act of faith that, as we have seen, changes things in an instant. Praise helps us to start magnifying God more than the circumstances in our lives. It brings a spiritual alignment, that recentres us with the Lord.

Praise is something that often make us feel good, as it shakes us out of our circumstances, and causes us to feel emboldened, encouraged and faith filled. What we must always remember though is that in terms of worship, praise is just a starting point.

In the Book of Hebrews we see that praise is linked to the thought of sacrifice.

> *By him therefore let us offer the **sacrifice of praise** to God continually, that is, the fruit of our lips giving thanks to his name. (Heb 13:15)*

As we have seen earlier in this study, sacrifice is an outer court activity. Sacrifice was that which only happened in the Outer Court of the Tabernacle. But it was also that which marked the start of the approach unto the Lord in the Holy of Holies. Sacrifice had to occur before one could move forward into the presence of God.

Praise is like that for the believer. It is a sacrifice as it is not something we solely do when we are on the mountain tops, but also when we are in the valleys and the circumstances of life try to hinder us from lifting His name up. It is the starting point of our worship of the Lord. Praise it not the fulness of worship but a part of it, that leads us further into the presence of the Lord.

2. Worship

Worship is an awe filled reverence for who God is. Whereas praise is upbeat and loud, worship is generally slower and quieter. Worship involves a stillness as we enter into and bask in the presence of the one true God. In worship, the focus is solely on the Lord and the majesty of who He is. There is no focus on self, but just a reverence and Holy fear for who God is.

We see a great example of this in Revelation Chapter 7. There we read:

> *After this I beheld, and, lo, a great multitude, which no man could number, of all nations, and kindreds, and people, and tongues, stood before the **throne**, and before the Lamb, clothed with white robes, and palms in their hands; And cried with a loud voice, saying, Salvation to our God which sitteth upon the **throne**, and unto the Lamb. And all the angels stood round about the **throne**, and about the elders and the four beasts, and fell before the **throne** on their faces, and worshipped God, Saying, Amen: Blessing, and glory, and wisdom, and thanksgiving, and honour, and power, and might, be unto our God for ever and ever. Amen. (Rev 7:9-12)*

Here we have a heavenly scene, but notice the place where it is set. The word throne is mentioned four times in this passage. This scene takes place before the very throne of God, in the very presence of the Almighty. This is a Most Holy Place scene. This is not an Outer Court scene, but a Most Holy Place scene.

In this scene there are two keys that we can learn about worship.

I) The Stance

> The first thing that we can glean from this is that of our stance. Praise builds us up as we declare the truths of who God is and what He has done. We are joyful, enthusiastic, and often move and dance. We find ourselves refuelled as we declare and recall the truths of God. But in worship we fall in humility before the presence of the living God. In worship we bow. In worship we reverence our indescribable God.
>
> > *And all the angels stood round about the **throne**, and about the elders and the four beasts, and **fell before the throne on their faces**, and worshipped God, Saying, Amen*
>
> Worship causes us to fall on our faces, as we bask in the presence of our Lord.

II) The Focus

> The second thing we can learn is that of focus. Notice the words that are proclaimed:
>
> > *Blessing, and glory, and wisdom, and thanksgiving, and honour, and power, and might, be unto our God for ever and ever. Amen. (Rev 7:9-12)*
>
> Every word is ascribing glory unto the Lord. There is nothing remotely about self, or what we need. In worship our words are focused on ascribing glory solely unto Him. It is all about Him. Worship shifts the focus of what God has done in and for us and focuses in on the glory of who God is.

With praise we noted the sacrificial element and how that was linked to the Outer Court. Here we see how worship is linked to the throne of the Lord, that is the Most Holy Place. What starts with praise leads us into worship where we are able to enter into the very presence of the Lord.

Worship and praise at their core lift our gaze. Praise takes our eyes off the natural circumstances and causes us to focus in on Him who rules above our circumstances. Worship engages us with the Lord, and when we are engaged we enter into His presence and we open ourselves to be able to receive from Him. What starts as praise leads us to worship.

B. What Worship does

   Having looked at what worship is and how praise and worship work together, let us look at a scriptural example that shows us just what worship does in the life of the believer.
   In 2 Kings 3, the account that this study was born from, we see that when the three kings were seeking answers for the situation that they found themselves in, they decided that they needed a prophet of the Lord. As a result of this decision, they sought out Elisha. Elisha was not overly keen on helping because of the deeds of the men and had it not been for the uprightness of Jehoshaphat king of Judah, Elisha possibly would not have helped at all.

   Elisha though agreed to help, but before he could seek a word from the Lord for them, Elisha asked for a minstrel to be brought who could play music for him:

   > *But now bring me a minstrel. And it came to pass, when the minstrel played, that the hand of the LORD came upon him. (2Ki 3:15)*

   Elisha was a mighty prophet of the Lord. He knew the Lord's voice! So why did he call for a minstrel to come before he gave a prophetic word to the three kings? Why would Elisha ask for music before bringing the word of the Lord? Could it be that the music helped Elisha engage with the Lord? The writer believes so. In this account we see that Elisha understood the way of approach.

   What we have seen so far is that praise and worship lead us into the presence of the Lord. It takes us from the Outer Court in the Most Holy Place. That is exactly what happened here with Elisha. It was during this time of worship that the hand of the Lord came upon Elisha (2 Ki 3:14-15). As Elisha pressed in in worship, the Spirit of the Lord flowed upon him. Worship took Elisha into the presence of God where he could receive from the Lord. Worship connected Elisha with the Lord and allowed Elisha to receive from Him. So too does our worship engage us with the Lord and allows us to receive from Him as His Spirit flows freely.

   It was after this time of Worship that Elisha gave the prophetic word that would see the deliverance and victory of the three kings from the situation that they were in.

   Through this example we see that the Holy Spirit was able to flow freely as Elisha pressed in, in worship. This is exactly what we have been looking at in terms of our wells. When we worship, we open up the pipe that allows His Spirit to flow. Worship is a well that allows for the infilling of the Lord.

C. Application

   Much more could be said on this topic, but that is not the focus of this text. From what we have discovered we see that worship causes our focus to shift and narrow in on the Lord. It is through this engagement that we are then able to receive from Him.

Worship connects us to Him by helping us focus our attention on Him. In worship everything else falls away as we engage with our Heavenly father. Worship causes our attention to focus in on the Lord and as we do this we enter into His presence where we commune with Him. Praise and worship lead us into the presence of God where we connect with Him in a deeper way.

As believers and churches we need worship. We need praise and we need worship. It is not about lights, songs and entertainment. It is about approaching the Lord in praise and worship according to His Word. It is moving from the Outer Court into the Most Holy Place and engaging in His presence. Scripture lays out for us a way of approach and ours is to follow the Word. We approach God in praise, but we enter His presence in worship. Praise stirs our soul, but worship transforms our lives. In our lives and in our Churches, we need both. We need the wells of worship and praise.

SUMMARY OF THE WELLS

In this section we have sought to define what the seven Golden Pipes of Zechariah's vision were. As we did this, we noted that the seven Golden Pipes are what connects the Church (The Golden Lampstand) to Jesus (The Golden Bowl) and allow the Holy Spirit to flow from our Great High Priest unto His Church. In doing this we saw how these related to the wells from our 2 Kings account. Without the wells in 2 Kings 3 the infilling and reflection that followed would not have occurred. Similarly, without the pipes in Zechariah's vision, the infilling and shining of the Golden Lampstand also wouldn't occur. The pipes and the wells speak of one and the same thing, they are the means by which infilling occurs. Without these, the process does not work. For the pipes to be open and the wells to be operational though, there is effort that is required on the part of man. As we saw in the account from 2 Kings 3, the responsibility for digging lays solely with man. Ours is to dig in accordance to the Word of the Lord, before the Lord steps in and does His part. We dig in faith and anticipation of what the Lord is going to outpour. In these days, the Lord is calling His people to dig into those areas He has outlined through His Word so that we may receive the fulness of the Holy Spirit that He has for us. We need each and every one of the seven wells.

In considering what these wells are the writer, after much prayer and study, has put forward what he feels, and that which he believes scripture would point to, are the wells. These seven wells are ways through which scripture clearly demonstrates that we connect to the Lord and receive from Him. The wells that we considered are:

A. The well of prayer.
B. The well of reading and meditating on the Word.
C. The well of sensitivity to the Holy Spirit.
D. The well of faith.
E. The well of obedience.

F. The well of speaking in tongues.
G. The well of worship and praise.

These are those connection points that allow the infilling of the Holy Spirit to occur. Whilst we have done more of an overview of these topics, the reader should be able to see that these are all things that connect us to the Lord and allow us to receive from Him. As we 'dig' into these, we connect with the Lord and then receive from Him. These are the wells that allow Him to infill. Just as the kings had a specific place where they were to dig, so to do we. Each of these wells need to be operational individually and corporately if we as individuals and the Church are to fully and completely reflect His glory. Each of these wells allow us to receive a portion of His Holy Spirit. When all seven wells are dug, it allows Him to fully infill and reflect. What we have learnt from Zechariah's vision is illustrated below:

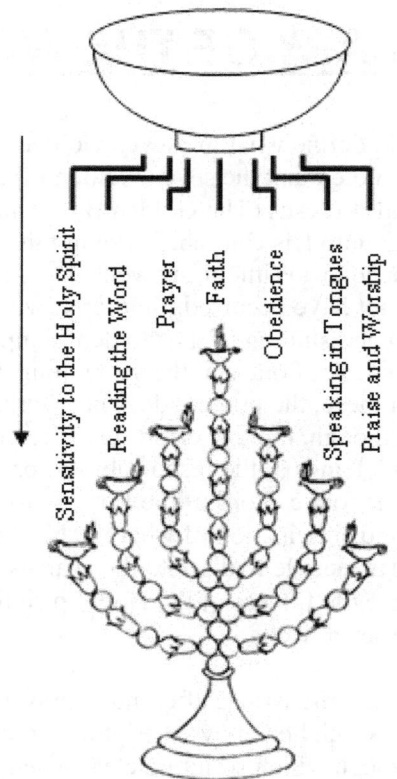

It should be noted here that what we have been looking at are the precursors. These are those things that have to be done before the infilling can occur. The wells in 2 Kings 3 had to be dug before the Lord could pour in. Likewise, these wells have to be dug in our lives and churches before the Lord can fill them. The infilling doesn't come, until the digging has occurred. If there are no wells, then there is nothing to catch that which the Lord is wanting to pour out and bless us with. There is an onus and a responsibility on the part of man to dig. Just as the armies had to dig in faith according to the Word of the Lord, holding on to the promise of infilling so too do we. The reader is encouraged to look back over our notes on digging where we considered just what it means to dig and what is involved in the process in the natural. The lessons we learnt have direct application to what we have just considered. As the reader looks back over those notes, it should further confirm the onus that is upon man in regard to digging these wells.

The writer's conviction is that these are the wells that the Lord is crying out for His people to dig. These are the first steps for us to be able to reflect His glory and to shine for Him. It takes effort on the part of man. These wells will not just dig themselves! There is a responsibility upon us as individuals and congregations to make sure that we are completely and fully pressing into God. One or two wells are good, but that is not the heart of the Father, and it is not the way He has created man and His Church to function. The image of the Golden Lampstand had seven pipes for a reason. One or two pipes would have meant partial light and our Lord is not into partiality. The Lord's purpose for His Church and His people is for them to shine brightly and fully and this can only happen when man puts the effort into digging the wells. Believers and the Church are only ever fully shining when each of the seven wells have been dug and are filled!

In each of the wells that we have considered, we have seen how they connect us to the Lord and enable us to receive from Him. Hopefully enough scriptural evidence has been put forward for the reader to see and understand that these are all ways in which man connects to God. If there is any doubt in the mind of the reader over what has been put forward, they are encouraged to put them on the shelf so to speak, and seek the Lord about them rather than just brush them aside. The writer is aware of his own inabilities to fully comprehend the Word of God, but firmly believes that that which has been put forward is a message and call of the Lord to His people. Whilst the writer's inadequacies may come across in trying to convey that message, the reader is encouraged to look beyond those and seek the Lord to confirm in His Word that which has been put forward.

From Zechariah's vision we see that these seven wells connect us unto Jesus and allow us to receive the Golden Oil from the Golden Bowl. The natural points to the spiritual. These are seven spiritual wells that allow our Heavenly Father to fill us. Before He can pour into us though, we must dig. Responsibility lies upon the part of man to make sure that the wells have been dug. Just as with the armies of 2 Kings 3, if we want the fulness of what the Lord has for us, we need to dig the valley full of ditches. If we truly desire the fulness of blessing that our Heavenly Father has for us, then we need to dig the wells. We need to be obedient unto His Word and dig those wells that allow Him to infill. We need the seven wells open so that the Golden Lampstand may shine brightly and fully. This world needs to see the fulness of light shining out from the Church of God and the people who make it. We need to be a people who in faith dig the wells of prayer, reading and meditating on the word, obedience, faith, sensitivity to the Holy Spirit, speaking in tongues and worship and praise.

Digging

THE IMPORTANCE OF MAINTAINING THE WELLS.

In our previous points, we have looked at the need to dig and where we are to dig. We have discovered that before infilling can occur, digging has to happen. The first step is to dig. Following on from digging though and of almost equal importance is the need to maintain the wells. In this section we are going to look at a scriptural example that shows the need to not only dig wells, but also the need to maintain those wells once they have been dug. Digging a well is not a one and done job. It is a process that requires continual attention to make sure that those wells that have been dug stay open and operational. What starts with digging is kept operational through maintenance. In considering the application of maintenance to us, we will look at an example of Isaac from Genesis 26. Before moving forward here the reader is encouraged to read over this chapter to familiarise themselves with its content.

In Genesis chapter 26 we read that a famine had come upon the land where Isaac dwelt. Scripture tells us that this was a different famine to that which Abraham had experienced in the land in his days.

> *And there was a famine in the land, **beside** the first famine that was in the days of Abraham. And Isaac went unto Abimelech king of the Philistines unto Gerar.(Gen 26:1)*

The mention of Abraham here would seem to reinforce to the reader that Isaac was still dwelling in the land of his father. Although it was the same place it was a different time, hence the mention of two different famines. There was a famine in the land during the time of Abraham and then there was a famine in the land in the time of Isaac. It was the same land, but two distinct time periods.

In the midst of this famine in Isaac's time, the Word of the Lord came to Isaac and reassured him that he should not go down to Egypt but remain in the land that the Lord had sworn to give to his father. The Lord then went on to confirm with Isaac the covenant that He had made with Abraham. This was a reassurance to Isaac that the Lord would be with him and the Lord would look after him.

Isaac remained in the land, but we read that he moved from his residence of Beer Lahai Roi (Gen 25:11) to that of Gerar (Gen 26:6) It should be noted here Isaac remained faithful to the Word of the Lord and remained in the land, but the move that he undertook within the land had effects that we will see shortly. Whilst he was faithful, his decision had consequences.

Gerar was a city that was ruled by Abimelech, king of the Philistines. From a reading of scripture, it would seem that this city was surrounded by agricultural and grazing lands.

Digging

The city itself possibly represented a place of safety and security for Isaac in the time of famine. During Isaac's time in Gerar we are told in verse 12 that the Lord blessed him exceedingly. In one year Isaac reaped a hundredfold and was blessed by the Lord. In the next verse of Genesis 26 the New King James reads;

> *The man began to prosper, and continued prospering until he became very prosperous. (Gen 26:13)*

The Lord's hand was indeed upon Isaac, and He blessed him as He had promised. This though brought with it jealousy from the Philistines who also inhabited the same land. The success of Isaac aroused the envy of his neighbours. This led to Abimelech, king of the Philistines, telling Isaac to depart from his territory and to go somewhere else.

> *And Abimelech said unto Isaac, Go from us; for thou art much mightier than we. (Gen 26:16)*

Isaac now found himself moving from the city of Gerar to the valley of Gerar. He had left the place of security and gone to one of isolation. This valley though, had previously been a place that Abraham had inhabited. Unfortunately for Isaac though, things had changed since the last time he had been there. In verses 15 and 18 we read of the actions the Philistines after the passing of Abraham:

> *For all the wells which his father's servants had digged in the days of Abraham his father,* **_the Philistines had stopped them, and filled them with earth_**. *(Gen 26:15)*

> *And Isaac digged again the wells of water, which they had digged in the days of Abraham his father;* **_for the Philistines had stopped them_** *after the death of Abraham: and he called their names after the names by which his father had called them. (Gen 26:18)*

It is not immediately clear exactly when the Philistines filled in these wells, but from what we can deduce from scripture this occurred after the death of Abraham and up to the time of the second famine in the land during the days of Isaac. What is clear though, is that this was a time when Isaac had the responsibility of looking after and maintaining the wells. The filling of the wells occurred during Isaac's watch.

The wells were dug by Abraham and his servants as a means of supporting life. The establishment of a well allowed Abraham to literally possess that plot of land as it provided water for his house, his servants and his flocks. Just as with the armies of Israel at the start of this study, the digging of a well provided water that restored and supported life. But in the case of Abraham, the establishment of a well also allowed the person who had dug it to claim that source of life and with it, a securement of the land upon which it had been dug.

The wells that had been dug in Abraham's days though, were filled in during the days of Isaac. That which had been toiled and sweated over was not maintained by the next generation. Whilst Isaac was in the region of Gerar, he was being blessed and possibly didn't have the need or see the importance of the wells. During his days of blessing, Isaac neglected the wells of his father. Now though, having been asked to leave Gerar by Abimelech, Isaac once again found himself in need of the wells that his father had dug. The problem was though, the Philistines saw the neglect of Isaac and took an opportunity to fill in the wells of Abraham while Isaac's focus was elsewhere.

Isaac now found himself in the valley of Gerar, with his household and flocks and no ready supply of water. The wells of his father had been filled in, so he set about re-digging the wells of Abraham. Because Isaac didn't maintain, he had to re-dig. Whilst this seems like a straightforward task, it was one that would not be easy and one that would attract its fair share of opposition.

Isaac started by digging in the valley and there he found a spring of water. The herdsmen of Gerar though heard of this and contended with Isaac's servants over the water. They claimed it was their water and strove with Isaac and his herdsmen (Gen 26:20). What would have seemed a simple task in Isaacs's mind to re-dig the wells of his father proved to be otherwise. It was not an easy task to re-establish the wells that had once been in operation.

Isaac then moved on and dug another well, but the herdsmen of Gerar also strove for that well (Gen 26:21). The herdsmen of Gerar were not going to just readily give up their grazing ground. The rights to the well brought with it the rights to graze and the right to water the flocks. The well bought with it ownership of that piece of land. Water was power and the herdsmen of Gerar were not just going to let Isaac reclaim it.

Isaac removed himself a third time and dug another well. This time though, there was no striving. The well was Isaac's and he called it Rehoboth which means "part". Note in verse 22 where Isaac gave it this name:

> *...and he called the name of it Rehoboth; and he said,* **_For now the LORD hath made room for us_**, *and we shall be fruitful in the land. (Gen 26:22)*

The well established Isaac's allotment within the promised land. The well was more than just a source of water it was a claim upon the land. This was Isaacs's territory, and this was his well.

Shortly after this Isaac went up to Beersheba. While he was there, his servants came to him reporting that they had dug another well and found water again. Isaacs's territory had been extended within the land.

Whilst we have taken a quick overview of Chapter 26 of Genesis here, we have seen that Isaac learned the hard way that re-digging a well is a far greater task than maintaining one. For Isaac the task of re-digging was not a simple one and certainly was not one that came about hassle free. Isaac faced constant opposition as he attempted to re-establish the wells of his father.

Digging

In this section we have considered the spiritual application of maintaining the wells through looking at the account of Isaac. From this account we see a number of points that are pertinent to us as believers, individually and corporately.

A. Digging requires maintenance

So far in our study, we have seen the requirement that is upon the people of the Lord to dig wells. Digging is the first step that allows infilling. Just as with the armies of Israel we have to dig wells in faith, trusting God's Word and that He will infill them. But it is not just a once off activity. That which is dug has to be maintained. We have to dig, and we have to maintain what we have dug. It is not enough to be filled, we have to maintain the well so that the infilling can continually occur. Maintenance of the wells requires our attention and dedication. When the wells aren't attended to, they slip into disrepair. Digging is vitally important, but of equal importance is maintenance. We need to maintain that which we have dug. The same effort that goes into digging needs to be also given to maintenance.

Maintenance naturally occurs when the wells retain their value and importance in our lives. Complacency and blessing can cause us to forget our need of these life-giving sources. Ours is to ever remember that the Lord's ability to fill us is measured by how operational the wells are. We learn from Isaac that we are not only to dig, but we are also to maintain. We need to value that which the 'fathers' have dug for us.

B. The enemy will fill in neglected wells to try and reclaim territory.

The Philistines didn't fill in the wells during the days of Abraham because they were being utilised and attended to. They Philistines waited until the death of Abraham and a time when Isaac was not focused on that which his father had established. It was during a time of neglect that the enemy saw an opportunity to fill in the wells to try and claim back territory from the family of Abraham.

Whilst this is a natural example, we see the spiritual reality so prevalent today. It is the classic battle between light and darkness. When the wells aren't being attended to, the enemy will move in and fill those wells in. His goal is to shut off those things that bring life and light to the people of God and the Church. As we neglect the wells of our fathers, the enemy fills them in with the purpose of reclaiming ground that had once been lost to our fathers in the faith.

This is a truth that we must grab hold of and one that we must pass on to the next generation. It is so much easier to maintain than to re-dig. The importance of the wells and their maintenance in the lives of believers and the Church can never be over emphasised. We need the wells that the fathers have dug open and made operational. We need to honour that which the fathers in the faith have contended for. The moment we relegate things to being old-school, or not cool or not service friendly, is the moment the enemy moves in to fill in the wells. The indifference of believers to the works of our forerunners causes the advancement of the enemy.

C. The enemy will oppose the re-digging of wells that previously existed.

As Isaac attempted to re-dig the wells that Abraham had dug, he was met with opposition. It was not just a case of "these used to be mine, now I am taking them back". There was resistance to what Isaac was trying to do. In many ways Isaac had forfeited part of his inheritance and what he found was that trying to claim it back was no easy feat. Isaac was met with opposition as he tried to re-establish the wells. There was a battle for territory.

Spiritually we are going to face opposition as we re-dig in areas that we have neglected. The enemy isn't going to easily give up the ground he has gained. Opposition will come, distraction will come, apathy will attempt to rise. Our call though is to endure. We need to understand the vital need we have for the wells. It is only when each of the wells are open in our lives and churches, that we then reflect the glory of the Lord in the capacity we have been called to. We have to focus on our call and endure through the opposition.

D. Life is maintained through wells that have been dug.

For Abraham, the wells were a source of life to his family, flocks and servants. For Isaac, he was searching for a source of life for his family, flocks and servants. Isaac was not able to support life until the wells of his father had been re-dug.

The life of believers and the Church is maintained through the wells that have been dug. We need to understand the vital importance of these wells and ensure we maintain them. When the wells are open and operational it is then that the people of God and the Church are walking in the fulness of life that the Lord has for it. The wells of the Lord bring spiritual life to the people of God.

E. The blessing of the Lord doesn't mitigate the need to maintain the wells of our predecessors.

Isaac was blessed beyond blessing. In a single year the Lord caused him to reap a hundred-fold. Despite this incredible season of blessing, Isaac still found himself in a place where his need rested on that which had been dug for him. In his time of blessing Isaac didn't look for or value the wells, but their vital importance never changed.

Prosperity can cause apathy and that is a dangerous place for believers to be. We ever need to walk in humility and understand our utter reliance upon the wells. We cannot ever let blessing negate the need in our minds for the wells of the Lord.

The land had been promised to Abraham. It had been promised to Isaac. But the wells had been neglected. During the time that Isaac was prospering, the wells hadn't seemed to be of importance. What we see from this example is that the wells that the previous generations have toiled over can be neglected by the next generation. Sadly, it is often not until the point of absolute need that we find ourselves in search of the wells of our forefathers. Pride and arrogance keep us from truly honouring that which has been dug for us and sadly through neglect, the enemy takes the opportunity to fill in these spiritual wells. How much time and effort could be saved if we would honour the wells of our forefathers rather than have to re-dig them ourselves? How much advancement for the Kingdom of God could occur if we simply maintained that which our fathers had toiled for?

Digging is a simple action, but one that requires effort, endurance and faith. Digging is something that does not bring an immediate reward, but it is done with a purpose for what is to come. Digging is required of us by the Lord so that He may fulfil His promise to us. The level to which we dig directly determines how much we can be infilled by the Lord. In these days the writer believes that the call of the Lord is for us to re-dig any of these wells that have been neglected and to dig deeply. Having done that we are called to maintain them and ensure that they can ever function as the life-giving source that they are intended to be. In our previous section, we considered what the seven wells of the Lord are. The question for us as individuals and Churches is have we maintained these wells or do we need to re-dig them? Have we forgotten that which our fathers toiled for, or have we honoured and respected that which they dug for us?

We are called to not only dig but also to maintain the wells. We do this not just for our benefit but also for the benefit of the generations to come. As we dig and maintain the wells, we ensure that their operation remains and that we and those that follow us can fully receive all that the Lord has for us. To neglect a well is to close a well and rob ourselves of its infilling. To maintain a well is to make sure that infilling can continue to occur. We are called to dig and part of that call involves maintenance. As we dig and maintain that which we have dug, we ensure that we receive all the infilling that the Lord has for us.

DIGGING SUMMARY

In this section we have focused in on digging. Digging was the first part of the process that we observed from the 2 Kings 3 account. In looking at this we discovered that in the overall four stage process from 2 Kings 3, digging is the only one upon which the responsibility lies solely with man. Digging is not only the start of the process it is something that only man can do. The Lord doesn't dig for us! It is a task that lies upon man and man alone.

As we examined the thought of digging in relation to 2 Kings 3, we saw that digging is an act of faith in response to the Word of God. Digging is a choice, shown through action and one that takes time, effort, endurance, repetition and faith. The kings and their armies were at a point of desperation when the Word of the Lord came to them to dig. Their act of faith though, saw their circumstances completely change. They not only received life giving waters from the Father, but they also walked in the victory that He had promised. All of this occurred because they dug. Just as the kings and their armies had to respond in action to the Word of the Lord through Elisha, so too do we as New Testament believers need to respond to the Word of the Lord to dig.

But where are we supposed to dig? For the kings and their armies, the call was to fill the valley full of ditches. The Lord told them where to dig. The question is though, has the Lord told us where we are to dig so that we might receive His infilling? In answering this we considered the vision of Zechariah concerning the Golden Lampstand. This vision showed a Golden Lampstand, which as we have already considered, represents the Church. Above this was a Golden Bowl and connecting the two were seven Golden Pipes. On either side of the Golden Bowl were two Olive Trees, which through two Golden Pipes, poured their Golden Oil into the Golden Bowl. As we interpreted this vision, we saw that this was a picture of flow. The vision shows Jesus, our Great High Priest as the Golden Bowl and it is through Him that the Golden Oil flows through the seven Golden Pipes unto the Church. The Church, as the Golden Lampstand, operates through the Golden Oil that He infills us with. The measure with which we shine directly relates to how much oil we receive!

In looking at the seven Golden Pipes of the vision we saw how these speak of seven wells that need to be dug. As we compared the vision of Zechariah to the account of 2 Kings 3, we observed that both the pipes and the wells are vessels that allow infilling to occur. They are the precursors to what happens next. If the pipes aren't open, there can be no flow and reception of the Golden Oil. The pipes allow infilling when they are open. Likewise, if the wells have not been dug and maintained there can be no reception and infilling of the life-giving water. Infilling only occurs when digging has been done. The pipes and the wells speak of the same thing. The seven Golden Pipes in Zechariah's vison show us seven wells that need to be open and operational for the Church to receive the infilling of the Holy Spirit and consequentially be able to shine. We need all seven open in order to receive the fulness of infilling of the Spirit that the Lord has for us.

What has been put forward in this section is that there are seven wells which connect us to the Lord and allow us to receive from Him. The wells we considered were those of prayer, His Word, sensitivity to the Holy Spirit, faith, obedience, speaking in tongues and worship and praise. As we examined each of these, we saw how they not only connect us unto the Lord, but how they allow us to receive from Him.

We need to remember here that the wells require action on the part of man before the Lord can respond and infill. The responsibility for these lies upon us. The call for us is to dig and once we have dug, we are then to maintain. Whenever the wells are neglected, the enemy will come and cut them off. Wherever infilling can be hindered, the light will begin to fade, and darkness will creep in. Digging and maintenance ensure that the Lord can continue to infill fully and that we can shine as brightly as we have been called to.

In our personal lives and in our churches, we need these pipes open and the wells dug so that infilling can occur. But that cannot happen until we put things into action. The call to the armies was to fill the valley full of ditches. It wasn't to dig one or two, it was to fill the valley full of ditches. It is the writer's belief that the call of the Lord is for His Church, not a Church or a few churches, but for all of His Church, to start digging ditches where they are. We need to be digging, re-digging and maintaining that which the Lord has called us to. We are to apply the lessons from 2 Kings 3 and from the example of Isaac and not only dig deep wells, but ensure they remain operational not just for ourselves, but for those that follow us.

We are in a time when we need to honestly look at our wells and consider their state. We need to look at prayer, His Word, sensitivity to the Holy Spirit, faith, obedience, speaking in tongues and worship and praise . We need to take an honest account of these in our personal lives and in our churches. If we truly want the fulness of what the Lord has for us, then we need to dig and maintain these wells. It will take effort, consistency, time and endurance. These are all things that each of us have in our possession. The question we need to ask ourselves is that if we are not spending these on the things of the Lord then what are we spending them on? The writer firmly believes that we are in a season of spiritual realignment, where the Lord is bringing His people back to the truths of His Word. This is not written as a condemnation to any Church or believer, but as an encouragement. As the writer has prepared and thought on this study, he has felt convicted about wells that need to be given attention in his own life.

This section has been written with possibly the same emphasis that Elisha felt as he gave the prophetic word to the three kings. Now is the time to dig. God's Word is for us and it is for now. The Lord is calling His people to dig, because the infilling is coming. When it does, we will not have time to react. We need to be prepared. We need to step out in faith, just as the three kings and their armies, and respond to the Word of the Lord. We need to dig. We need to dig deep, and we need to maintain. The wells need to be open and operational for all that the Lord wants to do. In order for us to be able to receive the fulness of infilling that the Father has for us as individuals and congregations, we need to dig. We need to fill the valley full of ditches. We need the wells of prayer, His Word, sensitivity to the Holy Spirit, faith, obedience, speaking in tongues and worship and praise fully open. It is only when we in faith are obedient unto the Word of the Lord, that He then can infill us to a level beyond our understanding or imagination. There is much that the Lord has for us, but it starts with digging.

INFILLING

We now turn out attention to the second step that we discovered from the account of 2 Kings 3. In our look at that account, we saw that the Word of the Lord through the prophet Elisha was for the kings and their united armies to fill the valley full of ditches. After they had done this, the Lord would fill that which had been dug. They would not see wind or rain and yet the Lord would fill the wells full of water.

> *And he said, Thus saith the LORD, **<u>Make this valley full of ditches</u>**. For thus saith the LORD, Ye shall not see wind, neither shall ye see rain; **<u>yet that valley shall be filled with water</u>**, that ye may drink, both ye, and your cattle, and your beasts. (2Ki 3:16-17)*

The call was for the armies to dig in faith in response to the Word of the Lord. Once the united armies had dug, it was then that the infilling occurred. Before a well can be filled it first has to be dug! Once digging has been done, then the Lord provides the Infilling.

Infilling is a gift from the Lord. Infilling provides life and sustenance to spiritual man. It is God's blessing unto man, and it is by this, and by this alone that we are then able to reflect. In our 2 Kings 3 account we saw that it was the infilling that allowed the reflection which then brought about the victory for the united armies. The armies had to be faithful in digging, and as they did this, the Lord blessed them with an infilling that restored life, restored hope, restored faith and allowed the reflection to be seen by the enemies of Israel, ultimately bringing about the victory.

Infilling is the response of God to the actions of man. When we first come to the Lord we receive a filling of the Holy Spirit, but the Lord has more for us than a onetime blessing. Infilling is to be a continual experience for New Testament believers.

In this section we are going to look at some scriptural truths that reveal how infilling occurs, what its purpose is and some lessons that we can learn about its importance to us as believers and New Testament churches. The truths that we will discover here build off the ones we have observed in our previous section and further emphasise their importance. This is the next progressive step for us to be able to reflect His glory and fulfil revivals call.

HOW INFILLING WORKS

Our purpose here is to gain a proper understanding of how we receive infilling from the Lord. Infilling is absolutely necessary if we are to reflect His glory. If we as believers and churches are to fulfil the call of the Lord to shine, then we need to have a biblical understanding of how infilling occurs.

In this section, we are going to examine a few examples from scripture which highlight the truth that the infilling of the Lord is always in **response** to the activities of His people on earth. This will not only reaffirm the importance of the truths of digging that we have already seen, but it will also highlight again the truths of 2 Kings 3 and the call to the Church and believers in this season. Infilling is the next progressive step, but is completely dependent on the step preceding it, digging. The infilling of the Lord is always dependant on the faithful actions of man in response to His Word.

The message of the Lord is not that He will infill so His people are then strengthened to be able to dig, the call of the Lord is for His people to dig so that He can infill. So often we ask the Lord to pour out His Spirit when in reality all we have done is sing a few songs. We ask for infilling, but we haven't truly dug. We expect the Lord to do His part when we haven't done ours! The truth of scripture is that the Lord always responds to the actions of man. If we want His infilling, then we need to have dug! Let's consider how the Word establishes this truth.

A. Jacob's Ladder

The first example for us to consider comes from Jacob, the grandson of Abraham. We read of this account in Genesis Chapter 28. The reader is encouraged to read this chapter in its entirety before moving forward here. Within Genesis Chapter 28 is contained a message which shows just how the Church and we as believers are infilled by the Lord.

In Genesis 28:10, we are introduced to Jacob as he prepares to leave Beersheba for Haran. As a quick background to this, in the previous chapter (Genesis 27), Jacob, with the aid of his mother, Rebekah, had tricked his father Isaac into giving him the blessing that belonged to his brother Esau, who was the firstborn son. Esau was enraged by his brother's deceit and spoke out against him, threating his life. Having heard of Esau's plot to kill Jacob, Rebekah arranged for Jacob to be sent away to the land of her family, under the pretence of finding a wife. It is worth noting here that scripture records Jacob as being a quiet man who dwelt in tents. He wasn't an adventurer like his brother, but more of a homebody (Gen 25:27). Yet suddenly he was being thrust out of the care of his family, away from the watchful eye of his mother to a foreign land. This would be Jacob's first trip away by himself and would have been something of a shock to the young man.

Whilst Jacob was travelling from Beersheba to Haran, he decided to stop for the night. He set up camp and fell asleep. Whilst asleep Jacob had a dream. Jacob saw a ladder set up on the earth reaching to heaven. On this ladder the angels of God ascended and descended. At the top of the ladder, in heaven, stood the Lord. The Lord then spoke to Jacob, asserting who He was and confirming the Abrahamic covenant to Jacob. Jacob then awoke in fear, astonished that he had been unaware that the Lord had been there. Jacob called the place the House of God, the gate of Heaven. In the morning, Jacob rose early and set up an altar to the Lord, pouring oil out upon it and renamed the place Bethel (House of God). He then went on to make a vow unto the Lord, promising servitude, worship and tithes if the Lord would go with him.

It is easy to skim over this passage and move on to the next chapter, thinking nothing more than Jacob simply had a personal vision from the Lord. But there is much more to this passage of scripture and to see the fullness of what's contained in it, we will spend some time considering it in more detail.

If we slowly work through the verses of Gen 28:10-19, we can more fully see what the Lord revealed here.

(Gen 28:10) And Jacob went out from Beersheba, and went toward Haran. (Gen 28:11) And he came upon a certain place, and tarried there all night, because the sun was set; and he took of the stones of that place, and put them for his pillows, and lay down in that place to sleep.

Jacob set out from Beersheba and headed towards Haran.

> Beersheba – well of an oath, well of the sevenfold oath.

> Haran – parched, mountaineer.

These two thoughts stand in complete contrast to one another. Jacob was leaving a well and heading to a parched land, leaving water for dryness. Jacob was leaving security behind, everything he had ever known, his whole life, his friends and his family.

So often God takes individuals out of places of abundance and leads them to their personal Haran's in order to deepen their understanding of Him and strengthen their relationship with Him. Think of Moses leaving Egypt for the desert or Joseph leaving his father's care for Egypt. There are lessons that we cannot learn in our personal Beersheba's. God needs to take us out to Haran, where our reliance is completely upon Him. He needs us in a place where we are ready, willing and able to hear what He is speaking to us.

On this first day of his journey, we read that Jacob stopped for the night. The sun had set and darkness had set in. It was night time. All that would follow happened after the setting of the sun. This would was a night time event.

Jacob then took stones for his pillows and laid down for the night to sleep. His head rested upon the stones. He lay down to sleep in an unknown place, his head resting upon the rock.

(Gen 28:12) And he dreamed, and behold a ladder set up on the earth, and the top of it reached to heaven: and behold the angels of God ascending and descending on it (Gen 28:13) And, behold, the LORD stood above it, and said, I am the LORD God of Abraham your father, and the God of Isaac: the land on which you lie, to you will I give it, and to your descendants;(Gen 28:14) And your descendants shall be as the dust of the earth, and you shall spread abroad to the west, and to the east, and to the north, and to the south: and in you and in your descendants shall all the families of the earth be blessed.(Gen 28:15) And, behold, I am with you, and will keep you in all places wherever you go, and will bring you again into this land; for I will not leave you, until I have done that which I have spoken to you of.

That night as Jacob lay asleep, he had a Godly dream. He saw a ladder standing on the earth and reaching to Heaven. The foot of the ladder rested upon the earth. The base rung of the ladder rested upon the earth, while the top rung was in the heights of Heaven. The ladder was the connecting point, it connected heaven to earth, and it allowed the movement of the angels. The ladder was the central point of the vision. Without it there was no connection, nothing joining heaven and earth. Without the ladder a gulf existed, there was heaven and earth but nothing connecting them. The ladder bridged the gap between heaven and earth.

On the ladder angels were ascending and descending. Note the order that was stated here, they were going up and then down, going from the earth to heaven and then back again. They weren't coming from heaven down to earth and going back up again, they were going from earth to heaven and returning to earth. Ascending and descending. Their focus was on the earth. Whatever it was they were doing it was earth centric. They would go from the earth and return to it.

Hebrews 1:14 in speaking of angels states 'Are they not all ministering spirits, sent forth to minister to them who shall be heirs of salvation?' There is a ministry of angels that is earth focused involving the heirs of salvation. They ascend from and return to the earth.

At the top of the ladder stood the Lord. What a dream, what a vision. To see the Lord!! How did Jacob determine it was the Lord? Just what did he see? How

Infilling

magnificent must this revelation have been to leave Jacob in no doubt that he had seen God? What a vision! What a life changing event!

So within this vision of Jacob, we see the earth and we see heaven. Connecting the two was a ladder. The ladder stands upon the earth and reaches to heaven. On the ladder the angels ascend from the earth to heaven and descend again from heaven to earth. The angels ascend and descend. At the top of ladder stood the Lord. That was the vision that Jacob had. What he saw is represented below, very much simplified.

Having received the vision, the Lord then spoke and went on to confirm the Abrahamic covenant to Jacob. This was the covenant that the Lord had given to Abraham, confirmed to Isaac and now confirmed to Jacob. Whilst Jacob had to trade to receive Esau's birth right and had to deceive his father to receive Esau's blessing as firstborn son, he was clearly the man for the covenant in the eyes of the Lord. Even though Jacob was the second born, he was God's choice. It was to Jacob that the Lord confirmed the Abrahamic covenant not Esau. The lineage that we know is Abraham, Isaac and Jacob. The Lord is no respecter of persons, and regardless of who had the birth right and blessing, the reason that the Abrahamic covenant was confirmed to Jacob and not Esau was because Jacob was the Lord's choice.

The Lord then went on to give personal assurance to Jacob about his travels. He promised to not only keep him safe wherever he travelled but He also promised to bring him back to this land. This was something that must have been of great comfort to Jacob, who was leaving everything that he had ever known. He had set out in great uncertainty, not knowing the people to whom he was going or for how long he would be there. But the Lord came to him and reassured him, "I will be with you".

What a powerful message this must have been to a person who had just walked away from everything they had ever known. What a comfort.

(Gen 28:16) And Jacob awaked out of his sleep, and he said, Surely the LORD is in this place; and I knew it not. (Gen 28:17) And he was afraid, and said, How dreadful is this place! (Gen 28:17) this is none other but the house of God, (Gen 28:17) and this is the gate of heaven.

Jacob awoke out of his sleep and realised that the Lord had been there and he hadn't known. He had been unaware of the presence of the Lord in the place where he was. The Lord had always been there, but previous to his vision, Jacob was unaware of that fact. It is a scary thought that one can be in the very presence of the Lord and yet be unaware of it.

A fear came upon Jacob, a Godly fear, a reverence for who God is compared to a knowledge of who He was. The Hebrew word for dreadful as used here is also translated as reverence. This was not a casual respect that Jacob offered unto the Lord, but a Godly reverence. It is a reverence that every believer should have.

Jacob then declared this to be the 'House of God'. This is the first use of the term 'the house of God' within the Word of God. Jacob called this place 'the house of God' because the Lord had been there, the presence of the Lord had been there. This was where He had dwelt, it was His house. What a revelation!

This was not only the House of God but also, the gate of Heaven. A gate is an access point. A gate either allows access or prohibits it. Here the gate provided access to heaven. An open gate means an open heaven. Jesus refers to himself as the gate, and no one comes to the Father except through Him (John 10:9). Jesus is the gate through which we have access to an open heaven!

(Gen 28:18) And Jacob rose up early in the morning, and took the stone that he had put for his pillows, and set it up for a pillar, and poured oil upon the top of it.

Jacob rose early in the morning. Note the language, "early" in the morning. He didn't just wake in the morning, but in the early morning. There is an emphasis added. The word for morning in Hebrew means 'dawn, at the break of day'. The word for early in Hebrew means 'to incline, to start early in the morning. So for Jacob this was an early dawn experience.

After lying down after the sun had set, Jacob rose early, before the sun came up. So the events we have just looked over happened between sunset and sunrise. In between those times of sunset and sunrise Jacob received this dream. That is the timeline we have for Jacob's vision.

(Gen 28:19) And he called the name of that place Bethel: but the name of that city was called Luz at first.

Luz: almond tree
Bethel: Beth – El, House of God.

Jacob renamed the place the House of God, Bethel. So strong was the experience that Jacob had with the Lord in this place that he renamed it. It would be known as Beth-El, the House of God.

To summarise what we have discovered from looking through these verses and considering Jacobs vision:

> This passage starts as the sun is setting and night is coming. As it is late, Jacob laid down for the night and set up a stone as a pillow for his head. After his vision, we are told that Jacob rose early. Jacob lay down after the sun had set, had the vision, and then rose early the next day. From these two points we can ascertain that the events in this passage occurred between sunset and sunrise, during the night time. This was not a day time event, but a night time one, between the setting of the sun and the rising of the same.

> As Jacob rested, the Lord gave him a vision. Jacob saw a ladder sitting upon the earth and reaching to Heaven. There was the earth, there was heaven and connecting the two, and bridging the gap, was the ladder. Upon this ladder Jacob saw that the angels were ascending and descending. They were going from earth to heaven and then from heaven to earth. The angels' starting point and finishing point was the earth, indicating that the earth was the focus of their ministry. At the top of the ladder, in heaven, stood the Lord.

> Jacob is overcome with reverential fear and suddenly realised that he had been in the presence of the Lord even though he was unaware of it. Jacob then renamed the place the House of God and the gate of Heaven.

So having looked at the encounter that Jacob had, the question remains what possible application does this have to the Church of today and the infilling we are considering in this section?

The time frame as we have discussed was between sunset and sunrise. It was between these two points that Jacob received the vision, and he also became aware that he was in the House of God. Interesting to note for the reader is that Paul, under inspiration of the Holy Spirit, references this vision of Jacob as he applies the truths of the House of God to the New Testament Church.

> *But if I tarry long, that thou mayest know how thou oughtest to behave thyself in **<u>the house of God, which is the church of the living God, the pillar and ground of the truth</u>**. (1Ti 3:15)*

The sun setting and the sun rising marked the starting and end points for the vision given to Jacob and the revelation of Bethel, the House of God.

After the death and resurrection of Jesus, we know that over a period of days Jesus appeared to individuals, before ascending to heaven. Shortly after this, as the apostles met in the upper room, the Holy Spirit was sent as promised by Jesus, and the Church was born. As has been discussed previously in this study, we are living in the Church age and the dispensation of the Holy Spirit. Since its birth on the Great Day of Pentecost the Church, as the New Testament House of God, has continued for the last 2000 years and will do so until our Lords return. The Church age continues until Jesus returns.

And so, in a snapshot we see that after Jesus Death, i.e. the Son Set, the Church, the New Testament House of God, came into being and continues until Jesus return, i.e. Son Rise.

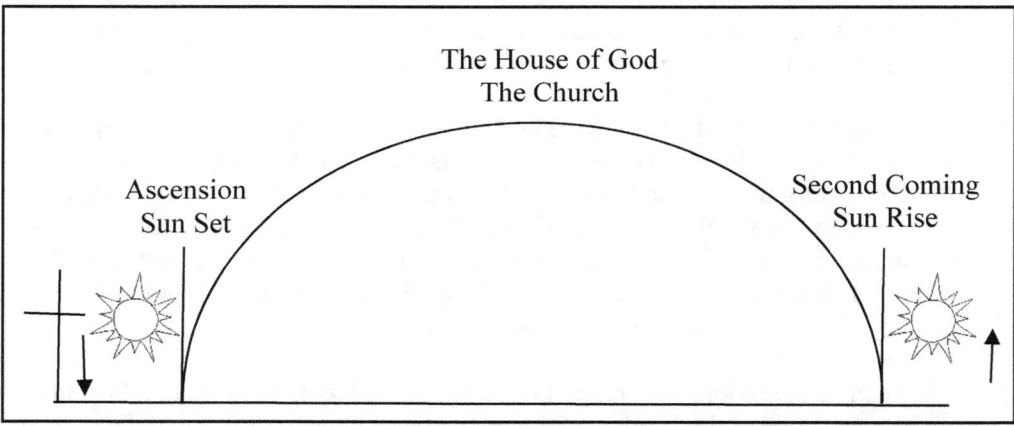

In our look at 'The Call to the Church', we noted that Jesus declared that He was the light of the world. In John 9 Jesus says:

> '*As long as **<u>I am IN the world, I am the light of the world</u>***'. *(John 9:5)*

When Jesus ascended to heaven, His light left, and the world entered its night season. He is no longer in the world, He is now in heaven! During this period of darkness, it is the Church, the Golden Lampstand, the House of God, that exists to shine, reflecting Jesus' glory, much like Moses face.

Infilling

Just as the vision Jacob received was between sun set and sun rise, so too does the Church exist, between the Son set and Son rise. This not only further confirms our earlier thoughts, but the linkage of these two time frames highlights the importance of Jacobs's vision to the Church. Jacob's vision of the House of God, speaks truth to the Church, the New Testament House of God.

Just as the time frame applies to the Church age so do the elements of the vision. Jacobs vision was compromised of a ladder that connected earth and heaven. Upon that ladder the angels ascended and descended. In John Chapter 1, we read of Jesus talking to Nathaniel and in that conversation He stated,

> *"And he said unto him, Verily, verily, I say unto you, Hereafter you shall see **heaven opened**, and the angels of God **ascending and descending** upon **the Son of man**." (John 1:51)*

Notice the language that Jesus used here. He said to Nathaniel three key things:

1. You shall see <u>Heaven Opened.</u>
2. You shall see the angels of God <u>ascending and descending.</u>
3. They will be ascending and descending upon <u>The Son of Man.</u>

In this short excerpt Jesus interprets for us that the ladder in Jacobs's vision represents Him. Jesus is the ladder of Jacob's vision. He is the One who bridges the gap between heaven and earth. He is the connection point.

Compare the language used by Jesus here to that used in the description of Jacobs's vision:

> You shall see Heaven Opened – Jacob saw an open Heaven. He saw the Lord standing atop of the ladder.
>
> And the angels of God ascending and descending – the exact same language and order as used in Jacob's dream. Heaven is opened and the angels ascend and descend upon the Son of man. They don't descend and ascend but **ASCEND** and **DESCEND**. Again, note where the focus is. The angels go from earth to heaven and then return. They ascend and then descend. It is the exact same direction as described in the vision of Jacob.
>
> Jacob saw a ladder connecting heaven and earth and the angels ascending and descending upon that. Here Jesus interprets the ladder as Himself. Jesus is the connection for man between earth and heaven. It is upon Him that the angels ascend and descend. Jesus is the ladder, Jesus is the gate.

JACOB'S VISION	JOHN 1:51
Open heaven	Heaven opened
Angels ascending – up	Angels ascending – up
Then descending - down	Then descending - down
The ladder – connecting earth and heaven	Jesus – connecting earth and heaven

The connecting point for the Church on earth to God in Heaven is Jesus Christ. Jesus is the connection! He is the One who bridges the gap. Where two or three are gathered in His name, there He is in the midst, as the connection, the ladder. It is He who provides the link. No man comes to the Father except through Him. Without Him we have no connection! With Him, we have access to the Father, an open Heaven! He is what connects us. He bridges the gap. Jesus is the fulfilment of the prophetic vision that Jacob saw.

At the start of this section, we stated that the infilling of the Lord is always in response to the digging of man. The actions of heaven respond to the actions of man on earth. In 2 Kings 3, the Lord infilled the wells because they had first been dug. Man had to step out and fulfil his part, before the Lord could do His. Heaven then responded to the actions of man on earth.

The key for us in the vision of Jacob is to understand where the focus is. Jesus, as we have established is the one who bridges the gap between heaven and earth, He is the ladder. But the focus is on earth. There is an ascending from the earth through Jesus to the Father **before** there is a descending from the Father through the Son to the earth. It is the activities of earth that precede the response from heaven.

Jesus is our mediator, He is the One that Job cried for, the one that stands between man and God. As we are faithful in prayer, in worship and praise, in speaking in tongues and so forth, these things rise to the Father through the Son. The Son, as our Great High Priest, presents them to the Father on our behalf. They rise from the earth, through the Son to the Father. It is then after this, that the response of Heaven descends from the Father, through the Son to man on earth. Earth is the focus. Jesus is the connection. The flow is that of ascending and **THEN** descending. Infilling doesn't come that we may be strengthened to dig. Infilling is always the response of heaven to the actions of man on earth. The descending blessing of the Lord happens **after** man has pressed in and dug the wells. The truths of Jacobs vision are the same as what we observed from Zechariah's vision of the lampstand. Man has to open the pipes upward before the oil can flow downward.

If we truly want to receive the fulness of the infilling that the Father has for us, then we need to dig in the areas that He has directed us to. We need to be digging the wells that we considered in our previous section. As the desperation of man for the Lord rises unto Him through the Son, His infilling flows via the Son and into the wells that man has dug. The descension follows the ascension. The infilling follows the digging. Just as it was with the kings, so it is with us.

Infilling

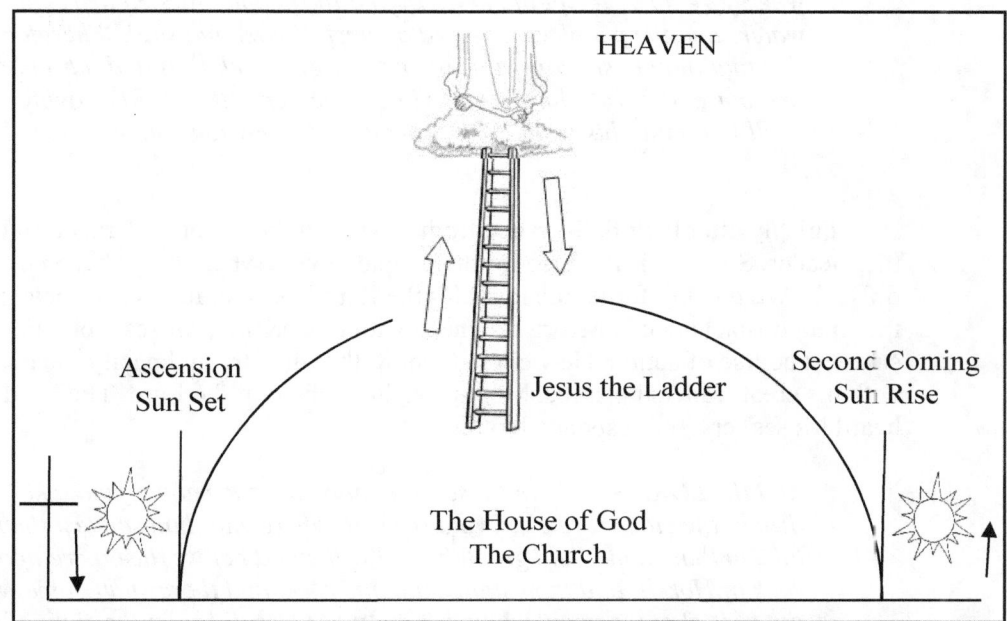

The key to remember is that what flows from heaven is a result of what ascends from man on earth. The truth of this is that the response of God is always unto the actions of man. This is what Jacob saw and this is what Jesus confirmed. Jesus is the ladder just as He is our Golden Bowl. The infilling we receive directly relates to what we do as believers and congregations. If we are faithful in having each of the seven wells we have considered previously open, then the promise of the Lord is that His infilling will follow. Heaven responds to that which ascends from the earth. Infilling always follows the obedient digging of the people of the Lord. When we dig in obedience and faith, heaven responds, and the Lords fills that which has been dug.

B. Moses and the Rock

The second example for us to consider is that of Moses and the rock. In scripture we are given two separate examples where Moses brought forth water from the rock. For our purposes here we will consider these individually, before bringing their truths together to again highlight our point for this section, that infilling is a result of digging.

1. Exodus 17

    The first example for us to consider is found in Exodus 17. This event occurred shortly after Israel's deliverance from Egypt, just after they had entered the wilderness. There we read that the people of Israel started to grumble against Moses.

    > *Wherefore the people did chide with Moses, and said, Give us water that we may drink. And Moses said unto them, Why chide ye with me?*

> *wherefore do ye tempt the LORD? And the people thirsted there for water; and the people murmured against Moses, and said, Wherefore is this that thou hast brought us up out of Egypt, to kill us and our children and our cattle with thirst? And Moses cried unto the LORD, saying, What shall I do unto this people? they be almost ready to stone me. (Exo 17:2-4)*

How quickly after their deliverance from Egypt did the nation of Israel turn on their leader. So often is the case for the people of God when things become difficult. We quickly forget the miracles the Lord has done for us and focus in on the small obstacle that is before us. Faced with an uprising, Moses took the smartest course of action. He went to God. Rather than try and pacify the people with his great leadership skills, Moses sought the help of the Lord. The Lord heard Moses' cry and responded to him.

> *And the LORD said unto Moses, Go on before the people, and take with thee of the elders of Israel; and thy rod, wherewith thou smotest the river, take in thine hand, and go. Behold, I will stand before thee there upon the rock in Horeb; and thou shalt smite the rock, and there shall come water out of it, that the people may drink. And Moses did so in the sight of the elders of Israel. (Exo 17:5-6)*

The Lord's response to this uprising was that Moses should take his rod, the same rod that he had used to perform the miracles in Egypt, and deliver the nation of Israel. He was to take this rod and go and smite the rock. As Moses acted in faith and obedience to the Word of the Lord, the Lord would cause water to flow out of the rock so that the people of Israel could drink. The promise of the Lord was that as Moses acted in faith with this, the Lord Himself would stand before Moses.

Moses acted in obedience and that day the nation of Israel experienced the miraculous provision of the Lord as the waters poured forth out of the rock.

2. Numbers 20

Sometime later in the journeying of Israel, after the death of Miriam, Moses found himself in a similar situation. There was no water for the congregation and so they gathered themselves together against Moses and Aaron. Note the similarities of the complaint of the people all of these years later.

> *And the people chode with Moses, and spake, saying, Would God that we had died when our brethren died before the LORD! And why have ye brought up the congregation of the LORD into this wilderness, that we and our cattle should die there? And wherefore have ye made us to come up out of Egypt, to bring us in unto this evil place? it is no place of seed, or of figs, or of vines, or of pomegranates; neither is there any water to drink. (Num 20:3-5)*

This time Aaron and Moses went before the Lord. Moses and Aaron, in unity, went to the Tabernacle of the Lord and fell upon their faces. The glory of the Lord appeared before them and the Lord said unto them:

> *Take the rod, and gather thou the assembly together, thou, and Aaron thy brother, and speak ye unto the rock before their eyes; and it shall give forth his water, and thou shalt bring forth to them water out of the rock: so thou shalt give the congregation and their beasts drink. (Num 20:8)*

The word this time to Moses and Aaron was for Moses to again take his rod, but this time he was to speak unto the rock before the eyes of the nation of Israel. As Moses would do this, the Lord would bring forth water from the rock for the congregation as well as their flocks and herds. We then go on to read:

> *And Moses took the rod from before the LORD, as he commanded him. And Moses and Aaron gathered the congregation together before the rock, and he said unto them, Hear now, ye rebels; must we fetch you water out of this rock? And Moses lifted up his hand, and with his rod he smote the rock twice: and the water came out abundantly, and the congregation drank, and their beasts also. (Num 20:9-11)*

Moses and Aaron headed out from the presence of the Lord and gathered the congregation before the rock. Moses addressed the congregation and in their presence he lifted his hands and struck the rock twice with his rod. As he did this water came out, water in abundance. Enough for the people of Israel, their herds and their flocks.

In the very next verse, we come to a conversation that seems out of place. In response to Moses actions at the rock, the Lord addressed him and said:

> *And the LORD spake unto Moses and Aaron, Because ye believed me not, to sanctify me in the eyes of the children of Israel, therefore ye shall not bring this congregation into the land which I have given them. (Num 20:12)*

The Word of the Lord here was that because of Moses' lack of belief, Moses would not lead the nation of Israel into the promised land. The way Moses interacted with the rock the second time, was not according to the will of the Lord and brought with it a consequence. The action of Moses caused him to fall under the judgement of the Lord. The judgement of the Lord may seem rather harsh here, but there is a truth involved in all this that we will explain shortly. What is evident though, is that in this encounter Moses erred in some way. Whilst the water was still provided from the rock by the Lord, the Lord was displeased with Moses on account of something that Moses had done.

Infilling

Through these encounters what we see is a progressive revelation of truth regarding the Rock. It is once we understand what this truth is that we better understand the Lord's judgment on Moses and again see the truth of infilling that we are establishing in this section.

Paul in 1 Corinthian 10, under inspiration of the Holy Spirit interprets for us some of the experiences of the nation of Israel. Of particular interest to us is what Paul says in verse 4:

> *And did all drink the same spiritual drink: for they drank of that spiritual Rock that followed them: and that Rock was Christ. (1Co 10:4)*

Paul stated that all of Israel drank the same spiritual drink, for they all drank of the spiritual Rock that followed them. Twice we have seen that the entire nation of Israel was nourished by the Lord through the provision of water from the Rock. On two occasions every man, woman and child drank the same spiritual drink from the same Rock that followed them.

Paul then went on to say that that Rock was Christ. The Rock that followed Israel, that supplied them with supernatural water, was Christ. All drank of the water from the Rock. There was only one source of the water, and all partook of that spiritual drink. Christ alone is the source and it is from Him that the people of God receive their infilling. Christ is the Rock and source.

It is when we understand this truth, that the rock of Exodus and Numbers speaks of Christ, that we are then able to better understand the fulness of these examples (1 Corinthians 10:11).

In the first instance the Word of the Lord for Moses was to **strike** the rock and then the water would flow. This points to Jesus, our Rock, on the cross of Calvary. Jesus was struck once for the sins of all mankind, and it was from His side upon the cross that blood and water flowed. Christ had to be struck for the life-giving waters of the Father to flow. The first example in Exodus speaks of Christ the rock who was struck.

In the Numbers account we see that the Word of the Lord was similar, but different. Moses was again told to go before the rock with His rod, but this time Moses was to **speak** to the rock and the waters would flow. Moses was **not to strike** the rock as he did the first time, he was to **speak** to the rock. The Word of the Lord was to **speak** to the rock. The truth that the Lord was seeking to communicate to man was that once the rock had been struck for the waters to flow then all that was needed from then on was for man to speak to the rock for the waters to flow.

EXODUS	NUMBERS
Strike the Rock	Speak to the Rock
Water will flow	Water will Flow

Christ was struck **once** for the remission of all sins, so that the life-giving waters of the Father may flow. After that we need only to speak to the rock for the water to flow. This was a truth that Moses violated when he struck the rock the second time. God, in His sovereignty, still delivered the nation of Israel through Moses' hand, but of necessity Moses received a punishment to highlight how great his error was. The Lord had to establish the truth He was setting forth to man, that the Rock would only be struck once and then after that it just had to be spoken to. Moses violated the truth God was establishing and that was why the Lord's judgement was so harsh. The judgement had to highlight the error of Moses.

Christ our Rock has been struck. He was struck at calvary where He died in place of us all. The truth is now, that Christ does not need to be struck again for the water to flow. All that is required for the water to flow from the Rock is for man to speak to the Rock. All that is required of us is to speak to Christ for the water to flow.

And whilst that process sounds simple, what it again illustrates is that infilling follows after the actions of man. Before the water flows from the Rock, we have to speak unto it. Before water flows from Christ, we have to raise our voices and speak unto Him. The words that rise from earth are met with a response from heaven. The infilling follows from the actions of man. Infilling again follows digging. It is the response of the Lord unto the actions of His people. The water flows after we speak. Infilling follows as the natural progression as heaven always answers the call of earth.

C. Daniel

The next example for us to consider is with the prophet Daniel. Daniel was a faithful servant of the Lord, whose ministry occurred while the nation of Israel was in exile. In the book of Daniel, we are given two examples where we read that Daniel received an answer from the Lord after he had sought Him. The truth that we have seen from Jacob's ladder and with Moses and the rock, we see demonstrated in the life of Daniel. We will consider these examples individually, and in doing so will see how the experience of Daniel confirms how infilling is a response of heaven to the actions of earth.

The first instance for us to look at is found in Daniel Chapter 9. There we read:

> *In the first year of his reign I Daniel understood by books the number of the years, whereof the word of the LORD came to Jeremiah the prophet, that he would accomplish seventy years in the desolations of Jerusalem. And I set my face unto the Lord God, to seek by prayer and supplications, with fasting, and sackcloth, and ashes: (Dan 9:2-3)*

Daniel had been studying the Word of God and whilst doing this he received a revelation from the Lord that Israel's exile in Babylon would last for seventy years. In the verses that follow, we read that this revelation caused Daniel to seek the Lord.

Infilling

Daniel humbled himself and laid out his prayer and petition before the Lord interceding on behalf of the nation. Notice the words of Daniel in regard to this:

> And **_I set my face unto the Lord God, to seek by prayer_** and **supplications**, with **fasting**, and **sackcloth**, and **ashes**: *(Dan 9:2-3)*

Daniel set his face to seek the Lord. This was not a one line and done prayer situation. Daniel was digging! He was pressing into the Lord in prayer, with focus, dedication and sacrifice. The prayer and intercession of Daniel continues down to verse 20, where we read that Daniel had an encounter with the angel Gabriel.

> *And whiles I was speaking, and praying, and confessing my sin and the sin of my people Israel, and presenting my supplication before the LORD my God for the holy mountain of my God; Yea, whiles I was speaking in prayer, even the man Gabriel, whom I had seen in the vision at the beginning, being caused to fly swiftly, touched me about the time of the evening oblation. And he informed me, and talked with me, and said, O Daniel, I am now come forth to give thee skill and understanding. At the beginning of thy supplications the commandment came forth, and I am come to shew thee; for thou art greatly beloved: therefore understand the matter, and consider the vision. (Dan 9:20-23)*

Notice again the actions of Daniel here. He had been speaking, praying, confessing, interceding and presenting his supplication before the Lord. Daniel's whole focus was on seeking the Lord. It was then after Daniel had been praying, fasting and seeking the Lord that Gabriel appeared unto him. Gabriel came and spoke to Daniel and went on to give unto him the notable seventy week prophecy. Of particular interest to us in this section, are the words of Gabriel in verse 23.

> *At the **beginning of thy supplications the commandment came forth**, and I am come to shew thee; for thou art greatly beloved: therefore understand the matter, and consider the vision. (Dan 9:23).*

Gabriel said to Daniel that at the beginning of Daniel's supplications the commandment came forth for Gabriel to come unto Daniel. Daniel humbled himself and set himself to seek the Lord on behalf of his nation. At the beginning of Daniel's supplications there was a response in heaven. It wasn't before Daniel's supplications, but at the **beginning** of them. In other words, the response from heaven came after Daniel's supplications had started. The response of heaven came because of the actions of Daniel on earth. The infilling came after the digging. Daniel set himself to seek the Lord, he was digging deep and as he did so, the infilling of the Lord followed.

We see this same truth again displayed in the life of Daniel in Daniel chapter 10. There we read again that Daniel was seeking the Lord:

Infilling

In the third year of Cyrus king of Persia a thing was revealed unto Daniel, whose name was called Belteshazzar; and the thing was true, but the time appointed was long: and he understood the thing, and had understanding of the vision. In those days I Daniel was mourning three full weeks. I ate no pleasant bread, neither came flesh nor wine in my mouth, neither did I anoint myself at all, till three whole weeks were fulfilled. (Dan 10:1-3)

Daniel was again in a time of fasting and seeking the Lord in humility. Daniel here fasted for three weeks, eating no pleasant food or flesh and did not anoint himself. Daniel had received a vision of the Lord, but it troubled him, so he fasted and sought the Lord regarding this vision. Note the response to the actions of Daniel in verse 12:

*Then said he unto me, Fear not, Daniel: for **<u>from the first day</u>** that thou didst set thine heart to understand, and to chasten thyself before thy God, **<u>thy words were heard, and I am come for thy words.</u>** (Dan 10:12)*

From the first day that Daniel set his heart to seek the Lord, Daniel's words were heard and there was a response from Heaven. Notice his words were heard. Daniel wasn't just fasting as outlined in vs 3, he was praying and seeking the Lord. His words were rising to heaven. It was on the first day that his words were uttered that they were heard in heaven and a response was sent. For us to note though is the order here.. It is again the actions of earth that initiate the response from heaven. There was an ascending from earth before there was a descending from heaven. The response that Daniel received was because of the words that he had offered up in prayer. Daniels words couldn't be heard until they had been uttered. Daniel had dug and the Lord again infilled.

We go on to read in this passage that this angel was delayed for three weeks in a spiritual battle before he could get to Daniel (v13). It is interesting that this delay was the exact same amount of time that Daniel was fasting for (compare vs 2 and vs 13). For us to note, is that whilst there was a delay in the answer coming, the moment Daniel set himself to seek the Lord, there was a response from heaven. His words were heard, and the angel was sent forth. Again, we see that the response from heaven occurred after the actions of man on earth. Daniel set himself to seek the Lord and **THEN** heaven responded. There was first digging and then there was infilling.

The truths of these two encounters are summarised below:

	DANIEL CHAPTER 9	**DANIEL CHAPTER 10**
ACTIONS OF EARTH	Vs 1-21 Daniel prayed, fasted and sought the Lord.	Vs 2,3 - Daniel fasted for 3 weeks, prayed and sought the Lord.
RESPONSE FROM HEAVEN	Vs 23 – At the **beginning** of Daniel's supplications the response was sent.	Vs 12 – From the **first day** Daniel's prayers were heard, and the angel was sent.

Infilling

In both cases heaven responded immediately to the actions of Daniel in prayer, fasting and humility. And in both cases it was just that, a response. Heaven responded to the actions of Daniel on earth. The infilling followed the digging. Just as with the kings and the wells, as Daniel in these chapters dug in faith the Lord then infilled. Earth initiated, Heaven responded.

D. The Words of Jesus

In Luke chapter 11 we read that Jesus was teaching His disciples to pray. In verses 1-8, in response to the disciples question of how to pray, Jesus gave them the model of the Lord's prayer. Continuing on the theme of prayer, Jesus then went on to give two illustrations in order to broaden our understanding of prayer. Our particular focus for this section is on Jesus' words in Luke 11:9-13. There we read:

> *And I say unto you, Ask, and it shall be given you; seek, and ye shall find; knock, and it shall be opened unto you. For every one that asketh receiveth; and he that seeketh findeth; and to him that knocketh it shall be opened. If a son shall ask bread of any of you that is a father, will he give him a stone? or if he ask a fish, will he for a fish give him a serpent? Or if he shall ask an egg, will he offer him a scorpion? If ye then, being evil, know how to give good gifts unto your children: how much more shall your heavenly Father give the Holy Spirit to them that ask him? (Luk 11:9-13)*

In this passage there are three actions of man that are highlighted. These actions are highlighted twice in this passage by our Lord. There is a double emphasis placed here. Jesus said we, as believers, are to ask, seek and knock. These are actions that we are to undertake. He then goes on to tell us that these actions have a response:

ACTION	RESPONSE
Ask	Receive
Seek	Find
Knock	Door opened

In each case there is an action and there is a response. Jesus then closes this discourse by applying this truth to believers and their Heavenly Father in terms of prayer. Notice the words of Jesus here:

> *If ye then, being evil, know how to give good gifts unto your children: how much more shall your **heavenly Father give the Holy Spirit** to them **that ask him**? (Luk 11:9-13)*

The words of Jesus here are that our Heavenly Father will give the Holy Spirit unto them that ask Him. Our Heavenly Father gives when we ask. In other words, there is a requirement upon man to ask, to seek and to knock. It is man who initiates the action. We seek the Lord and the Lord answers. The result though is dependent upon the action. There is a twofold truth in this example of Jesus:

TRUTH – POSITIVE SIDE	TRUTH – NEGATIVE SIDE
He who asks receives.	He who doesn't ask doesn't receive.
He who seeks finds.	He who doesn't seek doesn't find.
He who knocks has the door opened.	He who doesn't knock doesn't have the door opened.
He who asks for the Holy Spirit receives.	He who doesn't ask doesn't receive.

Through this study we have seen that Jesus is the Golden Bowl through whom the Holy Spirit flows unto the Church through the seven golden pipes. This discourse of Jesus again highlights the truths of flow that we have been discussing. It is when man digs the wells, opening the pipes, through asking, seeking and knocking, that the Father then responds and the Holy Spirit flows to His people. It is the actions of earth that determine the response from heaven. If we want His infilling, then we must of necessity have dug the wells. This was the truth for the kings, and it is the same truth for us. Our Heavenly Father is a good Father, and He always responds to His people when they ask, seek and knock. It is up to us though to ask, to seek and to knock. It is up to us to dig!

E. The Upper Room

At the start of Acts chapter 2, we read that when the day of Pentecost came all of the disciples were of one accord and in one place. The reason they were here was because they were being obedient unto the words of Jesus recorded in the gospel of Luke:

> *And said unto them, Thus it is written, and thus it behoved Christ to suffer, and to rise from the dead the third day: And that repentance and remission of sins should be preached in his name among all nations, beginning at Jerusalem. And ye are witnesses of these things. And, behold, I send the promise of my Father upon you: but tarry ye in the city of Jerusalem, until ye be endued with power from on high. (Luk 24:46-49)*

Jesus appeared here to His disciples, after his crucifixion and subsequent resurrection, and commissioned them. Having opened their understanding to the scriptures, He then gave them the mission that they should go to all nations preaching the good news, beginning at Jerusalem. Jesus threw in a but though. He said that before they were to do this, that they should tarry in the city of Jerusalem until they were endued with power from on high. Jesus had spoken to them about the promised sending of the Holy Spirit. Although it is possible that the disciples did not fully comprehend what this enduring of power meant, they knew they needed to be obedient unto the words of Jesus and "tarry".

We know from the book of Acts that as the disciples tarried in Jerusalem in obedience to the Word of God, that on the day of Pentecost the Holy Spirit descended as tongues of fire and they were all filled with the Holy Ghost (Acts 2:4). This was the fulfilment of what Jesus had spoken about.

Infilling

Between this encounter with Jesus in Luke and the infilling of the Holy Spirit as recorded in Acts, the disciples tarried. In Acts chapter 1 we read that during this time:

> *... when they were come in, they went up into an upper room, where abode both Peter, and James, and John, and Andrew, Philip, and Thomas, Bartholomew, and Matthew, James the son of Alphaeus, and Simon Zelotes, and Judas the brother of James. These all continued with one accord in prayer and supplication, with the women, and Mary the mother of Jesus, and with his brethren. (Act 1:13-14)*

It is the writer's opinion that this was not a once off event. As the disciples were waiting in Jerusalem in obedience to the Words of Jesus, they were pressing into God. They were gathered together of one accord and with one focus. They were united in prayer and praise. They were seeking the Lord for the promised outpouring of His Spirit and the enduing of power from on high. It was through their obedience to the Word that the Holy Spirit was poured out on the great day of Pentecost. Obedience to the Word and pressing into the Lord again preceded His infilling. The infilling of Heaven was as a result of the actions of earth. The Lord poured out as the disciples pressed in, in obedience to the words of Jesus. They tarried in Jerusalem and dug, before the Lord infilled them.

F. Behold I stand at the door and knock

In Revelation chapter 3 Jesus addressed the Church at Laodicea. Whilst we have considered this passage in our look at the well of prayer, here we will recap those thoughts to see how this passage also highlights that the actions of heaven respond to those of earth. In verse 20 of Revelation 3 we read:

> *Behold, I stand at the door, and knock: if any man hear my voice, and open the door, I will come in to him, and will sup with him, and he with me.(Rev 3:20)*

Here we read that Jesus stands at the door and knocks. He doesn't just knock though! His Words are that if any man hears My voice. Jesus stands and knocks but He also calls so that man may hear His voice. Jesus is at the door knocking, calling out. But notice the burden of responsibility in this verse. Jesus says that if any man hears My voice and opens the door, then I will come in and sup with him and he with Me. Jesus is wanting to come into our lives, into our houses and have relationship with us, but the onus is on us to open the door. It is not just that we hear His voice, we also have to open the door.

In the natural when there is a knock at the door, we have to stop what we are doing, get up and turn our attention and effort to going to the door and opening it. If we don't make the effort then whoever is at the door can't get in. They may be ready and willing but their ability to enter is dependent on us.

This again is the truth that we have been talking about. The ability of Jesus to infill us is determined by our action. The infilling comes after we take the initiative to open the door. It is again the actions of man that determine the response of heaven. We either open ourselves to the blessing of infilling or rob ourselves of it. It is our actions that determine the outcome.

God is ready and waiting, but His ability to connect depends on us. How often does God knock at the door of our lives and churches and we don't take the necessary actions to answer? We have to respond to His Words and put in the effort to open the door, before He can come in. We have to dig if we truly want His infilling.

Throughout the examples that we have looked at we have seen time and time again that infilling is always the response of the Lord to the actions of man on earth. What we have discovered in this section is summarised in the table below.

	JACOB'S LADDER	**WATER FROM THE ROCK**		**DANIEL**	**JESUS'S WORDS**	**UPPER ROOM**	**STAND AT THE DOOR**
ACTIONS OF EARTH	Angels Ascend from	Strike the Rock	Speak to the Rock	Daniel sought the Lord	Ask, seek, knock	Gathered in unity in obedience	Man responds and opens the door
RESPONSE OF HEAVEN	Angels Descend from	Water Flows	Water Flows	Heaven heard and responded	Receive, find, door opened	Outpouring of the Holy Spirit	Jesus comes into the House

We see from all of these examples the truth of what we discovered in 2 Kings 3, that the infilling of God is in response to the actions and obedience of man. The response of heaven is determined by the actions of earth. If we truly want the fulness of infilling that the Lord has for us then it is our responsibility to press into the Lord and dig. God is always faithful to His Word and He will always respond to the actions of man. The blessing though, is dependent upon the obedience of man to the Word of God. We need to understand that the infilling of the Lord, the filling of the Holy Spirit doesn't occur to stir the hunger of the people, but rather it occurs because the people have been stirred to press into the Lord. The question is are we thirsty enough to dig, knowing all that it involves? Are we prepared to invest the time, effort and sacrifice continually so that we may be infilled? That is the question that lays upon each individual and Church. Yes we want the infilling, but are we prepared to do the work of digging. The infilling we receive will always be measured against the depth of digging we have done. If we want the fulness of His infilling then we need to dig deep the wells.

What we have established so far is that the responsibility and call to dig is upon us as New Testament believers and churches. It is the first step and the part where the sole responsibility lies with man. The second part and the focus of this section is the infilling of the Lord. God will always respond to the actions of man be they in obedience or disobedience. Throughout the scriptural examples that we have considered in this section, we have seen the truth established that the actions of heaven are always in response to the actions of man. The angels, as ministering spirits, descend after they have ascended from the earth. The water flowed from the rock after it was struck/spoken too. Daniel sought the Lord in prayer and supplication and heaven heard and responded. We ask, seek and knock and we then receive, find and have the door opened. The disciples were filled with the Holy Spirit after they gathered in obedience to the Word of the Lord. Jesus comes into to sup with us after we open the door and let Him in. Infilling always follows digging. God always responds to the actions of man. If we want His infilling, then like the kings and their armies we have to dig where He has told us to. We need to dig deep the wells of prayer, reading and meditating on the Word, sensitivity to the Holy Spirit, faith, obedience, tongues and worship and praise. If we do this, then heaven will respond! Heaven always responds to the actions of earth. When His people dig, the Lord infills. It is a truth that is shown time and time again. We don't get infilled to dig, we dig so that He will infill. Infilling always follows digging.

THE PURPOSE OF IN-FILLING

Having seen how infilling works, we turn our attention now to its purpose. In our 2 Kings 3 example, we saw that the Word of the Lord for the kings and their united armies was for them to dig. They had to dig so that the Lord could infill. This infilling of the Lord then had a number of impacts upon the kings and their armies.

Our purpose here is to consider these impacts and gain a better understanding of why infilling is of such importance. The Lord didn't just infill their wells for the sake of it. He didn't just ask them to dig for the sake of it. There was purpose behind it and there was purpose to the infilling of the Lord.

Here we will work though our example from 2 Kings 3 identifying the purpose of the infilling of the Lord, before applying those lessons to the lives of believers and the Church today. In doing this we will hopefully gain an increased understanding of the importance and necessity for each of us to be infilled by the Lord.

A. Infilling is for the preservation and restoration of life

> *So the king of Israel went, and the king of Judah, and the king of Edom: and they fetched a compass of seven days' journey: and there was no water for the host, and for the cattle that followed them. (2Ki 3:9).*

The kings and their armies marched for seven days as they set out to meet Moab in battle. By the seventh day they had run out of water. Whether they had failed to take enough water with them, or whether they had expected to find water on the way we don't know. All that we know for sure is that the kings and their armies were out of water and there was obviously no ready source near them otherwise they would have sent for it or returned to it. The kings and their armies were in a situation where they had no ready and available supply of water.

The human body can go without food for a while, but water is an essential for life. This was the concern of the king of Israel. He understood that the lack of water would impede the ability of his men to function and that without it they would be handed over to Moab in battle.

In our 2 Kings 3 example, the Lord answered this need of the kings and their men. The Lord supernaturally provided water for them, miracoulsey filling the wells that they had dug.. This water restored their life, it preserved their life and it equipped them with strength to go and fulfil what the Lord had set before them. Without this restoration the strength of the army would have failed. The men would have been in a weakened state and vulnerable to the army of Moab. Water though restored life. It regenerated the life of the kings and their men.

Spiritually we have the same need for water. Our spiritual man needs to partake of the spiritual water that comes from the Lord. The infilling of the Lord is what gives life to our spiritual man. Without it, we find ourselves in a state of spiritual weakness and in a place of vulnerability to the enemy.

One of the major problems we face as individuals though is that we often don't realise that we are thirsty and in need of a drink. This can often be why individuals become dehydrated. They are unaware of their lack of water and their need for it. Spiritually we need to be aware that we need to be partaking daily of the spiritual living waters of the Lord. We need His infilling daily. We need to be speaking to the Rock on a daily basis and receiving the precious infilling of the Lord. His infilling is not a break glass in an emergency situation. His infilling is to be a daily staple in our spiritual lives. We need to be aware of our spiritual intake, we can't just presume we are ok. We need to pause and take stock of whether we are receiving enough of the Lord's water for us. It is when we neglect this that we risk becoming spiritually dehydrated. Jesus came that we may have life and life abundantly. The question is though, are we partaking of that which the Lord has provided for our spiritual life? Are we spiritually hydrated and is this the norm for our lives? Our spiritual man needs the Lord's spiritual water.

B. Infilling is for more than just us

> *For thus saith the LORD, Ye shall not see wind, neither shall ye see rain; yet that valley shall be filled with water,* **_that ye may drink, both ye, and your cattle, and your beasts_**. *(2Ki 3:17)*

The infilling of the Lord didn't just come for the kings. It didn't just come for the kings and their men. It didn't just come for the kings, their men and cattle. The infilling came for the complete congregation! It came for the kings, their men, their cattle and their beasts. There was not one amongst the congregation who missed out. The infilling of the Lord wasn't just for a special few, nor was it to be kept by a special few. There were not reserved wells or water that was off limits to some people. The infilling was for the common good of the entire congregation.

Such is true in our lives as well. That which the Lord infills us with is meant for more than just us. It is not to be a blessing that we guard and protect, but one that we share and as we do we impart spiritual life to those who partake of it. The infilling of the Lord is not meant to be hoarded, it is meant to be shared.

Whilst we unequivocally need the infilling of the Lord for our spiritual wellbeing, we must always remember that His infilling is never meant for just us. The blessing of life is meant to be shared with those that are with and around us. There is a blessing for others in what the Lord infills us with. Ours it to be faithful with what He blesses us with.

C. Infilling builds our faith

The infilling of the Lord creates the faith for the next step. The Word of the Lord through Elisha was that though the kings would not see wind or rain, yet the Lord would fill the ditches they had dug with water. Elisha then went on to say:

> *And this is but a light thing in the sight of the LORD: he will deliver the Moabites also into your hand. (2Ki 3:18)*

The kings didn't go in faith unto Elisha, they went in desperation! They were put in a desperate situation that caused them to seek out the Lord. Their armies were without water and death and defeat were what they imminently faced. It was not in faith that they sought the Lord but in desperation and urgent need. What we see though, is that the Lord said to the kings that if you think me providing water is a miracle, wait till you see what I do with Moab. The Israelites were in a place where they could maybe muster faith to believe God for His miracle of water, but to defeat the enemy was possibly still something they were not prepared for. Their focus at the time of Elisha's word was on saving their lives.

What we see here is that the infilling of the Lord built their faith for what was to come next. The Lord spoke to the kings and Israel that they would defeat Moab before the miracle of water was provided. It is the writer's opinion, that although the kings and armies may have initially struggled to fully grab hold of this, their faith in God's Word for the victory would have soared when they woke up to see how He had been faithful to His Word and provided water in abundance for them. The infilling of the Lord would have absolutely stirred the faith of the armies for the next thing that God had promised them. If the Lord provided the water according to His Word, then He could most certainly hand Moab over to them!

The Infilling of the Lord builds our faith for the next steps He has for us. As we dig and press into Him for His infilling, our faith and trust in Him also grows. As we are infilled we step out, faith filled, into what God has called us to.

D. Infilling is to have greater affects

> His infilling has a flow on effect, and this is something that we will consider more fully in our next sections. Suffice to say for now, we need to be aware that our need of infilling has greater consequences than just ourselves. Whilst infilling has personal benefits it is something that should never be done with a purely personal focus. Infilling is something that blesses us as we receive the Holy Spirit through the Son. Infilling revives us, it strengthens us, it imparts life and rejuvenates. But those personal benefits of infilling should never be our motivation for digging. Digging should never be done with a self-minded mentality. We can never afford to be a people who dig just to reap the feel good benefits of infilling, for when we do that we miss the purpose of the process. We dig to receive His infilling so that we might reflect His glory and see His Kingdom come. Infilling is an essential part of the process, but it is not the end of it.
>
> Just as the purpose of digging is to allow infilling, the purpose of infilling is to allow reflection. In our Kings example, we saw that the men dug, the Lord infilled and in the morning the sun reflected off of the water. The reflection could never have occurred if the infilling hadn't, just as the infilling could never have occurred if the wells hadn't been dug. The infilling was not just for the points considered above, it had a greater purpose. The infilling blessed the men and the armies, but that was not the fulness of what the infilling was for. The infilling was to have greater affects than just those personally reaped by the kings and their armies. This is something that we will consider in our next section.

God always does things for a reason and His infilling is always with a purpose. The infilling of the Lord is for the benefit of His people. It restores and preserves life, it is for those who are with us, it builds our faith and it serves a greater purpose than we can imagine. The Lord's infilling restores and nourishes our spiritual man, it blesses those around us and ensures that we walk in the fulness of spiritual health, ready and willing for what lays ahead.

His infilling allows us to walk in the fulness of what He has for us. His infilling is a progressive step for us to be able to reflect His glory. Infilling is absolutely necessary if reflection is to ever occur. Just as digging has a purpose, so too does infilling!

LESSONS FROM INFILLING

Having looked at how infilling occurs and what its purposes are, there are a couple of points for us as believers to keep in mind. Ours is to learn and apply the lessons learned from our predecessors, whether they be successes or mistakes. If we can do that, we can ensure that we and the Kingdom of God are always advancing and not just going round the mountain. When we learn from, rather than relearn ourselves, the Kingdom continues to move forward.

With that in mind, the following thoughts are ones that the Lord prompted the writer on in regard to infilling in the lives of believers and the Church.

A. Obedience

Our infilling is dependent upon our obedience to the Word of God. In 2 Kings 3 we saw that the Word of the Lord was for the kings and their armies to dig before the infilling of the Lord occurred. As we have already discussed digging was a faith step. The armies were already without water, exhausted and contemplating defeat. Then the Lord asked them to exert energy filling the valley with ditches. The test laid by the Lord through Elisha was obedience. Would the kings and their armies be obedient to the Word of the Lord? Would they dig in faithful obedience and trust the Word of the Lord?

The truth is, that the wells had to be dug so they could be infilled. The wells were the vessels to catch the infilling of the Lord. Without the wells the water would have passed through and all that would have been left would have been muddy ground. The promised infilling relied upon the obedience of the people.

For New Testament believers and churches, we can't expect the Lord to fill when we haven't dug. If we truly want the fulness of what the Lord has for us, we need to do the hard yards and press into the Lord seeking Him for it. Digging is not a Sunday event, it is a lifestyle! If we truly want the fulness of infilling that the Lord has for us we need to have a lifestyle of digging and maintaining spiritual wells. The infilling we will receive is based upon our obedience or lack of it to the Word of God. If we truly want the fulness of what the Lord has for us as His people, then we need to be walking in obedience and making sure those wells are open and ready. The Lord will always fill that which has been dug in obedience. In fact, He can only fill that which has been dug in obedience! His infilling rests on our obedience.

B. Depth

As already discussed, the Hebrew word for ditches in 2 Kings 3:16 means a well or a cistern. The kings and armies weren't asked to dig puddles, or shallow holes, they were asked to dig wells of depth. They had to dig deep so that there was sufficient depth to contain that which the Lord wanted to provide and infill them with. The measure of what they received would be determined by how deeply they dug. Shallow wells would have meant that they only received a fraction of the fulness of the Lord's blessing for them. The amount of blessing poured out by the Lord never changed, but their ability to receive it was determined by how deeply they dug. For Israel to receive God's infilling in its entirety, the armies had to dig deep.

For us, the level of infilling that we will receive is directly related to how faithful we have been to dig, and how deep we have dug. Shallow wells don't hold much water and quickly run dry. Our desperation for God to move will determine how deep we dig. God's supply is never limited, but the amount we receive is determined by how desperate and thirsty we are for it. If we are truly after the infilling of the Lord, our lives will be littered with the evidence of our digging. Prayer, His Word, sensitivity to the Spirit, obedience, faith, tongues, praise and worship are things that our lives should be marked by and things that overflow through our services. For us as His people and corporately as His Church, these cannot be things that we just encourage, they need to be wells that we dig deeply into. It is only as we dig deep and maintain these wells that we can receive the fulness of the infilling of the Lord. We need to be obedient to dig but we also need to be faithful to dig deep and maintain. God's hand is never short, but sometimes we limit our ability to receive.

The lessons for us to apply, as believers and churches, is that we are called to be obedient to dig and we are called to dig to a depth. The armies of Israel were obedient, even in a time of exhaustion and despair. They filled the valley not with holes, but with wells. Their obedience and faithfulness to dig deep saw them receive the fulness of the infilling that the Lord had for them. If we want to receive the same, then we need to act the same. We need to be faithful to the Word of the Lord and dig deep, maintaining the wells so that the Lord can infill us with the fulness of His Spirit. Ours is to dig and to dig deep. If we do that, then we will receive the fulness of God's outpoured Spirit. It is not an if or a maybe, it is a promise. God always responds to the actions of earth and if we have been faithful to dig deep then we can be assured of receiving the fulness of His infilling.

INFILLING SUMMARY

In this section we have considered the second point from our 2 Kings 3 example, infilling. Through this we have seen that infilling always follows digging. Infilling is the response of the Lord to the obedience of man. Through the examples of Jacobs ladder, Moses and the rock, Daniel and the Words of Jesus, we established that heaven always responds to the actions of man on earth. As we step out in faith according to the Word of the Lord, the Lord is always faithful in His response. The actions of heaven are always in response to the actions of earth. When we dig, the Lord infills. We do our part and He then does His.

Infilling is needed by the people of God for the sustaining and preservation of life. Just as the natural body needs water to survive, so too does our spiritual man. The infilling of the Lord is for the spiritual life of His people. It restores and strengthens us, it builds our faith, it is used to bless those around us, and it also serves a greater purpose, it enables reflection. Just as digging allows infilling, so too does infilling allow reflection. These are progressive steps, each of which is dependent upon its predecessor. Infilling isn't the end of the process, it's a part of it and one that leads us to our next section.

Infilling

For now though, the points for us to grab hold of and remember are that the requirement for us is to be obedient to dig and be faithful to dig deep. The measure of faithfulness that we demonstrate in these will determine the level to which we are filled. If we truly want to see the Lord pouring out His Spirit upon our lives and our churches we need to be digging deep the wells.

It is the writer's prayer that the reader understand his heart in this. The entirety of this study has been born out of a word that the Lord has stirred within the writer's heart. It is something that the writer believes that the Lord is wanting His people to truly grasp hold of. The Lord is wanting to infill His people. He is wanting His Church to walk in the fulness of what He has for it, but He needs His people and His Churches to be digging the seven wells that we have considered. The Lord will always infill that which has been dug to the measure of which it has been dug. The actions of heaven are always in response to the actions of earth. The promise of the Lord is that He will infill, but the responsibility lies upon us to dig. Let us be faithful in digging that He may infill us with the fulness of His Spirit. We dig the wells and the Lord them infills them beyond measure!

REFLECTION

In this section we consider the third aspect of what 2 Kings 3 reveals to us, reflection. In our 2 Kings 3 account we read:

> *And it came to pass in the morning, when the meat offering was offered, that, behold, there came water by the way of Edom, and the country was filled with water. And when all the Moabites heard that the kings were come up to fight against them, they gathered all that were able to put on armour, and upward, and stood in the border. And they rose up early in the morning, **and the sun shone upon the water**, and the Moabites saw the water on the other side as red as blood: (2Ki 3:20-22)*

After receiving the Word of the Lord through Elisha, the kings and the armies dug the wells in the valley in faith and obedience. The Lord, according to His Word, then supernaturally filled these wells with water. The next day, as the sun rose, it shone upon the wells that had been infilled with water and caused a reflection. This reflection occurred because of the infilling. The infilling was enabled because of the digging. The writer cannot emphasise enough the progressive revelation we are seeing from this 2 Kings 3 account. Digging leads to infilling which then leads to reflection. The latter cannot happen without the former. Each progressive event is completely dependent upon the one that precedes it. The reflection occurred here because the wells had been infilled.

In this section we are going to consider in detail how reflection works, how it is maintained, what we reflect and finally what is seen when we reflect. Reflection is really a pivotal moment, as it is an outworking in the world of the steps that have preceded it. For believers and the Church, there are lessons within this section that we need to apply so that we reflect as fully as we have been called to.

Reflection

OUR TWO EXAMPLES

At the beginning of this study the reader will remember that we looked at two examples in regard to whether or not there existed a call to shine within the Word of God. These two examples were of Moses and the Golden Lampstand. We will quickly spend a few moments recapping these as they will be referred to throughout this section.

The first example we considered was in regard to the call to the individual to shine where we looked at the words of Paul in 2 Corinthians where he stated:

> *But we all, with open face beholding as in a glass the glory of the Lord, are changed into the same image from glory to glory, even as by the Spirit of the Lord. (2Co 3:18)*

We noted that the context of this passage was in reference to the example of Moses who would speak to the Lord face to face, as a man does his friend. During this encounter Moses' countenance was literally enlightened by the presence of the Lord. When Moses would step out of God's presence, he shone so brightly that the people of Israel asked him to place a veil over His face. Moses' face was an outworking of that which he was living. The closeness of his relationship with the Lord was evident upon his face. The words of Paul in Corinthians are that we have the same call, to shine as Moses did, but without the veil. We are called to shine as Moses did, but not hide it from the world.

The second example we considered was the corporate example of the Golden Lampstand. We saw from Jesus's words in the book of Revelation that the Golden Lampstand speaks of the Church.

> *The mystery of the seven stars which thou sawest in my right hand, and the seven golden candlesticks. The seven stars are the angels of the seven churches: and the seven candlesticks which thou sawest are the seven churches. (Rev 1:20)*

The Church, as the Golden Lampstand, is called to shine. In this Church age during which we live, the Church is to be the vessel of light that the Lampstand was in the Holy Place. The Church stands upon this earth and is to shine forth the divine glory of the Lord. The Church is to be a vessel of light in a world of darkness.

HOW REFLECTION WORKS

Reflection is something that we all understand and are familiar with. Our purpose here is not to reinvent the wheel here, but it was through this point that the Lord possibly spoke the most to the writer as he meditated upon the account of 2 Kings 3. It is the writers hope that he will be able to adequately convey the thoughts and message that the Lord spoke to

Reflection

his heart. We will start by considering our passage from 2 Kings, before seeing how these truths are confirmed by our two examples.

A. 2 King 3

   As a recap, in 2 Kings 3 we read:

   > *And it came to pass in the morning, when the meat offering was offered, that, behold, there came water by the way of Edom, and the country was filled with water. And when all the Moabites heard that the kings were come up to fight against them, they gathered all that were able to put on armour, and upward, and stood in the border. And they rose up early in the morning, **and the sun shone upon the water, and the Moabites saw the water on the other side as red as blood**: (2Ki 3:20-22)*

   The reflection that we read of here is quite interesting when we start to break it down. Within it we see a number of things:

   1. The Human Aspect.

      The purpose of the wells was so that the water could be caught. The Lord was going to provide, but in order for the armies to receive they had to be faithful to dig. The first thing that we see is that the valley had been dug full of wells. It was this digging of wells that allowed them to be filled with water.

      The digging and the wells are the human aspect. These are the responsibility of man and act as the vessels to be able to allow and hold the infilling that God promises. In the wells we see the human aspect.

   2. The Heavenly Response

      The second thing we see is the response of Heaven to the actions of earth. The Lord was faithful to His Word and filled each and every one of the wells that had been dug. Here we see the divine response, infilling, which fills the human aspect. The wells were filled with the divine, that which came from God.

      It was the water from the Lord that filled the wells that man had dug. Here we have wells that were filled.

   3. The Divine Light

      Finally we see the divine aspect, the sun, or that which causes the reflection. The sun was created by God and given by God as a source of light upon the earth. It was as the sun shone upon the infilled wells that the reflection occurred.

Reflection

> The wells were dug by man, they were filled by the Lord in response to the actions of man. To this point though all that there were was wells filled to the brim. The reflection didn't and couldn't occur until the sun shone upon them. It is when the divine touches that which has been filled on earth that a reflection occurs. It is when the glory of heaven hits that which has been filled by the Lord on earth that we see the glorious reflection.
>
> The important part to notice here is that the wells acted almost as a mirror. They reflected that which shone upon them. The wells took the glory of the sun and reflected it out to the world. The wells weren't the source, they were vessels of reflection.

So within this we see that there are three aspects that are required for the reflection to occur as God has purposed it. Man has to dig the well and those wells have to be infilled. It is then, and only then, that as the glory of the Lord shines upon the infilled wells that the world sees the reflection of glory. The reflection cannot occur if the first steps are lacking. Reflection is completely dependent upon the first two steps being completed in a full measure. Anything less and the reflection is not what it should be.

Having seen this truth from the 2 Kings 3 account, let us consider how it is confirmed through our two examples.

B. Moses

> In our example of Moses, we noted that his countenance was changed after he had been in the presence of Lord. Exodus tells us that:
>
> > *But when Moses went in before the LORD to speak with him, he took the vail off, until he came out. And he came out, and spake unto the children of Israel that which he was commanded. And the children of Israel saw the face of Moses, that the skin of Moses' face shone: and Moses put the vail upon his face again, until he went in to speak with him.(Exo 34:34-35)*
>
> From this we see the same truths presented to us.
>
> 1. The Human Aspect.
>
> > It was Moses who went in unto the Lord. Moses made the effort to go and stand before the presence of the Lord. He made the choice, followed through with effort and saw the choice through to completion. No one made Moses do this. This was a choice on Moses behalf and showed his faith and obedience. He understood his need of the Lord and had the faith to believe that God would come and meet him.
>
> 2. The Heavenly Response
>
> > As Moses dug, the Lord responded. Exodus 33 tells us that:

Reflection

> *And it came to pass, as Moses entered into the tabernacle, the cloudy pillar descended, and stood at the door of the tabernacle, **<u>and the LORD talked with Moses</u>**. (Exo 33:9)*

As Moses sought the Lord, the Lord responded. The actions of heaven again are in response to the actions of earth. As Moses dug into the Lord in relationship, the Lord would always faithfully respond.

Further on in Exodus 33 it tells us that:

> *And the LORD spake unto Moses face to face, as a man speaketh unto his friend. (Exo 33:11)*

As Moses pressed in to seek the Lord, he received from the Lord. As the Lord spoke to Moses, he was infilled by the Word and Spirit of God. In these encounters that Moses had with the Lord, Moses was infilled by God. As Moses dug, the Lord infilled.

3. The Divine Light

   It was after these encounters with the Lord, that when Moses left the Lord's presence, Moses' face shone with the glory of God. This had absolutely nothing to do with Moses! Moses was reflecting the glory of the Father. Moses dug, making the effort to go in unto the Lord. In speaking with the Lord Moses was infilled by His Word and Spirit. It was after this infilling that Moses went out reflecting the glory of the Lord to the nation of Israel. Moses' face was reflecting the glory of the Lord that he had been in intimate fellowship with. His face reflected the divine light. The presence of God was the light. It was His brilliance that lit up the Most Holy Place. Moses left, reflecting this glory to a nation that wasn't yet ready for it.

Again, we see the same truth emphasised. Man has to dig before he is infilled. In this case Moses had to go unto the Lord before he could speak and receive from Him face to face. It was only after this infilling that the reflection could occur. Having been infilled by the Lord, Moses left His presence, reflecting the very glory of God to the nation of Israel. Moses needed to dig and be infilled before he could reflect. Without digging and infilling the reflection couldn't occur.

C. The Golden Lampstand

Our next example is that of the Golden Lampstand. The reader is encouraged to look back on our section on this, particularly Zechariah's vision, as a prompt to their memory before moving forward here. We see with this example the same truths we have been considering.

Reflection

1. The Human Aspect.

   The Golden Lampstand was an instrument made entirely of gold. It was a beautiful ornament, but in and of itself it had no ability to shine. In order for the Golden Lampstand to be able to shine it required oil. In our investigation of the Lampstand, we noted that the responsibility for the provision of oil lay with the people of Israel.

   > *Command the children of Israel, that they bring unto thee pure oil olive beaten for the light, to cause the lamps to burn continually. (Lev 24:2)*

   The children of Israel weren't asked to bring olives to the priests so that the priests could do the work of extracting the oil. The children of Israel were commanded by the Lord that they do the work of extracting the oil! The children of Israel were to bring the pure, beaten olive oil unto the Tabernacle for the priests to use. The people were responsible for the supply of oil.

   In the vision of Zechariah, we noted the seven Golden Pipes that connected the Golden Bowl to the Golden Lampstand represent seven connection points or wells, that allow the Spirit to flow from Jesus, our great High priest, unto His body, the Church. The onus, or responsibility, lies upon man to make sure that these seven Pipes are open and fully operational. Seven in scripture is the number of fulness, perfection. In order for us to be receiving the fullness of the Spirit that the Lord has for His Church, it is the responsibility of His people to be making sure that these wells are dug and that they are maintained. There lies upon the people of God, both the Church in the Old Testament and the Church in the New Testament, the responsibility to ensure that the oil can flow. The people of God have a responsibility for the flow of oil.

2. The Heavenly Response

   The people were responsible for the supply of oil, but it was the priest who would administer the oil to the Golden Lampstand. Morning and evening the priest would tend the Golden Lampstand, responding to its needs. The priests were able to administer the oil, so long as the people continued to provide it. The priests were able to operate based upon the faithfulness of the people.

   The Old Testament priesthood points to Jesus. Jesus is both our Great High Priest after the order of Melchizedek and the Golden Bowl in the vision of Zechariah. To Jesus the Spirit was given without measure. Jesus is ready, willing and waiting to pour His spirit out on His people. He will always respond to the actions of earth. If the pipes are open, He will infill through them. If we do the digging for the supply of oil, He will always administer it.

Reflection

3.   The Divine Light

After the Tabernacle of Moses had been built and set up, we read in the book of Leviticus of the consecration and ordination of Aaron and his sons into the roles of priests for the nation of Israel. This was really the last step before the Tabernacle become operational. In Leviticus 9, we read that after seven days of consecration Aaron stepped into the role of High Priest and presented offerings before the Lord on behalf of the nation of Israel. After doing this Aaron lifted his hands and blessed the people and then went with Moses into the Tabernacle itself. Upon coming out, the glory of the Lord appeared unto the nation and we then read:

> *And there came a fire out from before the LORD, and consumed upon the altar the burnt offering and the fat: which when all the people saw, they shouted, and fell on their faces.(Lev 9:24)*

This fire was God's confirmation of His acceptance of the offerings, the Priesthood and the Tabernacle system. What is interesting for us to note is the direction of this fire. The Word says that this fire came out from before the Lord. The presence of the Lord resided upon the Ark of the Covenant in the Most Holy Place. This fire came out from the Lord in the Most Holy Place, through the Holy Place, where the Golden Lampstand resided and ended upon the Brazen Altar in the Outer Court. This fire was a divine fire from the Lord and consumed the offerings upon the Altar. This was Holy fire and it lit the fire upon the Brazen Altar, a fire that was to never go out according to the Word of the Lord. There is little doubt amongst expositors that this same divine fire was used to light the Golden Lampstand, either by the priests or by the Lord as it passed through the Holy Place. The operation of the Tabernacle system, the Church of the Old Testament, was based upon the divine fire of the Lord. The people brought the oil, they supplied it. The priest administered the oil to the Lampstand according to the people's supply. The fire though was divine. The Golden Lampstand only shone when the fire of the Lord came upon that which had been filled. Man supplied, the priest filled and God lit.

We see this truth echoed in the birth of the early Church. On the great day of Pentecost as the disciples were gathered together in the upper room, waiting in obedience to the Words of Jesus, the Holy Spirit descended upon them as tongues of fire. The disciples had dug, they were filled with the Spirit and the Lord lit them with His divine light. The New Testament Church was lit by the divine fire of the Lord as He descended upon His people. The light is always divine.

The scriptural law of witness is that any matter is established in the mouth of two or three witnesses. That is what we have sought to do here, provide scriptural examples that agree and testify of the same truth. Reflection occurs when the divine ignites or shines on that which has been filled on earth. Through the three examples we have considered we have seen that as man digs in obedience and faith, the Lord will always respond and fill. Whilst we are infilled, we are simply vessels though, the light is always of divine source and origin. What we have seen can be summarised as below.

	2 KINGS 3	MOSES	THE GOLDEN LAMPSTAND
EARTH'S ACTIONS	The valley dug full of wells.	Moses would go into meet with the Lord.	The people had to bring the pure, beaten, olive oil.
HEAVEN'S RESPONSE	No rain, no wind, yet the Lord provided water.	The Lord would speak with Moses face to face.	The High Priest would administer the oil.
DIVINE LIGHT	The Sun.	The glory of God upon Moses.	The Divine Fire of the Lord.

What we see is that the light is always divine. That which digs and receives infilling is simply the vessel. The glory is always the Lord's, but the responsibility to be filled lies with us. What this speaks to us is that the illumination of God is not for the glorification of man or our local churches. God's light shines upon us so that we may reflect His light to a world that is otherwise in darkness. Any reflection we shine that does not have its source from the divine light of God is a wrong reflection. We are not called to manufacture and project an image to the world that we think it will accept and want to see. Our focus should never be on projecting an image. We are called to be the light of the World by being vessels that reflect His light. The world does not need another substitute. The world needs to see the unadulterated light of God reflecting off of His people and His churches. The world needs to see His light reflected through His vessels that have been infilled.

We press in, heaven responds and we shine the glory of the Lord forth. We reflect His glory. That is the call and the truth of scripture. Whilst we are called to shine, the revelation we see here is that it is not actually us or our churches who shine! It is the Lord who shines. Ours is to be the vessels who are filled to enable this to happen. We are called to reflect His glory, His light, His fire. The reflection is always of divine origin. That which is meant to shine is always of divine origin. The shining is always Him. It is all about Him. The Church and we as His people, fulfill our call to be the light of the World when we are fully reflecting His glory to the world around us. We are His vessels, called to reflect His glory. But this can only happen when we dig and receive the infilling of His Spirit.

HOW REFLECTION IS MAINTAINED

Having seen that reflection occurs when the divine shines upon that which has been filled on earth, we now turn our attention to the thought of maintaining that reflection. With our main example from 2 Kings 3 what we read of essentially was a one-off event. The armies were obedient to the word of the Lord and filled the valley full of wells. In response to this act of faithful obedience the Lord infilled the wells that had been dug and in the morning, as the sun rose it shone upon the waters causing the reflection to be seen by the world. In considering this, the writer was prompted upon the thought of what would need to happen if this was to be more than just a one-day event. The reflection that happened in a day for the kings is something that is meant to occur over a lifetime in believers! How can a reflection be maintained over this period of time? The fact is that whilst the sun shines upon the water to cause a reflection, this same sun, over time, causes the same water it reflects off to evaporate. As the water evaporates, the level of the wells drops and the ability for the sun to reflect is diminished. The measure of brightness of the reflection is determined by the measure of fulness of the wells! If this reflection was to endure over many days then there would need to be a replenishment in the wells to lift their levels back up from that which had evaporated. A dry well does not reflect!

In order for the reflection to be maintained for an extended period, there would have to be a continual infilling, otherwise the reflection would diminish. A one-off infilling does not sustain a well over a great duration. For reflection to be maintained there must of necessity be continual infilling.

In considering this thought the writer was again drawn to the two examples we have been considering throughout this text. Let us turn to them now and see how this thought of a continual infilling to maintain reflection is confirmed by the truth of scripture.

A. Moses

    Moses went in unto the Lord and as the Lord spoke to him face to face, he came out with his countenance changed. Moses came out from the presence of the Lord, reflecting the glory of the Lord to the nation of Israel. The people though were not ready for this, they were scared and because of this Moses wore a veil to cover his face.

> *And when Aaron and all the children of Israel saw Moses, behold, the skin of his face shone; and they were afraid to come nigh him. (Exo 34:30)*

    It would seem though that this veil served a dual purpose. We noted in our investigation into Moses that Paul in Corinthians seem to imply that this glory, that was imparted to Moses, was temporary in nature.

> *And not as Moses, which put a vail over his face, that the children of Israel could not stedfastly look to the end of that which is abolished: (2Co 3:13)*

    The glory upon Moses' face was not a permanent transformation. It was a temporary one and one that diminished over time. The veil served both as to shield the people from the glory of God as well as conceal the diminishing glow of Moses. This truth

Reflection

would seem to be confirmed by what we read in Exodus. After Moses initially put the veil upon his face, we go on to read in the next verses that:

> *But when Moses went in before the LORD to speak with him, he took the vail off, until he came out. And he came out, and spake unto the children of Israel that which he was commanded. And the children of Israel saw the face of Moses, that the skin of Moses' face shone: and Moses put the vail upon his face again, until he went in to speak with him. (Exo 34:34-35)*

Moses would lift the veil every time he went in to speak to the Lord. As he spoke and was infilled, he would leave reflecting the glory of God to the nation of Israel. This reflection was a confirmation to the nation that Moses had been speaking with the Lord. The light upon Moses' face was a testimony of where Moses had been. Moses would then put the veil over his face. This covered the glory and also concealed the diminishing glow. The veil remained in place until the next time Moses went into the presence of the Lord.

Moses' countenance was changed every time he went into the presence of the Lord. While he was away from the presence of the Lord this reflection started to diminish. Moses was only able to reflect the fulness of the glory of God by continually going into the presence of the Lord. One visit was not enough. In order for the reflection to be maintained, Moses had to be continually infilled through speaking with the Lord face to face. When the infilling was not being attended to the glory of the reflection diminished. Reflection was maintained consistently though continual infilling from the Lord.

B. The Golden Lampstand

With the Golden Lampstand we saw that it was the responsibility of the Israelites to bring the pure, beaten olive oil in order for the priest to administer it to the Lampstand. This Golden Lampstand was then lit by the divine fire that fell on the day of dedication, as the fire of the Lord proceeded from the Most Holy Place and consumed the offerings that were upon the Brazen Altar.

In Exodus we read that the Lord said:

> *And thou shalt command the children of Israel, that they bring thee pure oil olive beaten for the light,* **_to cause the lamp to burn always_**. *(Exo 27:20)*

Here, whilst we see the Lord again mentions the responsibility that lay upon the congregation of Israel, we also see that the oil was to be provided so that the lamps would burn always. As we have discovered earlier, the Lampstand was the only instrument of light within the curtain of the Holy Place. Without this light the Holy place would have been plunged into darkness. It is for this reason that the lamps were to burn continually. They were to always be lit, so that there was light. This light could only be maintained though as long as there was oil for the fire to burn. The fire was only enabled whilst the lamp was filled with oil. As the fire burned, it consumed the oil, causing the infilling of the lamps to decrease. In order for this light to be maintained the priest would need to resupply the oil and he could only do this so long as the people of Israel continually brought in the pure, beaten olive oil. The light of the Lampstand, the reflection of the divine fire, was only able to be maintained so long as there was continual infilling of the oil.

The thing about reflection, is that that which causes the reflection, the divine, also causes the consumption of the infilling. The sun evaporates the water, the fire consumes the oil, Moses' face declined as he testified regarding the Word of the Lord to the people. The outworking consumes the infilling. In order for reflection to be maintained there has to be continual infilling. Moses had to continually go before the presence of the Lord. The Lampstand had to be continually tended to by the priest. The wells have to continually receive water.

Reflection is maintained when we understand that we need to be continually infilled by the Lord in order to reflect His light to the world around us. Burnout, or lack of reflection, occurs when we don't maintain the wells and continually press into the Lord for His infilling. A reflection can't shine off an empty well. A Lampstand can't provide light without oil. Reflection is maintained when we understand that we are here to reflect His glory and we can only do this as we continually receive His infilling. It comes back to the value we place on the wells. We need to dig and maintain that which we dig so that the Lord may continually infill us and we may continually reflect. As believers and churches, we are able to continually reflect His glory when we are continually receiving from Him.

WHAT IS SEEN THROUGH REFLECTION

Having seen what reflection is and how it is maintained, we will now spend some time considering what is seen when the glory of the Lord reflects off His people and His Church. Upon first thought the answer may seem fairly self-evident, i.e. that the world sees the effect of spiritual light when the Lord shines upon His people. Whilst that is true, there is also more to it than that. What we will focus on here is what the light reveals. Light in and of itself makes things visible. When we stop and consider what the light of the Lord does when it shines upon an infilled people, we see that it illuminates things that would otherwise be hidden. Our purpose here is to discover what these things are. These are truths that should be evident in each of our lives and churches. When the light of the Lord shines upon us, the truths that we will discover in this section are the truths that the world should be seeing. God's glory shines for a purpose and ours is to make sure that those things that should be being seen are being seen. These are not things that we should be forcing into our lives and churches in order to mark off a checklist. Rather these are the things that should be naturally evident when we have dug, been infilled and are reflecting His glory. These are the natural outworking's and if they are not being evidenced in our lives or churches, it may mean we need to take a step back to make sure all of the wells have been dug, so that there is a fulness of light shining out from us.

Reflection

As has been our approach in this section, we will work through each of our examples to see the truths revealed in each. The writer cannot emphasise enough that this is not meant to be condemnatory. The truth of scripture though is that there is a fulness of light that we have been called to reflect. If each of the wells are open and infilled, then each of the points we will look at should be evidenced in some way in our lives and churches. God's light exists to illuminate. If we only have one or two of the wells open, then we may well be operating with partial light and not illuminating all that we have been called to. The writer's encouragement would be for the reader to take this as more of a prompt from the Holy Spirit, as that is what has been spoken to him. The reality is that in each of our lives and churches, at various times, we neglect some of the wells. The call of the Lord, especially in these days, is for us to take stock and make sure that all of our wells are fully open and operational so that His glory may be fully reflected to a world that so desperately needs to see it.

Reflection is the natural progression from digging and infilling, but if we are not aware of what we are supposed to reflect we can lose our way. We can be under the impression that we are on the right track, when the reality may be that we are missing the mark. This was the case with some of the churches in Revelation 2 and 3! Knowing what we should be reflecting is a safeguard to ensure that we are always walking as we should and portraying to the world everything we are called to. With that in mind let us look at what His Word shows us should be reflected when His light shines fully upon us.

A. 2 Kings 3

> *And they rose up early in the morning, and the sun shone upon the water, and the Moabites saw the water on the other side as red as blood: And they said, This is blood: the kings are surely slain, and they have smitten one another: now therefore, Moab, to the spoil. (2Ki 3:22-23)*

What is interesting to note from these verses is that this was not a normal reflection! When the enemies of Israel, the world, saw the sun, the divine, shine upon the infilled wells, they did not see a normal reflection, they saw blood. This is not a normal occurrence. A normal occurrence would have been a reflection of light, but that is not what was seen. What was seen was blood. As the Lord shone upon the infilled wells, the world saw blood. Whilst we will talk about this more in our next section, it was the vision of blood that ultimately brought about the victory for the kings and their armies!

Throughout Israel's history, victory, preservation and deliverance have been associated with the blood being seen. During the final plague of the Lord upon Egypt, it was as the angel saw the blood on the doors of the Israelites that the plague of death passed over them (Exo 12:13). Similarly, it was the sight of blood that brought restoration of life and deliverance for Rahab. It was only upon the two spies seeing the scarlet thread tied in Rahab's window, that she and her family were spared (Jos 2:18-19). Finally, we as believers receive the fullness of life and deliverance as the blood of Jesus, the true Passover Lamb is seen upon us.

Our account from Kings shows us that as the glory of the Lord shone upon the wells that had been infilled, the resulting illumination caused the world to see blood. For us as believers, when we go out into the world, a normal reflection for the world to see is us. We may even think that the world should see a happy, upbeat version of us, as this would speak of the joy of the Lord! We are called to reflect more than that though. When we, as believers, are infilled with the Spirit, and God's divine glory shines upon us we don't reflect ourselves! When the glory of the Lord shines upon us the world should be seeing Jesus. That may seem like a big ask, but the fact of the matter is that the very name we call ourselves by, 'Christians', means little Christs, little anointed ones. We are called to represent Him to the world. When the world looks at us, they should see the reflection of Jesus.

In the book of Corinthians, the Apostle Paul puts it this way:

> *Now then we are ambassadors for Christ, as though God did beseech you by us: we pray you in Christ's stead, be ye reconciled to God. (2Co 5:20)*

An ambassador acts as a representative of their home country or kingdom in a foreign one. We through the blood of Christ are counted as citizens of heaven with the role of representing Christ on the earth. We carry our Kingdom's colours and present them to the lands in which we dwell.

The first thing that we see that gets illuminated by the reflection of His glory is Christ. Christ is the reason we receive salvation. Christ is the reason for everything we do. Christ is the cornerstone of our lives and churches. It is little wonder then that Christ should be illuminated through us. How can He not be! When we have dug, been infilled and His glory shines upon us all of those around us should be seeing Jesus.

B. Moses

From the example of Moses, we see that the reflection of the Lord had a twofold effect.

1. The reflection showed who Moses had been with

    Without wanting to repeat too much, we have seen that the countenance of Moses was changed as he literally reflected the glory of the Lord. This reflection was enabled from Moses receiving from the Lord through his face-to-face encounters. Over time, the reflection diminished, as the well decreased, until Moses went back into the presence of the Lord and received fresh infilling.

    With Moses we see that the reflection illuminated who Moses had been spending time with. There was a difference in the appearance of Moses. The people could tell when Moses had been associating with the leaders of Israel and when he had been associating with the Lord. There was a discernible difference in Moses.

Reflection

None questioned it, and all saw it. All were able to tell who Moses had been spending time with.

Such should be the same with us and our churches. When all of the wells are fully open there should be a discernible difference in our lives and in our churches. People should be readily able to see the difference. The life-giving power of the Spirit should be evident. We should look different. Individuals should be able to see the difference in us when we have a full, intimate relationship with the Lord. His glory should be a testimony of our intimacy.

2. The reflection highlighted the Word of God

But when Moses went in before the LORD to speak with him, he took the vail off, until he came out. And he came out, and **spake unto the children of Israel that which he was commanded. And the children of Israel saw the face of Moses, that the skin of Moses' face shone***: and Moses put the vail upon his face again, until he went in to speak with him.(Exo 34:34-35)*

The second thing that we see is that whenever Moses had spoken with the Lord, he would then come out and address the nation of Israel and speak to them the Lord's commands. From the reading of the above verses, it would seem that Moses would leave his face unveiled until he had given the Lord's command to the nation. It was after this that he would then cover his face again.

The reflection upon Moses validated and illuminated the Word of God to the nation of Israel. It was the reflection that caused the people to take heed of the Word of God. When the nation of Israel saw the glory reflected upon the face of Moses, they received the Words of God. With the unveiled glory of Moses' face, the Word of God shone forth. The reflection upon Moses face highlighted to the people the Words of the Lord.

With Moses we see that when the divine light reflected it illuminated the Word of God and it was also a testimony of who Moses had been spending time with. When His light reflects of us it should cause us to appear differently and to speak differently. The should be a difference that is obvious in us because of Him.

C. The Golden Lampstand

This is perhaps the example that provides us with the most information regarding what should be evident when the full glory of the Lord reflects upon His people and His Church. The Golden Lampstand was a vessel of light and its purpose was to illuminate. We will spend some time here, bringing out the truths of the Word in regard to the Golden Lampstand. As we do, the reader will hopefully not only see the above truths further confirmed, but also further truths revealed.

Reflection

As we look through scripture, we see that the theme of the Golden Lampstand is one that flows throughout the entire Bible. As we consider all of these references, we start to see that the light of the Lampstand illuminated a number of things. We will endeavour here to uncover what these were and how they apply to believers and the Church. The reader is once again reminded that what we are looking at here are those things that should be highlighted when the glory of the Lord is fully reflecting off our lives and churches. The evidence of these shows us that we are truly reflecting the fulness of the glory of the Lord as we have been called. If we are not seeing them then we possibly need to check our wells! Let us now look at scripture to see what it reveals to us in regard to reflecting His glory and the Golden Lampstand.

1. The Lampstand shone upon itself

    *And thou shalt make the seven lamps thereof: and they shall light the lamps thereof, that they may give **light over against it.** (Exo 25:37)*

    *Speak unto Aaron, and say unto him, When thou lightest the lamps, the seven lamps shall give light **over against the candlestick**. (Num 8:2)*

    Part of the purpose of the Lampstand was that it was to cause light to shine upon itself. The light caused by the divine fire of the Lord upon the infilled lamps caused the Lampstand itself to be illuminated. This light enabled the Lampstand to be seen. The Lampstand not only illuminated the Holy Place, it illuminated itself. The light of the Lampstand allowed the intricate work of the Lampstand to be seen and allowed the priest to minister unto it.

    When the Lampstand shone upon itself it caused all of its intricate work and craftsmanship to be seen. It allowed all that it was to be revealed to those that looked upon it.

    When we considered the design of the Lampstand, we saw that it was made according to the divine pattern of the Lord. This was a pattern that the Lord showed unto Moses when Moses received the revelation of the Tabernacle and its furniture. The Golden Lampstand was a divine design of the Lord. It was not an imagination of man, but a design of God.

    And look that thou make them after their pattern, which was shewed thee in the mount. (Exo 25:40)

    God revealed and spoke specifically to Moses about the construction of the Lampstand and that it had to be made exactly according to the Word of the Lord. There was a divine design and within that we see divine truth that the Lord was communicating to man. When the Lampstand shone upon itself it revealed the divine pattern that the Lord had spoken and shown to Moses.

Reflection

Here we will work through the revelation of the Lampstand in Exodus 25, looking at the construction of the Golden Lampstand and see what it reveals to us. As we do this, we will gain a fuller understanding of exactly what the light of the Lord reflected when the Lampstand shone upon itself.

I) Its Metal

*And thou shalt make a candlestick of **pure gold**: of beaten work shall the candlestick be made: his shaft, and his branches, his bowls, his knops, and his flowers, **shall be of the same**. (Exo 25:31)*

The Lampstand was made from pure gold. No other material was used in its construction. Throughout all of the Tabernacle furniture items only two were made from metals alone. These were the Brazen Laver and the Golden Lampstand.

Pure gold is that which has had all dross and impurities removed. It is completely pure. Pure gold is symbolic of the Lord, deity, the divine nature. Pure gold speaks to us of God. He who is completely pure.

The Lampstand was made completely of gold and when it was lit, its light would have reflected upon the gold and glistened. The light illuminated the pureness of the Lampstand's metal. As the Lampstand shone upon itself, its gold was front and centre. None would have been able to miss this beautiful reflection.

The Church, when it is lit, is to show forth the divine nature of the Lord as it glistens and reflects His divine design. The light of the Church is to show forth the Lord. His purity, His glory and His beauty. When we as individuals and corporately as the Church are looked upon, the world should see the Lord front and centre. We are to be vessels that show forth to the world the truth of our Lord. God should always be the central focus. From all that we do, people should be able to see and encounter the Lord. When the divine shines upon us, the Lord should be seen in everything that we do. When His glory reflects, people should not see monuments of men, they should see, and only see, the Lord.

II) Its Design

And six branches shall come out of the sides of it; three branches of the candlestick out of the one side, and three branches of the candlestick out of the other side: (Exo 25:32)

The Golden Lampstand consisted of one main, central shaft. This was the candle 'stick' if you will. From this shaft there extended branches on each side, three on the left and three on the right. These branches came out in pairs, one on the right and one on the left. Each pair ascended up the main shaft, so what was seen was the main shaft and three pairs of branches. There was a pair of branches at the bottom, a pair of branches in the middle and a pair of branches near the top. It was on top of the main shaft and on top of each of these branches that the seven lamps of the Lampstand sat. The amazing thing is that the entire Lampstand was made of one piece of gold, beaten out by the skilled craftsman. Parts were not added or welded on, it was all of one piece. Whilst there was one shaft and six branches, all were of the same piece of gold, perfectly united. There was oneness and wholeness in its design.

With the main shaft we see the number one. The number one in scripture speaks of the Lord. He is the beginning, the source, the alpha, the first.

With the branches we see the number six. There were three branches on one side and three on the other, six in total. Six in scripture is the number of man. Man was created on the sixth day of creation.

In the Lampstand we see the unity of one shaft and six branches to make a complete Lampstand, stamped with the number seven. One shaft plus six branches equals seven. Seven in scripture in the number of fulness, completion, perfection.

Such should be the case with the Church. Where two or three are gathered in Jesus' name, He is there is the midst. It is this gathering in Jesus name that forms the Church. It is the unity of the Lord (1) and man (6), which form the Church.

The Church is to show forth to the world, the unity of man with God. It is to fulfill the call of John 15 where Jesus says:

> *I am the vine, ye are the branches: He that abideth in me, and I in him, the same bringeth forth much fruit: for without me ye can do nothing. (Joh 15:5)*

The Church is to shine forth its oneness with Jesus. We are the branches, extended from the vine (the shaft) and completely dependent upon Him. It speaks of a complete, unified relationship with Jesus, where He is at the centre. When the Church is seen, people should see the people of God united in their Saviour, and He front and centre. He is the head, we are the body and together there is oneness and unity as we abide in Him.

The Church shines forth our unmistakable connection to Jesus. We are unmistakably connected to Him and it is through Him that we function. It is with Him at the centre that the Church exists and operates. If the vine or shaft isn't there, then there is nothing to hold up the branches. The Church only truly exists when Jesus is at the centre. When we gather together in His name,

Reflection

there He is in the midst. The churches relationship and dependence on its Saviour should be seen when the glory of the Lord reflects upon us.

III) Its Pattern

When it came to the actual making of the Golden Lampstand the Lord gave very specific instructions on how the branches and shaft were to look. What we see is that the Lord laid out a pattern that was to be followed when the Golden Lampstand was made.

> ***Three* bowls made like unto *almonds, with a knop and a flower*** in one branch; and ***three bowls made like almonds in the other branch, with a knop and a flower***: so in the six branches that come out of the candlestick. And in the candlestick shall be ***four bowls made like unto almonds, with their knops and their flowers***. *(Exo 25:33-34)*

We will discuss the outworking of this more in the below points, but what we see essentially here is a threefold pattern that was repeated varying times. This pattern consisted of a bowl made like unto an almond, then a knop and then a flower. The pattern speaks of fruitfulness. We have the bud (the knop), then the flower and then the fruit (the bowl).

It is interesting to note that this is the same pattern that was evidenced with the rod of Aaron. In Numbers 17 we read that each of the tribes of Israel were all to bring a rod before the Lord. Aaron was to be representative for the tribe of Levi. These rods were to be laid before the Lord and left. The Lord would cause one of these rods to bud and this would be a sign to the congregation of who the Lord had chosen. The intent of this was to clearly show God's choice of priest and to stop the murmurings of the children of Israel. The next day when they went to check the rods it was seen that Aaron's rod, not only budded, but blossomed and brought forth fruit.

> *And it came to pass, that on the morrow Moses went into the tabernacle of witness; and, behold, the rod of Aaron for the house of Levi was budded, and brought forth **buds, and bloomed blossoms, and yielded almonds**. (Num 17:8)*

Aaron's rod budded, flowered and brought forth fruit, almonds. It is this same threefold pattern that the Lord stamped upon the Lampstand.

AARON'S ROD	THE GOLDEN LAMPSTAND
Buds	Knop
Blossomed	Flower
Almonds	Almonds

Reflection

The number three in scripture speaks of the Godhead and perfect witness. We see this especially in the pattern before us. The threefold fruitfulness of Aaron's rod was God's testimony that He had chosen him.
If we consider this pattern in more detail, we can see that there is a distinction between each element of the pattern. Whilst all are related, they are all unique and clearly distinguishable. In this we again see the Lord communicating truth to His people.

The bud speaks of the Father God. He is the first, the source, the beginning of all things.

The Flower speaks of Christ. The flower comes from the bud and speaks of Christ who was crushed for our transgressions, emitting a sweet smell.

The Almond speaks of fruit and is representative of the Holy Spirit. The Holy Spirit is sent by the Father through the Son to create fruit in the lives of His people.

So within this pattern we see the tri-unity of God stamped: Father, Son and Holy Spirit. It is not one at the expense of the other, but all three in unity and harmony. When the Lampstand shone upon itself, this threefold pattern was clear and visible. There was no imbalance, but perfect representation. The knop, flower and almond were all clearly visible.

Such should be the case in our lives and churches. The foundation of the Father, Son and Holy Spirit should be evidenced. There should not be one at the expense of the other, but all should be seen in balance and harmony. There should be the perfect witness of the Father, Son and Holy Spirit.

This pattern we read was repeated in both the shaft and all of the branches. Within each of these we see that the Lord was again communicating further truth to us with this pattern.

a)   In the Shaft

    *And in the candlestick shall be **four** bowls made like unto almonds, with their knops and their flowers. (Exo 25:34)*

    Within the shaft the threefold pattern was repeated four times. That is, there was a knop, flower, fruit, knop, flower, fruit, knop, flower, fruit, knop, flower, fruit. The pattern was repeated four times. We see here in the shaft the number twelve stamped and imprinted. Three times four equals twelve.

    Twelve in scripture speaks of divine government or apostolic government. Within the Lampstand the Lord laid the truth and need of these. These form part of the central shaft of the lampstand. They are core, if you will, to the Lampstand's divine pattern.

When we are reflecting His glory, apostolic government should be evidenced in our churches. The Lord laid out His pattern in the Golden Lampstand. He then revealed the truth of this pattern in the early Church. Now more than ever, we need these truths applied and evidenced within our churches. If we are truly to be the Church we have been called to be, we need to be illuminating that which the Lord has told us to.

The New Testament Church is built upon the foundation of the apostles and prophets. The Lord has given unto the Church apostles, prophets, evangelists, pastors and teachers. The early Church was built on these giftings and such should be evident in the Church today. When we reflect His glory, these ministerial gifts of the Lord should be evident.

b) In the Branches

> ***Three*** *bowls made like unto almonds, with a knop and a flower in one branch; and **three** bowls made like almonds in the other branch, with a knop and a flower: **so in the six branches** that come out of the candlestick. (Exo 25:33)*

In each of the branches we see that the threefold pattern was repeated three times. There were three lots of three. In each of the six branches we see the number nine. Three times three equals nine. Nine in scripture speaks of the Holy Spirit.

As the light of the Golden Lampstand shone it illuminated the pattern of nine, the number that speaks of the Holy Spirit. When we consider the truth revealed by this, we see that there is a two-fold application.

In Galatians Chapter 5 we read of the fruit of the Spirit as detailed by Paul. There he said:

> *But the fruit of the Spirit is love, joy, peace, longsuffering, gentleness, goodness, faith, Meekness, temperance: against such there is no law. (Gal 5:22-23)*

Paul here listed nine fruits of the Spirit. These are fruits that should be evidenced in the lives of believers and Churches. If we walk in the Spirit, we will produce the fruit of the Spirit.

Paul also spoke in 1 Corinthians of nine gifts of the Spirit:
> *But the manifestation of the Spirit is given to every man to profit withal. For to one is given by the Spirit the word of wisdom; to*

> *another the word of knowledge by the same Spirit; To another faith by the same Spirit; to another the gifts of healing by the same Spirit; To another the working of miracles; to another prophecy; to another discerning of spirits; to another divers kinds of tongues; to another the interpretation of tongues: But all these worketh that one and the selfsame Spirit, dividing to every man severally as he will. (1Co 12:7-11).*

These are the spiritual gifts God has given unto man by the Holy Spirit as the Lord wills. These are different to the ministerial gifts we referred to earlier. The spiritual gifts should be, in one form or more, evidenced in each of our individual lives. Within our churches we should see all of these gifts in operation. These gifts are given by God for the benefit of His people, to profit all.

The fruit of the Spirit and gifts of the Spirit are a study in themselves which is not our purpose here. What the writer would put forth here though is that these fruit of the Spirit and gifts of the Spirit are to be equally as visible when His glory shines upon His Church and His people. The gifts are not more important than the fruit and the fruit are not more important than the gifts. Each validates the other and there is an equal call for both to be seen. When the Lampstand shone upon itself, it highlighted the pattern of nine. When the glory of the Lord shines upon His Church and His people the world should be able to see the fruit and the gifts demonstrated. The work of the Spirit should be visible when the Church, and the people who make it, are illuminated by the light of the Lord.

c) The Pattern Overall

So far we have considered the three-fold pattern, the pattern in the branches and the pattern in the shaft. When we consider the pattern in its entirety we see something incredible and something that is undeniably of God.

In the shaft we see that the pattern of three was repeated four times for a total of twelve. In the pattern of the branches we see that the pattern was repeated three times for a total of nine. But this pattern was repeated in each branch, a total of six times. If we multiple this out we see:

> 1 shaft x 3 fold pattern x 4 times repeated
> $1 \times (3 \times 4) = 12$
>
> 6 branches x 3 fold pattern x 3 times repeated
> $6 \times (3 \times 3) = 54$
>
> $54 + 12 = 66$

Reflection

In total we see that the threefold pattern is repeated twenty-two times giving a total of sixty-six. The number in and of itself may not mean much until we pause and reflect on all that we have seen so far of the Lampstand and how it speaks of the Church. In the Word of God, the Bible, there are exactly sixty-six books. There are thirty-nine Old Testament books and twenty-seven New Testament Books, making sixty-six books in total. The numbers in the shaft and three branches equal thirty-nine, (twelve + twenty-seven). The numbers in the remaining three branches equal twenty-seven. (three branches x pattern of nine). Overall, we see sixty-six. This overall pattern in the Golden Lampstand speaks of the sixty-six books of the infallible Word of the Lord. When the Lord gave the pattern of the Golden Lampstand, He did so in full knowledge of the Word of God being composed and finalised. He sees the end from the beginning and within the Lampstand He set forth the vital importance of His Word for His people.

When the glory of the Lord reflects upon His people and His Church the Word of God should be prominent. It is not mere words that people want to hear, or seeker sensitive sermons, that should be evident. What should be clearly and unmistakably seen is the complete, full, unadulterated Word of God. We do not just need the New, we cannot just rely on the Old. We need the Word of God in its **entirety,** and it should be visible in our lives and churches.

The first words of the Lord in the Bible are found in Genesis 1. There the Lord says, "let there be light". The Word of the Lord caused light to come into existence. Light and the Word always go together. His Word is light, it is a lamp unto our feet and as we go out reflecting His glory, His Word should be enlightened by us individually and corporately. We are to give light to His Word. His Word should be evident, all sixty-six books of it, when we are truly reflecting His glory.

IV) The Extra Knops

And there shall be a knop under two branches of the same, and a knop under two branches of the same, and a knop under two branches of the same, according to the six branches that proceed out of the candlestick. (Exo 25:35)

A careful reading of Exodus 25 would seem to indicate that under each pair of branches there was an extra knop that the pairs of branches joined to. There was a knop and then pair of branches, a knop and then a pair a branches, a knop then a pair of branches and finally the main shaft. In total there was three of these extra knops.
As stated earlier three is the number of the Godhead and perfect witness. The three knops here further confirm the truths we covered in the three-fold

pattern. The reader is encouraged to re-read our comments on these where we dealt with this thought.

V) Its Size

What is interesting to note from scripture is that the Golden Lampstand and the Brazen Laver as well as being the only pieces of furniture made completely of metal, are also the only two pieces of furniture which do not have any measurements recorded in the Word of the Lord. We know that the Lampstand was made of talent of pure gold, but we do not know its dimensions or size.

To the writer this speaks that the focus of the Lampstand was never to illuminate its size and grandeur, but rather those things that were at its core, as we have mentioned above and as we will cover below.

In a world where image and size are deemed as representative of success and favour in the things of God, the Lampstand, in the writer's opinion, highlights to us that this is not a factor that the Lord seeks to illuminate. When we are the reflecting the glory of the Lord it should not be on the things we deem important, but on those that He has shown us should be illuminated. The call of God is for the things of His divine pattern to be illuminated. In the writer's opinion, when we are given so much information and detail regarding the Tabernacle in scripture, there is possibly a reason as to why the Lord chose to leave this one out!

The Golden Lampstand was not thought up in the mind of man. The Golden Lampstand, like all of the Tabernacle structure and furniture, was made according to the divine pattern of God. The Lord God gave to Moses the exact blueprints for how the Golden Lampstand was to be made and how it was to look. It is when we stop and consider the design of God here, that we start to see the truth that the Lord contained within the Golden Lampstand. When the Lampstand shone upon, it wasn't doing so in a self-glorifying manner. As the Lampstand shone upon itself, it highlighted to all who saw the foundational, structural, truths that God had placed within it.

If this was true of the symbol, how much more should it be of the fulfillment of the symbol. The Church, as Gods true Lampstand, is called not to publicize itself to the world, but to highlight to the world the foundational, structural truths that God has put at its very core. When the Church shines upon itself, through reflecting His glory, we show forth the truths of: God the Father, Son and Holy Spirit; the gifts and fruit of the Spirit; the Church as the body of Christ, He the vine, we the branches; the Word of God.
In our account from Kings, the victory didn't come for Israel when their army was highlighted! The victory came when the world saw that which God intended them

to! How much more so for the Church!

The Golden Lampstand shone upon itself! In shining upon ourselves, as individuals and the Church, we see that our call is to show forth the truths within the Lampstand. When His glory reflects upon us, we are to show forth the divine truths that our Heavenly Father has laid out in scripture. It is all about Him. The world doesn't need to see us, it needs to see Him.

2. The Lampstand Shone upon the Table of Shewbread

And he put the candlestick in the tent of the congregation, over against the table, on the side of the tabernacle southward. And he lighted the lamps before the LORD; as the LORD commanded Moses. (Exo 40:24-25)

The second function of the Golden Lampstand for us to consider is that it shone upon the Golden Table of Shewbread. The Golden Table of Shewbread stood opposite the Golden Lampstand, just after the entry into the Holy Place, within the Tent. As we have already discussed in our look at the Lampstand at the start of this study, the Lampstand was the only instrument of light within the Holy Place. The sun gave light in the Outer Court and the glory of God lit up the Most Holy Place. The Holy Place though, was separated from both through the covering of the Tent and the Veils at its entrances, between the Outer Court and the Most Holy Place. The only thing giving light in the Holy Place was the Golden Lampstand and as it shone, it shone not only upon itself but upon the Golden Table of Shewbread. It provided the light to highlight this other piece of Tabernacle furniture.

The Golden Table of Shewbread was made of shittim wood and overlaid with gold. The Table measured two cubits long, a cubit wide and a cubit and a half high. It is significant to note thar this measurement of one and a half cubits in height is shared by the grate of the Brazen Altar, as well as Ark of the Covenant, upon which rested the blood-stained Mercy Seat. Such gives us an indication into the truth of the Table.

The Golden Table of Shewbreads sole function was to hold upon it the shewbread. Exodus tells us that:

And thou shalt set upon the table shewbread before me alway. (Exo 25:30)

The Table was to stand in the Holy Place and always have upon it the shewbread. The shewbread was made of fine flour. Flour is produced through a wheat kernel being crushed and beaten. This fine flour was taken and baked into twelve cakes, each cake having two tenths deal of flour. These were then placed into two stacks of six upon the Table and then anointed with frankincense. The Lord's instruction for this was that:

Reflection

And thou shalt put pure frankincense upon each row, that it may be on the bread for a memorial, even an offering made by fire unto the LORD. (Lev 24:7)

This was done every Sabbath. Each Sabbath the priests would take in fresh bread for the Table and partake. This was something that only the priests would do, and they would only consume it within the Holy Place. None was to be eaten in the Outer Court or the Most Holy Place. The shewbread was strictly something for the Holy Place.

The Shewbread points to Jesus who is the bread of life and the Table of Shewbread points to the Table of Communion. Jesus says in the gospel of John:

I am the living bread which came down from heaven: if any man eat of this bread, he shall live for ever: and the bread that I will give is my flesh, which I will give for the life of the world. Joh 6:51)

The link between bread and sacrifice that we see with the Golden Table of Shewbread we see fulfilled in Jesus. Jesus is the bread of life through His sacrifice on the cross (the Brazen Altar). It is His sacrifice in the Outer Court, that gives us the bread to consume within the Holy Place. What was the Golden Table of Shewbread in the Tabernacle of Moses is the Table of Communion in the New Testament Church. The Table points to the Table. As believer priests we are able to partake of the table and are to do so regularly.

When the Church is truly reflecting the glory of God, the Table of Communion, the body and blood of Jesus should be seen by all who look. Paul in his first letter to the Corinthians said:

For as often as ye eat this bread, and drink this cup, ye do shew the Lord's death till he come. (1Co 11:26)

The Greek word for 'shew' as used in this verse, means to proclaim or promulgate and is translated declare, preach, shew, speak of or teach. When we, as the body of Christ, partake of the Table, we are declaring, preaching, shewing, speaking of and teaching the truth of the sacrifice of Jesus to a world that so desperately needs to know it. It is an absolute foundational truth that needs to be highlighted. Whilst it's true that things can fall into religious tradition, the exact same can be said of worship, prayer and preaching and yet these are things we see in almost every service. The distinction comes with how we approach and present and teach about the Table. When we understand the call to illuminate the Table and the life it produces, we present a message of life. If the reason that we all gather is because of the sacrifice of Jesus, how can we not highlight this in our services! He is the bread of life and there is life in the bread.

Reflection

Just as the Golden Lampstand illuminated the Golden Table of Shewbread, so is the Church to illuminate the Table of Communion. For the writer, and this is opinion not interpretation, there would seem to be an interesting correlation here between illuminating the Table of Communion and highlighting Christ's death to what happened in the Kings account where when the sun shone upon the waters the world saw blood. Again, this is the writer's own thoughts, but in the account of 2 Kings 3, when the world saw the blood, victory soon followed!

3. The Lampstand shone upon the Golden Altar

And he put the golden altar in the tent of the congregation before the veil: And he burnt sweet incense thereon; as the LORD commanded Moses.(Exo 40:26-27)

The third, and only other piece of furniture, within the Holy Place in the Tent of the Congregation was the Golden Altar of Incense. This piece of furniture stood at almost the end of the Holy Place, just in front of the Veil that led into the Most Holy Place.

The Golden Altar, like the Golden Table, was made of shittim wood and overlaid with gold. Unlike the Brazen Altar of the Outer Court though, absolutely no sacrifice took place at this altar. The Golden Altar was a place where the Lord stipulated that incense alone was to be offered unto Him. The incense was offered upon the Golden Altar and as it burned, it would ascend and not only fill and permeate the Holy Place, but flow into the Most Holy Place as well.

It is interesting to note of the connection we read of between the Lampstand and Golden Altar in Exodus 30.

> *And thou shalt put it before the vail that is by the ark of the testimony, before the mercy seat that is over the testimony, where I will meet with thee. And Aaron shall burn thereon sweet incense **every morning: when he dresseth the lamps, he shall burn incense upon it**. And when Aaron **lighteth the lamps at even, he shall burn incense upon it,** a perpetual incense before the LORD throughout your generations. (Exo 30:6-8)*

We see here that the Golden Altar and the Golden Lampstand are linked. The two are tied together in their operation. When the priest attended to one, he would attend the other. The incense was to burn continually, with Aaron attending to it in connection with his attendance to the Lampstand. The Golden Lampstand not only illuminated the Golden Altar, but their ministry was also tied together.
In scripture incense speaks of the prayers of the people of God. The prayers of his people start on earth and ascend up into the Holy of Holies, in Heaven where the Lord dwells. Our prayers are presented upon the Golden Altar by our Great High Priest, the Lord Jesus Christ. It is He who intercedes with and for us. We see the truth of this in Revelation Chapter 8.

> *And another angel came and stood at the altar, having a golden censer; and there was given unto him much **incense, that he should offer it with the prayers of all saints** upon the **golden altar** which was before the **throne**. And the smoke of the incense, which came with the prayers of the saints, ascended up before God out of the angel's hand. (Rev 8:3-4)*

There is only one who intercedes between God and man, the Lord Jesus Christ. He alone is the one who can present our prayers before the Father. In Revelation, we see the fulfilment of the truth of the Golden Altar, as the angel, the Lord Jesus Christ presents the prayers of the saints upon the Heavenly Altar which stands before God's true throne. As Jesus presents the prayers of earth, they fill the Holiest of Holies in Heaven.

The Golden Altar speaks of the prayers of His people. The reason it is placed at the end of the Holy Place, in the writer's opinion, is to highlight the vital importance, need and relevance of prayer in the last days of this age in which we live.

When the Lampstand is illuminated, the world should be able to see the truth and fulness of prayer and intercession in our lives and churches. Just as the Golden Lampstands purpose was to highlight this, so too is it the purpose of the Church. Prayer should be a daily ministration. The two are unmistakably linked in the Tabernacle and the two should be unmistakably linked in the New Testament Church. The example and importance of prayer should be seen and evidenced in our lives and fellowships.

4. The Lampstand illuminated the Holy Place

Such has already been covered briefly in this section and more fully in our initial look at the Golden Lampstand and its application to the Church to shine. The reader is encouraged to re-read our comments there as we will be fairly succinct here.

The Outer Court was illuminated by the glory of the sun. The Most Holy Place was illuminated by the glory of the presence of God. The Holy Place had neither. It was separated from both and the only way that it had light was if the Golden Lampstand was functioning.
Without the light of the Lampstand the Holy Place would have been in perpetual darkness!

As we have seen earlier, the Holy Place of the Tabernacle of Moses speaks of the Church age. The words of Jesus were that as long as He was in the world He was the light of the world (John 9:5). With Jesus' death on the cross, and subsequent ascension, the dispensation of the Son ended, and the dispensation of the Holy Spirit began. On the great day of Pentecost, the Holy Spirit descended and divinely lit the New Testament Church. From that time to when Christ returns, the

Reflection

Church as the Golden Lampstand is the means of light for the age in which we live. The Church is God's vessel to reflect His glory to the world. If the Church isn't doing this then all we are left with is darkness.

The reason we had the religious dark ages was because the Church was not shining as it had been called. But praise God for the reformation saints who God used to bring back the foundational truths that would see the Church start to shine once again. Ours is to see this continue and increase as we press fully into all that the Lord has for us that we as the Church would reflect the Glory of God as we have been designed to. We are the light of the world, we are the city on a hill (Matt 5:14). Ours is to shine so that there exists light in the world in which we live.

Peter refers to the age we live in as God's period of longsuffering and likens it to the days of Noah when the door of the ark was available for the entire one hundred years that it took Noah to build. There came a day though when the door was shut, and the longsuffering of the Lord ended. The reality is that this age, and God's period of long suffering, will come to an end just like it did in Noah's. Currently the door of salvation, Jesus, is open for any who would receive Him. But one has to ask, if the vessel that was created to provide light in this Church age, the age of longsuffering, isn't shining, how are people supposed to find the door? If the way isn't made clear, how can they avail themselves of it?

Again, we see the Church doesn't shine for its own purposes. It shines because it is not only a vessel of light, but because it is the only vessel of light. God's Church is His Lampstand in this age. It is His vessel created to reflect His glory. If it isn't, then the result is darkness. As we noted earlier, darkness is simply the absence of light. It is the Church who determines the level of light in this age. We are called to shine, but how brightly we do is determined by us.

5. The Lampstand illuminated the path forward

When one studies the layout of the Tabernacle of Moses, it quickly becomes apparent that there was a way of progression from the entrance to the Tabernacle unto the Most Holy Place. This can particularly be seen in the fact that the entrance curtains to the Outer Court, the Holy Place and the Most holy Place were constructed of exactly the same material. The entrances were all alike, and highlighted to the individual the way to move forward in the things of God.

For the Priests and the people everything started in the Outer Court. One couldn't move into the Holy Place without having been in the Outer Court. The Brazen Altar and the Brazen Laver had to be passed before one could step into the Holy Place. There was no way around, no alternative route. There was one way forward. Such was exactly the same situation when one entered the Holy Place, there was only one way to enter into the Most Holy Place. The Great High Priest had to go through the Holy Place before they could enter the presence of the Lord.

Reflection

Lighting the way to the Most Holy place was the Golden Lampstand. It was the Golden Lampstand that clearly illuminated that path for the individual to be able to enter into the Most Holy Place and the presence of the living God.

As New Testament believers we know that when Jesus gave Himself upon the cross of Calvary that the curtain in the Temple, separating the Most Holy place from the Holy Place was torn in two, from top to bottom, from heaven to earth (Mat 27:51, Mar 15:38, Luke 23:45). God was removing the barrier that only allowed the High Priest to enter into His presence once a year. God was giving access to His people to enter into His presence for themselves. The sacrifice of Christ allows us as believer priests to experience at any time that which only the High priest used to experience once a year.

The key in all this is to understand that when the Lord tore the curtain in two, He allowed us access to His presence. We don't yet dwell in His presence permanently, that time is coming, but we have access to it whenever we choose, as Moses, to go in unto the Lord.

The Golden Lampstand shows us that we are not to just reflect the glory of the Lord we are to show to the world how they can experience it too! Part of the role of the Church is to illuminate to the world how they can experience that which we experience. We are to illuminate the path into the presence of the Lord. It is being in the presence of the Lord that will ultimately transform the lives of people. The Church is to uncompromisingly show the way into His presence. We are called to highlight this path. Part of our role is to show people how to enter and experience the life transforming presence of the Lord.

6. The Lampstand illuminated the Word

    We noted earlier how the Word was built into the Golden Lampstand through the threefold pattern of the knop, flower and fruit. The pattern through the shaft and branches represents the sixty-six books of the Bible. When the Golden Lampstand shines it reveals the Word of the Lord! Here we will look at another example that confirms that part of the purpose of the Lampstand is to illuminate the Word of the Lord.

    As we move through scripture, we read of an interesting occurrence of the Golden Lampstand in Daniel Chapter 5. The reader is encouraged to read over this chapter before moving on here.

    To give some background to this portion of scripture, the nation of Judah had years before been defeated and taken captive by the nation of Babylon. Upon their victory, Babylon plundered the nation of Judah and the people were taken captive to Babylon where they would dwell for 70 years because of their sins against the Lord. This was in accordance with the Word of the Lord spoken through the prophet Jeremiah.

Reflection

During this time of Judah's captivity, Belshazzar, king of Babylon, made a great feast for a thousand of his lords and governors. In all there were several thousand guests and during this time they feasted and indulged in wine. In the midst of the celebration, king Belshazzar commanded that the golden and silver vessels, which his father Nebuchadnezzar had plundered from the Temple of Solomon, be brought so that he and his guests might drink wine from them. These were the vessels that had been dedicated to the service of the Lord by Solomon when he made the Temple. This was the Temple that replaced the Tabernacle of Moses. This was the Temple that was the permanent House of the Lord, where His presence dwelt in the Holy of Holies.

At the kings command, the vessels that had been plundered from the Temple of the Lord were brought and as king Belshazzar and his guests drank from them, they praised the gods of gold, silver, bronze, iron, wood and stone.

> *Then they brought the golden vessels that were taken out of the temple of the house of God which was at Jerusalem; and the king, and his princes, his wives, and his concubines, drank in them. They drank wine, and praised the gods of gold, and of silver, of brass, of iron, of wood, and of stone. (Dan 5:3-4)*

The king of Babylon and his guests not only desecrated the vessels of the Temple by getting drunk with them, but whilst doing so they began praising idols and false gods. They used the instruments that were for the worship of the Lord and instead of honouring the Lord they indulged the flesh and engaged in worldly and false worship. What a horrific scene!

As they were in the midst of this desecration, the judgement of the Lord came forth. In verse 5 of Dan Chapter 5 we read:

> *In the same hour came forth fingers of a man's hand, and wrote opposite the lampstand upon the plaster of the wall of the king's palace: and the king saw the part of the hand that wrote. Dan 5:5*

Upon seeing this miraculous sign, the king's demeanour, and that of his lords, changed. We read that the king hips were loosed, that is they lost strength, and his knees knocked together. The king was in fear of not only the hand that appeared but also because of the message that had been left. In trying to seek an answer for what had just happened, the king sought his religious personnel, the astrologers, Chaldeans and soothsayers, but none could interpret what the hand had written. All of the wisdom of Babylon fell utterly short at interpreting the message of the Lord. Upon hearing of the king's distress, the queen mother came and reminded the king of Daniel and the abilities and qualities he had displayed when serving his father, king Nebuchadnezzar. Upon hearing this, and having got nowhere with his own wise men, king Belshazzar summoned Daniel. Daniel, as the faithful prophet of the Lord came before the king and all the nobles. Daniel started off by reminding the king how the Lord had humbled his father, king Nebuchadnezzar, until he knew that the Lord was the true God. Despite knowing what his father had been through, king Belshazzar had not humbled himself before the Lord. Daniel, as the voice of the Lord to the king, then said:

> *But have lifted up yourself against the Lord of heaven; and they have brought the vessels of his house before you, and you, and your lords, your wives, and your concubines, have drunk wine in them; and you have praised the gods of silver, and gold, of bronze, iron, wood, and stone, which see not, nor hear, nor know: and the God in whose hand your breath is, and whose are all your ways, have you not glorified: Then was the part of the hand sent from him; and this writing was written. And this is the writing that was written, MENE, MENE, TEKEL, UPHARSIN. This is the interpretation of the matter: MENE; God has numbered your kingdom, and finished it. TEKEL; you are weighed in the balances, and are found wanting. PERES; Your kingdom is divided, and given to the Medes and Persians. (Dan 5:23-28)*

Such was the judgment from the Lord that fell on king Belshazzar because of his proud, presumptuous, unholy and unrighteous actions. He had not learned from the experience of his father but had walked in complete pride and utter contempt for the Lord. The book of Daniel goes on to record that it was that very night that the king died according to the Word of the Lord.

What is clear from this chapter of Daniel, is that the message written on the wall was the Word of the Lord. It was a word of judgment, but it was a Word of the Lord to king Belshazzar and his guests. The wise men of Babylon couldn't interpret this. It took the prophet from Judah, Daniel, because it was a Word from God.

Back at the start of Daniel chapter 5 we read that this Word of the Lord was written opposite, or behind, the Lampstand.

> *In the same hour came forth fingers of a man's hand, and wrote over against the **lampstand** upon the plaister of the wall of the king's palace: and the king saw the part of the hand that wrote. (Dan 5:5)*

The Word of the Lord was written where the Golden Lampstand was shining. The Golden Lampstand highlighted the hand and the words that were written by it. The light of the Lampstand caused the Words of the Lord to be seen by king Belshazzar and his guests. Whilst scripture doesn't specifically state this to be the Golden Lampstand, when we consider the situation here, there is little doubt that this is the case. The following is presented for the reader's contemplation.

> According to the prophet Jeremiah [Jer 52:19] the Golden Lampstand was just one of the items taken as plunder from the Temple of Solomon.

Reflection

We know that the items from the Temple were treated with contempt and used as everyday items, as evidenced by the king and his guests using the vessels of silver and gold to drink from.

We know that the Golden Lampstand existed to give light, especially in regard to the things of God and the Word of God as we have already established.

A question to ponder is why did the hand write by the Lampstand? Why not somewhere else? If there is no significance in the Lampstand, why is it mentioned and why did the hand write near it? God didn't have to do the miracle there, but He chose to. There are no coincidences in the Word of God! The Word of the Lord was written there because the Golden Lampstand illuminates the Word of God.

The real indication that the Lampstand mentioned was in fact the Golden Lampstand, is the fact of what the Lampstand illuminated. The Lampstand mentioned, caused the Word of the Lord to be absolutely and unmistakably evident and visible, even to those who had been indulging in wine. The Golden Lampstand caused the Word of the Lord to be illuminated. There is a connection between the Word and the Lampstand. Why did the hand right there? Why not somewhere else in the palace?

In Psalm 119 we read

> *Your word is a lamp unto my feet, and a light unto my path. (Ps 119:105)*

The psalmist saw the connection between the Lamp and the Word. This same connection is evidenced in Daniel 5. The lamp of the Lord caused the Word of the Lord to be seen. The lamp highlighted the Word. It brought attention to the Word of God. It caused it to be recognised. It caused the world to stop and see the Word of God.

We see again from this example of Daniel that when the Church reflects the glory of God, part of its role is to highlight the Word of the Lord. Jesus was the Word made flesh and the reality is if we are not highlighting the full and complete Word of God, we are not highlighting our full and complete Saviour. The full and complete Word of God needs to be illuminated in our lives and in our churches. When His glory is reflected, the Word is seen.

Hopefully as we have moved through this section, the reader has seen that whilst the Church and believers are called to reflect the glory of God to the world, it should never be with a focus on illuminating self. When we are truly reflecting the glory of God, those around us shouldn't see us, they should see Him. Our call is to make sure we are reflecting all the things that the Lord has purposed. We are called to highlight these things to a people that need to see them. We should never project what we think the world needs or wants, it should always be what the Lord wants the world to see. Just as with Moses and the Lampstand, the call of God for His people and His Church is to illuminate those things that He has called us to. God has laid out in His Word those things that should be evident when we are reflecting His glory and it is these things that ultimately lead to victory. Reflection leads to victory, but we have to be reflecting the right things! Any time we dilute or shy away from that which we have been called to reflect in order to be less offensive to the world, or more palatable, all we really do is diminish the brightness with which we shine and hinder the victory that the Lord has for us. We are to unashamedly and boldly reflect all that the Lord has called us too.

REFLECTION SUMMARY

Through this section we have seen that reflection occurs when the glory of the Lord shines upon that which has been dug and infilled. Unless digging and infilling occurs, then there is nothing for the divine to shine upon. When the digging and infilling does occur though, the Lord is able to shine upon His people and Church and draw the attention of all those that are around them.

It is not enough just to dig and infill though, we need to maintain the wells and ensure the infilling continues to flow. The sun evaporates the water, the fire consumes the oil, the glory upon Moses' face declined as Moses spoke the Word of the Lord to the people. In order for reflection to be maintained there has to be continual infilling. Ours is not to just be infilled, it is to be continually infilled, that His light may shine always, wherever He has planted us.

We also saw that when the Lord reflects upon His people, the Lord does it with the intent not of highlighting the individual or Church to the world, but rather with the intent of causing the world to be able to see the truths that He is wanting them too. When we are truly reflecting the glory of God then His Word, His sacrifice, His Spirit, Prayer and Worship and all of the other points we looked at in this section are what should be illuminated. If each of the pipes are open and there is a fulness of His Spirit flowing into the seven lamps of the Lampstand, nothing should be hidden. If things aren't evident then it perhaps means that we need to check and clear the pipes so that we are shining as brightly as we are called.

Such may sound heavy, but it is not written with that intent. The fact is though if we want to see the resulting effect of reflecting His glory, victory, then the first three steps have to be fully operational in our lives and churches. The victory for the united armies came when they had dug deeply according to the Word of the Lord, had been fully infilled by the Lord and the glory of the heavens shone upon this. We cannot expect any different. Victory for the Church comes when we are shining as fully as God has called us to. Victory comes when all that God has purposed and designed to be illuminated is illuminated. We need to remember that we are just the vessels. We are called to be vessels that reflect His glory upon those things that He has spoken of. The Lord knows what will

Reflection

bring the victory for the people of God. Ours is not to try and reinvent the wheel, ours is simply to be faithful and obedient. When His light reveals what He has purposed it to, victory follows.

VICTORY

The final point from the 2 Kings 3 account for us to consider is that of victory. We saw in the Kings account that after the wells had been dug and infilled by the Lord that the sun rose and shone upon that which had been infilled. As the sun shone upon the infilled wells, the nation of Moab saw the reflection of blood and wrongly assumed that the united armies had turned on each other. Moab went down unarmed, expecting to plunder the slaughtered armies but were instead met with a rejuvenated army that they were not expecting. It was at this point that the victory began for the kings and their united armies. In a short amount of time the situation of the kings was turned from a place of defeat to a place of victory. The united armies arose against Moab and not only drove them out of the camp but pursued them into their own land as the Moabites fled for their lives. The battle was won, and the victory was attained.

The victory came, and was enabled only, because each of the previous steps had occurred. The victory that was experienced was completely dependent upon the steps that had occurred prior. If the sun hadn't shone upon the waters, Moab wouldn't have seen the reflection of blood and gone down unarmed and unprepared for battle. The sun was only able to reflect upon the water because the wells had been infilled. The wells were only able to be infilled because they had been dug in faithful obedience to the Word of God. Victory came only because of that which preceded it. There were no shortcuts. There was no 'plan B'. The Lord laid out for the kings how they would be victorious, it was up to them to follow the Word of the Lord.

Throughout this study we have emphasised that each of these steps are progressive in nature and utterly dependent upon the ones that preceded them. Such is the case seen again here. The victory experienced by the united armies was an outworking of what had previously been done and happened. There was no short cut to victory! There never is! Victory came, and only came, through what had been done prior. Victory is a result, not a starting point!

Victory

The victory in our Kings account is summed up for us in verse 24 of 2 Kings 3.

> *And when they came to the camp of Israel, the Israelites rose up and smote the Moabites, **so that they fled before them**: but they **went forward smiting the Moabites, even in their country**.(2Ki 3:24)*

Within this verse there are a couple of points for us to take notice of in regard to the victory that was experienced by the kings and the united armies.

A. Victory stopped the advancement of the enemy.

We read in 2 Kings 3 that when Moab heard that the three kings had marched out in battle toward them that the armies of Moab gathered together at the border of Moab. Moab set up camp at its border and opposite, in camp were the three kings and their united armies. There was essentially a face off, as each army stood in opposition to the other.

This was a common occurrence in Old Testament times. The two armies would set up opposite each other with the battle line in the middle. They would then come together in a struggle to gain an advantage. Think of the account of David and Goliath where we read that Israel was encamped opposite the Philistines. Each day Goliath would come out to the battle line and challenge the armies of Israel who subsequently fled back to their tents. These battles were an arm wrestle as both sides desperately tried to hold their ground and then gain the advantage, by pushing the enemy back and causing them to flee. Here though we see that the people of Moab fled without a battle. They didn't hold their ground, they retreated and retreated quickly.

It was because of what the Lord had caused them to see, that the people of Moab fled before the united armies. After initially advancing into the camp of the united armies, the enemy quickly abandoned their posts, their positions and fled. The opposition ceased and the struggle no longer existed. That which had stood to oppose the united armies, dissipated because of the reflection they had seen. All that had been a worry and fear to the united armies only a day ago, was suddenly fleeing before them. This mighty enemy was no longer hindering their progress but was instead fleeing before them in haste. Those whom the united armies had been afraid would take their lives, were now running in fear of their lives from the united armies.

The armies of Moab went from a place of looking to take territory from the united armies to quickly conceding ground to the united armies. The victory halted the advancement of the enemy and saw them flee before the kings and their united army.

B. The people of God took back territory

The second thing that we see is that the united armies were not only able to move forward, but they were also able to go into the territory of Moab.

> *but they **went forward smiting the Moabites, even in their country**. (2Ki 3:24)*

The united armies advanced into enemy land. Land which they had previously not been able to enter, they were now freely taking. That which had once been off limits and protected, was now being taken as the united armies advanced. As the people of God moved forward, the hold of the enemy began to shrink. As the united armies advanced, the army of Moab was pushed back further and further. The enemy's territory began to shrink as the people of God walked in the promise of His victory.

The victory that occurred here, and all that it involved, all happened according to the Word of the Lord that was given through Elisha to the three kings.

> *And he said, Thus saith the LORD, **Make this valley full of ditches**. For thus saith the LORD, Ye shall not see wind, neither shall ye see rain; yet that valley shall be filled with water, that ye may drink, both ye, and your cattle, and your beasts. And this is but a light thing in the sight of the LORD: **he will deliver the Moabites also into your hand. And ye shall smite every fenced city, and every choice city, and shall fell every good tree, and stop all wells of water, and mar every good piece of land with stones**. (2Ki 3:16-19)*

The Word of the Lord was that victory would come if the armies started the process of digging. The amazing thing with all this is the speed of the turnaround for the united armies. The united armies were downtrodden and in despair, without water and expecting to be defeated and given into the hands of Moab. They were expecting to be overrun and destroyed. Then they received a Word from the Lord! If they would dig then the Lord would infill, but He wouldn't just do that, He would then give Moab into the hands of the united armies. The Lord would turn the tables, but the united armies had to start the process. The armies had to dig.

The victory came for the kings when the sun shone upon the infilled wells. It was a battle strategy that made absolutely no sense but highlights the truths that the battle is the Lord's (1 Sam 17:47, 2 Chron 20:15). The battle is always the Lords. The requirement upon man is not to come up with the best battle plan, the requirement upon man is simply summed up with the word obedience.

We see a very similar example of this with Gideon in the book of Judges. In Judges 6 we read that Israel was oppressed by the Midianites. Every year the Midianites came up with the Amalekites and the people of the East and destroyed all of the produce of the land, leaving the Israelites nothing. These nations came up as locusts and the Israelites would retreat and hide in the dens and caves in fear of their lives.

In verse 11 we are introduced to Gideon who was threshing wheat, hidden away in a winepress, in fear that the enemy might see him. The people of Israel were oppressed, and things were done behind closed doors and hidden away as the nation of Israel lived in fear of their lives.

Victory

Fast forward a couple of chapters and we see that after Gideon had encountered, been strengthened and filled by the Lord, that the Lord gave Gideon a battle plan. Having already reduced Gideon's army down to three hundred men, the Lord then told Gideon that the enemy would be handed over to Him that night. The Lord instructed Gideon to have every man grab a trumpet and a torch, but to cover the torch with a pot. Initially the light was to be hidden. The army was divided into three companies and on Gideon's command they were to do as he did. We go on to read:

> *So Gideon, and the hundred men that were with him, came unto the outside of the camp in the beginning of the middle watch; and they had but newly set the watch: and they blew the trumpets, and brake the pitchers that were in their hands. And the three companies blew the trumpets, and brake the pitchers, and held the lamps in their left hands, and the trumpets in their right hands to blow withal: and they cried, The sword of the LORD, and of Gideon. And they stood every man in his place round about the camp: and all the host ran, and cried, and fled. And the three hundred blew the trumpets, and the LORD set every man's sword against his fellow, even throughout all the host: and the host fled to Bethshittah in Zererath, and to the border of Abelmeholah, unto Tabbath. And the men of Israel gathered themselves together out of Naphtali, and out of Asher, and out of all Manasseh, and pursued after the Midianites.(Jdg 7:19-23)*

Again, we see that as the light of the Lord was revealed that the enemy fled and was pushed back, and the people of God were able to advance into territory that had previously been hindered to them. The battle plan made no sense! But God didn't need it to make sense to man, He just needed man to be obedient.

When the pitchers were broken and the light of the torches were seen, the enemy fled, and Israel pursued. That which had previously caused the people to hide in caves and Gideon to thresh in a winepress, was now being driven back because the light of the Lord had been unveiled. The victory for the people of God comes when His light shines forth. The battle is His, the victory is His, ours is to allow His light to shine forth. The united armies experienced this, Gideon experienced this, and the same promise exists for His people and His Church if we will be obedient.

For believers and the Church our victory will come when His light shines forth brightly. The requirement for this, like with the united armies and Gideon, is a call to obedience. As we are faithful in digging the wells and seeking the Lord's infilling, we will see the Lord win the battle. As we press deeper into Him, He will cause our light to push back the enemy and cause us to start taking land that was previously blocked to us. Victory comes as a result of obedience. As the light of the Lord is able to fully reflect off His infilled people and churches, the Church will start to see the enemy retreat and the light of His glory extend across the areas where the Lord has placed us. There is a victory at hand, but it starts with complete and total obedience. When we dig, are infilled and allow His divine light to reflect that which He wants the world to see, then the victory comes. When we as individuals and churches are walking in obedience, that is when we will start to see the kingdom of God advance in our streets, towns, cities, states and nations. If we truly want to see His victory here on earth, we have to be fulfilling the prior steps. The fulness of victory is determined upon how fully the previous steps have been attended to. Partial obedience means partial victory. If we want the fulness of victory we need to be walking in a fulness of obedience. Victory is a natural progression when the previous steps have been fulfilled.

As the people of God and as those who form His Church, if we want to see the darkness of the enemy not only halt, but be driven back in our towns, cities, states and countries then we need the victory of the Lord. When we are faithful unto His call, just as the kings were to the Word of the Lord through Elisha, then we will likewise experience the victory of the Lord. The victory is there if we will be obedient.

Victory

Part B Summary

PART B SUMMARY

Throughout this section we have focused in on and broken down the main points of the 2 Kings 3 account. As we have looked at these points of digging, infilling, reflection and victory we have hopefully not only grown in our understanding of the 2 Kings 3 account but also in the application that it has to us as believers and as the New Testament Church. It is the writer's belief that there is a message in this that is applicable to believers today. When we understand these steps and their progressive nature, we can then step into that which the Lord is calling us unto.

In our look at digging, we learned that this was the first part of the process. The Word of the Lord to the kings and the united armies was to fill the valley full of ditches. This call to dig lies solely on the part of man and requires his time, effort, endurance and commitment to dig where the Lord has commanded him to. As we considered our examples of Moses and the Golden Lampstand in regard to digging, we saw that just as the kings were given a specific place to dig, so too have we been. As believes we are called to dig the seven wells that were revealed through the vision of Zechariah. These are the wells of prayer, reading and meditating on the word, sensitivity to the Holy Spirit, faith, obedience, speaking in tongues and worship and praise. These seven wells connect us to the Golden Bowl, and it is only when these are open and operational that the oil can flow from our Great High Priest unto us as believers. The call to believers and the Church today is to dig these wells and having dug them to continually maintain them. We are to dig so that the Lord may infill, and we are to learn from the mistakes of Isaac and maintain the wells that have been dug so that the enemy cannot cut them off. It is only when we have dug all of these wells that we allow ourselves to receive the fulness of infilling that the Lord has for us. Zechariah's vision showed us that there were seven pipes and seven lamps. In order for the Lampstand to shine as fully as it was created each well has to be dug. Partial digging results in partial light. If we are to have the fulness of light that the Lord has for us we have to dig completely.

Part B Summary

When we have dug the Lord then infills. Infilling naturally follows digging. The promise of the Lord is that He will provide the infilling, ours is to be faithful to His Word and dig the wells so that we may be able to catch that which He pours out. As we looked at Jacob's dream of the ladder and our other examples, we saw that Heaven always responds to the actions of earth. That which ascends from the earth is always met with a response from heaven. As we are faithful to dig the wells (plural), the Lord is faithful to fill them. If we as believers and the Church are going to shine with the fulness we have been created to, then like with the vision of Zechariah, we need to make sure all of the wells are open. The Lord will always fill, but He can't fill a well that hasn't been dug. When we are faithful in digging, He will always infill. The Lord matches our digging with His infilling. Heaven responds to the actions of man on earth.

The third part of the process that we looked at from 2 Kings 3 was that of reflection. When that which has been dug in obedience is filled by the Lord, it allows His divine light to shine off it. The light is always divine and its purpose is always to highlight the things of the Lord to the world. Reflection is never to highlight an individual or a particular Church! Reflection should always show the Lord to the world. We are called to reflect His glory and be beacons of His light to a world that so desperately needs to see Him. As the Lord reflects off His vessels that have been filled by His Spirit, the world should see the things of God. They should see His Word, His sacrifice, His Spirit, His purity and so forth. Everything that is seen should be God focused. There should be absolutely no evidence of self, for it is only when the divine reflection occurs that the victory comes. In the Kings account, when the reflection occurred the world saw blood and then the victory came. When we reflect His glory, the world sees Him and His kingdom advances. It is a divine reflection.

Finally, we saw that after digging, infilling and reflection, victory was the result. When the people of God are faithful to dig and allow the Lord to infill the wells, He shines off them and causes His people to walk in victory. The victory not only stops the advancement of darkness, it pushes it back as the people of God advance and retake territory in the light of their Lord. Victory is the natural outcome of the steps that have preceded it. When we dig, are infilled and reflect, then victory comes as His light expands across our town, cities, states and countries.

The key for us as believers in all this is to remember that each of these steps are progressive. Digging leads to infilling which leads to reflection which leads to victory. Each step is completely dependent upon the ones that precede it. If we as the people of God want to reflect His glory and walk in the victory that brings, then we need to be faithful to the call to dig. We need to give constant attention to the wells that we have been called to dig, and ensure they are operational and maintain them for the generations that follow us. How much spiritual ground could His people take if we would be faithful to the call to dig. The writer believes that the account of Kings is very much prophetic for the people of God today. There is a spiritual victory available in our towns, cities, states and countries if we can follow the example of the kings and the united armies. If we can be faithful to the Word of God to dig the wells, He will bring the victory for us. The method may not make sense. It may not answer the questions we have. It may be opposite to modern day thinking, **BUT** it is the Word of God. Like with the kings and with Gideon, ours is to not necessarily to understand the battle plan, ours is simply to be obedient to the call. If we can follow His Word, then we shall reflect His glory and experience the victory that it brings.

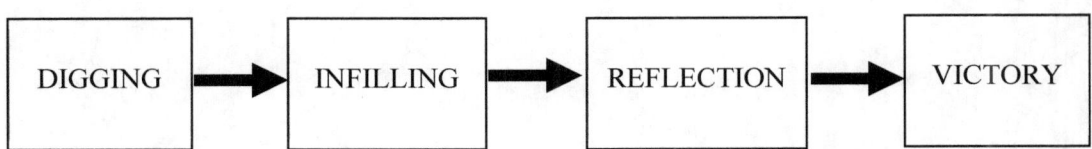

The path to spiritual victory is clear, the responsibility however lies upon the people of God and the Church to start the process! This is what the writer has sought to convey in this section. When we fulfil the process, we reflect His glory as we have been called to. This fulfils the first part of the title of this book, Reflecting His Glory. The second part of the title leads us to our next section, Revivals Call. Having seen the call to shine and the process to fulfil that, we will turn our attention and look at the impetus that exists for New Testament believers and the Church to take hold of the truths of this message. It is the writer's belief that the Lord is stirring His people for what He is going to in the days ahead. Revivals Call is sounding.

Part B Summary

PART C
REVIVALS
CALL

Part C Introduction

PART C INTRODUCTION

This study was brought about by the Lord impressing upon the heart of the writer a message from the account of 2 Kings 3 which we have been studying. Throughout the preparation of this text, the writer has continually been drawn to the thought of revival. It is the writer's belief that the overall theme that the Lord is wanting to communicate through this text is that of revival. The four points that we have constantly spoken of and reaffirmed of digging, infilling, reflection and victory are summed up by the word revival. These four points can actually be split into two groups. These two groups are united and yet there is a distinction that exists. A coin has two sides, and each presents its own unique picture, but the two are still completely united and speak one truth overall. There is distinction between the head and the tail of a coin, but its value neve changes. Such is the case with the groups we are discussing here. Each group presents its own side of revival, but the two are completely united and speak the same overall truth of revival.

With digging and infilling we see the 'Process of Revival'. The kings and the united armies were in a place where naturally they needed reviving. They were without water and faced the very real possibility of death. The Word of the Lord to them was that if they were faithful to dig then the Lord would provide that which would revive them. The kings and the armies experienced revival in the natural once the Lord had infilled that which they had dug. There was a process for the kings and their armies to be revived. Digging and infilling show us the process of revival.

For us as New Testament believers, we need the spiritual reviving of the Lord. Just as with the united armies the process of revival starts with us. Revival starts when the people of the Lord, act in obedience to the Word of the Lord and dig deep the wells that we have been called to. It happens when His people become not only aware of their spiritual need of infilling but develop a desperate thirst for it continually. The process of revival starts when we, the people of God, are desperate enough to dig and maintain the wells that we have been called to. Once we have dug the Lord is always faithful to infill. As we press

Part C Introduction

into Him, we receive spiritual reviving as the Lord pours His spirit out upon us. Digging and infilling show us the process to receive revival.

The second side of the coin that we see, and the one we probably more readily identify with revival, is the 'Fruit of Revival'. It is through reflection and the victory that we see the fruit of revival and those things we so commonly associate with it. The reflection and the victory are the visible outworking's of revival. When the glory of the Lord shone upon the water of the wells the united armies were able to push the enemy back and take land that they had previously faced resistance with. We see the light of God shining and the people of God taking ground because of it. With the fruit of revival we see the advancement of the people of God.

As believers we readily identify with the fruit of revival. We long to see the light of the Lord shining off us and starting to expand in the streets, towns and communities in which we live in, as the enemy is pushed back. We look for the mighty moves of God. We look for His Spirit to move in might and power and possibly wonder at times why we don't see it.

For us as New Testament believers the key for us to understand in all of this is that there can only ever be the fruit of revival if the process of revival has first been carried out. Whilst we are looking at two sides of the same coin, the fruit always follows the process. Without the process there is no fruit. Often we pray and ask the Lord to send revival, understanding the need we have of the Lord to move, but we perhaps do not fully grasp that revival actually starts with us! Revival starts with man, not with God!

In the 2 Kings 3 account the victory came because the glory reflected. The glory reflected because the wells had been filled. The wells were filled because they had been dug. The wells were dug because the people acted in accordance and obedience to the Word of the Lord. Man started the process and then the fruit came. If the digging hadn't occurred, the fruit wouldn't have been possible. The fruit cannot happen without the process!

It all starts with us! The fruit of revival is only possible when we start the process through digging. Heaven will always respond to the actions of earth! If we truly want to see revival, if we want to see the glory of the Kingdom of God expand across this world, then we need to understand the truths of digging and infilling.

It is the writer's belief that the Lord has given us a prophetic picture of revival through the 2 Kings 3 account. This picture shows the process of revival and the fruit of revival. Within this account is a message that if we as believers, and corporately as the Church, can grasp hold of, then God will be able to do incredible things to extend His Kingdom. The account of 2 Kings 3 speaks to us a message of revival.

At the same time that the writer was given the picture of revival from the 2 Kings 3 account, the Lord also impressed upon the writer that the call for revival was and is for now. It is the writer's belief that the Lord is calling and stirring His people at this moment

Part C Introduction

to go deeper into the things of the Lord. Throughout the preparation of this text, this has been something that the Lord has continually put on the writer's heart.

The Lord is calling His people to a new depth of relationship. This call to revival is one that has impetus. In the Kings example, there was a window for faithful obedience that the united armies had to respond to the message of the Lord. They had to dig immediately if they were to receive the infilling of the Lord and all that would follow. There was an urgency to the call, and the writer would put forth that the Lord has issued a call to revival to His people in this day that holds the same urgency. The Lord is wanting to move upon His people and have His glory reflected throughout the regions where we dwell. The Lord is calling His people so that we might step out of our winepresses and shine brightly, that there may be spiritual victory all around us.

As the writer thought upon and contemplated this call to revival, he felt directed by the Lord to two passages of scripture. Through these the Lord confirmed both the call to revival and the urgency that the writer had felt.

In this section we will spend some time investigating these passages and see what the Word of the Lord reveals to us about revival and the call to the Church in the time we are in. As we move through these examples, the reader will hopefully see that the Lord is wanting His people to not only understand the process of revival but the need to start digging into it. It is the writer's sincere hope that as the reader contemplates what is presented in the following pages that they will be likewise stirred by the Lord to press deeper into Him, that we may see Him move like never before.

Part C Introduction

THE PARABLE OF THE 10 VIRGINS

The parable of the ten virgins was given to us by Jesus in Matthew 25. For our purposes here, we will spend some time working through the parable itself, before considering its interpretation and application.

A. The Parable

In Matthew 25:1-13 we read of the parable of the ten virgins. The reader is encouraged to read over this passage several times before moving forward. Here we will provide a short summation of what Jesus said rather than quoting the whole passage.

The parable of the ten virgins is one of the "Kingdom of Heaven Parables". In total there are twelve of these parables given in Matthew's gospel and all are used by Jesus to highlight a particular truth about the Kingdom of Heaven to believers. In this case, Jesus said that the Kingdom of Heaven is like ten virgins who took their lamps and went out to meet the bridegroom. Five of these virgins were wise and five of these virgins were foolish. The wise took their lamps and extra oil with them but the foolish took only the oil in their lamps. As they all waited for the bridegroom to come, they slipped into slumber and fell asleep. At the midnight hour, a cry went out that the bridegroom was coming. All of the virgins awoke and started tending to their lamps. The foolish quickly realised that they needed more oil and asked the wise to share some of their oil with them. The wise replied that they did not have enough oil to share and that the foolish should go and buy some oil for themselves. As the foolish were out buying oil, the bridegroom came and he went in with the five wise virgins unto the feast. The doors to the feast were then shut. When the foolish eventually arrived, they pleaded to come in, but were met with the response "I don't know you". The foolish had missed the opportunity because they had insufficient oil. In applying this to believers, Jesus then closed off this parable with the warning for believers to keep watch, for we do not know the day nor hour when the Son of man cometh.

B. Interpretation

When we first read this parable it can seem rather heavy, but what we need to remember here is that these were and are the Words of Jesus. Whilst the parable may seem heavy, it is really a warning for believers to take hold of. These were words spoken in love that we may take hold of the warning within.

Within this parable there are a number of truths that we must understand before we can fully grasp what Jesus was saying in it. In order to discover these we will focus in on some of the verses of this passage and take some time to bring out the truths that were being communicated. As we do this the reader should start to see the fulness of revelation contained within this parable.

Then shall the kingdom of heaven be likened unto ten virgins, which took their lamps, and went forth to meet the bridegroom.(Mat 25:1)

Within this verse there are a few things for us to take note of:

1. Then

    'Then' sounds like a fairly innocuous introduction to this parable, but it actually provides the timeframe for what we are looking at. Matthew 25 is a continuation of Jesus' discourse in Matthew 24, where Jesus had been speaking about the 'days' and the 'day' of the Lord. There is a distinction in these that we must recognise. The 'days', plural, refer to that time leading up until the return of the Lord. The 'day', singular, however refers to the actual day when Jesus does return. There are the 'days' leading up to His return and then there is the 'day' of His return.

    Matthew 24 closes with the parable of faithful and slothful servants, where the focus is on the 'days' leading up to the master's return. The focus is on that period preceding the return of Jesus. It is from here that Matthew 25 picks up. It refers to the same period. The parable of the ten virgins refers to that time, just before the coming return of the King. It is referring to the 'days' leading up to Jesus' return.

2. The 10 Virgins

    Notice here that that the Kingdom of Heaven is likened unto ten virgins who went forth to meet the bridegroom. There is no mention of a bride! The parable speaks of the bridegroom coming and being greeted by the 10 virgins who were waiting for Him. This scene speaks of an old Jewish custom, where the brides attendants, the virgins, would go out and meet the bridegroom, bringing him in to the house of the bride.

For us to note here is that the parable speaks of ten virgins. What we see here is one class of individuals. A virgin in scripture speaks of believers. It speaks of the purity of the individual. We are made pure through the precious blood of Christ, and as believers are to be presented to Christ as a chaste virgin (2 Cor 11:1-3).

The ten virgins speaks of those who have accepted and believe in Christ. They speak of New Testament believers. This is a point that needs to be fully grasped. This is **one** classification of individuals spoken of by Jesus here.

3. The Lamps

The lamps were the vessels of light that the virgins needed to have shining when the bridegroom arrived. With the Golden Lampstand, each of the seven branches had a lamp at its end. Here each virgin had their own lamp. The lamps are vessels of light and are meant to shine in the darkness until the rising of the sun. It speaks to the necessity of light and that light to be always shining in the lead up to the bridegroom's return.

4. The Bridegroom

The Bridegroom is unmistakably Jesus. There is no mistaking the interpretation here, compare verses 5 and 6 with verse 13.

> *While the bridegroom tarried, they all slumbered and slept. And at midnight there was a cry made, Behold, the bridegroom cometh; go ye out to meet him. (Mat 25:5-6)*
>
> *Watch therefore, for ye know neither the day nor the hour wherein the Son of man cometh. (Mat 25:13)*

The bridegroom comes, Jesus comes, but in both cases the hour is unknown. Jesus is the bridegroom! His believers are to be ready and waiting with their lamps for His return. This is what the first verse of the parable shows us. There is a meeting to come between Christ (the bridegroom) and His followers (the virgins). In preparation for this, His followers (the virgins) are to be ready with their lamps shining through a ready supply of oil.

These four points are ones we need to understand and grasp in order to be able to understand the truth of this parable. This parable is about believers and their lamps in the days that lead up to the day that Jesus returns.

The Parable Of The 10 Virgins

And five of them were wise, and five were foolish. They that were foolish took their lamps, and took no oil with them: But the wise took oil in their vessels with their lamps. (Mat 25:2 -4)

In verse one we noted that there were the ten virgins and that this spoke of a single class of individuals. These were the bride's attendants. There were not believers and unbelievers. There were not sinners and saints. There were just believers, one classification of individuals. There were ten virgins. All were classified the same. It is one group of the same individuals.

Here though, we see that Jesus made a distinction in this singular group. Jesus identified a difference that existed and separated this one classification of individuals into a group of wise virgins and a group of foolish virgins. Again, the reader is reminded that Jesus was talking about believers here. In the days leading up to the return of Jesus there will be a distinction between wise believers and of foolish believers. This is the warning of Jesus in this parable.

One of the keys in understanding all this is to distinguish the difference between the two groups. What made the wise wise, and what made the foolish, foolish? To understand the difference will help us to understand how we can be wise and not foolish! If we understand what differentiates the two then we learn how not to make the same mistakes as the foolish.

Verse 3 tells us that the foolish took their lamps with them, but they took no extra oil.

> *They that were foolish took their lamps, and took no oil with them.*

The foolish had their lamps and their lamps only.

The wise on the other hand we are told in verse 4 took their lamps and also took extra oil in their vessels.

> *But the wise took oil in their vessels with their lamps.*

The wise had their lamps and then they had an extra supply of oil to be able to top up their lamps as needed.

The difference between the wise and the foolish was in their supply of oil. This is what differentiated this one group into two categories. The foolish had a lamps worth of oil, but the wise had their lamps full of oil and then an extra portion of oil on top of that.

In the words of Jesus in this parable, the wise were wise because they had an extra portion of oil. They had oil in their lamps plus they had extra oil. The supply of oil is what separated the wise from the foolish. It is the point of distinction between the two. This one group is divided into wise and foolish based on whether or not they had extra oil. The wisdom of the wise is seen in that they not only had oil for their lamps, they also had an extra supply of oil.

While the bridegroom tarried, they all slumbered and slept. (Mat 25:5)

The bridegroom tarried in coming! To tarry means to take time, to linger, to delay. For the virgins, the bridegroom took longer to come than they first thought. The virgins were waiting, but they had to wait longer than they thought they would. On this thought Peter said:

> *The Lord is not slack concerning his promise (his return), as some men count slackness; but is longsuffering to us-ward, not willing that any should perish, but that all should come to repentance. (2Pe 3:9)*

The Bridegroom will come exactly when the Lord has foreordained Him to. What seems as tarrying to us is actually a period of longsuffering for the Lord. Within this tarrying period the call for the virgins was to be ready with their lamps. Here though we read that the virgins all slumbered and slept. Rather than being ready, the virgins slept and their lamps went unattended.

Again it should be noted the time element here. We see in this parable the days leading to the return of the bridegroom and then the day of the bridegroom's return. This parable is referring to the days immediately preceding the coming of Jesus. It is a parable to the last days Church. It is a message of warning for us to grasp hold of. The greatest danger for the Church today is complacency. Complacency causes us to slumber and sleep, but we are not called to that. We are called to be ready and shining!

And at midnight there was a cry made, Behold, the bridegroom cometh; go ye out to meet him. (Mat 25:6)

At the midnight hour the cry went out that the groom was coming. At midnight the angel went through Egypt where a great cry was heard(Ex 12:29). At midnight Boaz woke to find his bride at his feet (Ruth 3:8). At the midnight hour Christ returns!

Then all those virgins arose, and trimmed their lamps. (Mat 25:7)

The bridegroom hadn't arrived yet, but his coming was imminent. This parable would indicate that there will be a stirring amongst believers just before the return of the bridegroom.

At the sound of the cry, the virgins were all stirred from their slumber and tended to their lamps. This again highlights the fact that believers are to be ready and waiting for the return of Jesus.

What we see here is an awakening. There was a call that stirred the virgins from their place of slumber and sleep. They not only awoke though, they also trimmed their lamps. The call wasn't just to be 'awake', the call was also to be prepared. It was a call to action and a call to prepare. There was a call to the virgins in the days leading to the bridegroom's return.

The writer is not saying that we are at the 'day' of the Bridegroom's return, but would put forth that in these days leading up to His coming there is a renewed call and stirring going out to the people of God and His Church worldwide. There is a spiritual awakening occurring as the Lord calls His people to stir from the place of rest to a place of preparedness. It is a call to shake off all distractions and focus in on that which we have been called to. These virgins were called to be prepared and to wait. They were to be on duty and committed to that task, but they had allowed themselves to become distracted from this. There is a call today for us to have an ear to hear what the Spirit says to the Church and His people. It is a call to stir from our spiritual slumber and be spiritually awake and prepared in these days.

And the foolish said unto the wise, Give us of your oil; for our lamps are gone out. But the wise answered, saying, Not so; lest there be not enough for us and you: but go ye rather to them that sell, and buy for yourselves. (Mat 25:7-9)

As the foolish tended to their lamps, they immediately became aware that they needed oil! They did not have enough. Some versions translate "our lamps are gone out" as "our lamps are going out". The foolish found themselves in a position where they weren't ready and did not have the means to tend to their lamps. They did not have the oil to supply their lamps so that they were ready for the bridegroom's return.

The foolish then demanded that the wise share their oil. The wise replied that they did not have enough to be able to supply their lamps and the lamps of the foolish. Such speaks to the fact that no one else's supply of oil can be used to sustain another. We each need our own supply of oil. We can't rely on others or feed off them.

The expectation here was for each virgin to be standing ready with their lamp shining. The foolish couldn't use the oil of the wise nor could they rely on the light provided by the lamps of the wise. Each virgin had to be there shining with their own lamp. There is personal responsibility seen here. Someone else's oil won't do. Someone else's light won't do. Each individual needs their own supply of oil and to be standing ready with their own lamp shining.

Here the wisdom of the wise is displayed. They not only had oil in their lamps, they had extra oil so that they could maintain the flow to the lamp and allow it to continually burn. Their extra oil allowed them to be ready and shining when the bridegroom arrived. The extra oil allowed the lamp to continually burn. The extra oil allowed them to be ready and waiting for the bridegroom.

And while they went to buy, the bridegroom came; and they that were ready went in with him to the marriage: and the door was shut. Afterward came also the other virgins, saying, Lord, Lord, open to us. But he answered and said, Verily I say unto you, I know you not. (Mat 25:10 - 12)

While the foolish were off trying to find oil to supply their lamps, the bridegroom came. The wise virgins went in with him unto the wedding and the doors were shut. When the foolish eventually returned they found themselves locked out, and unknown. They missed out on the wedding supper because they weren't ready when the bridegroom came. Their lack of oil caused them to miss out.

Notice in this verse the different terminology that is applied to the virgins. Here the wise virgins are referred to as 'those that were ready', whereas the foolish virgins are referred to as the 'other virgins'. When the Bridegroom returns, He is looking for those virgins that are ready, waiting and shining for Him. Shining, through the extra provision of oil, is what separates the 'ready' virgins from 'the other' virgins. There was an expectation for the virgins to be ready and waiting with their lamps shining. The wise were ready for the bridegrooms return, the foolish were not.

Watch therefore, for ye know neither the day nor the hour wherein the Son of man cometh. (Mat 25:13)

Here we have the warning of Jesus. There is a day and a set hour when He will return. Whilst we do not know when this is, scripture does tell us what the days leading up to it will be like. The virgins time was in those days.

We as believers are the virgins and we are in the days imminent to our Bridegroom's return. The call of Christ is for His people to be ready, waiting and shining in the days leading up to His return. When He comes, He comes for a people that are ready, shining and waiting for Him. This is the message of the parable. What we have learned is illustrated below:

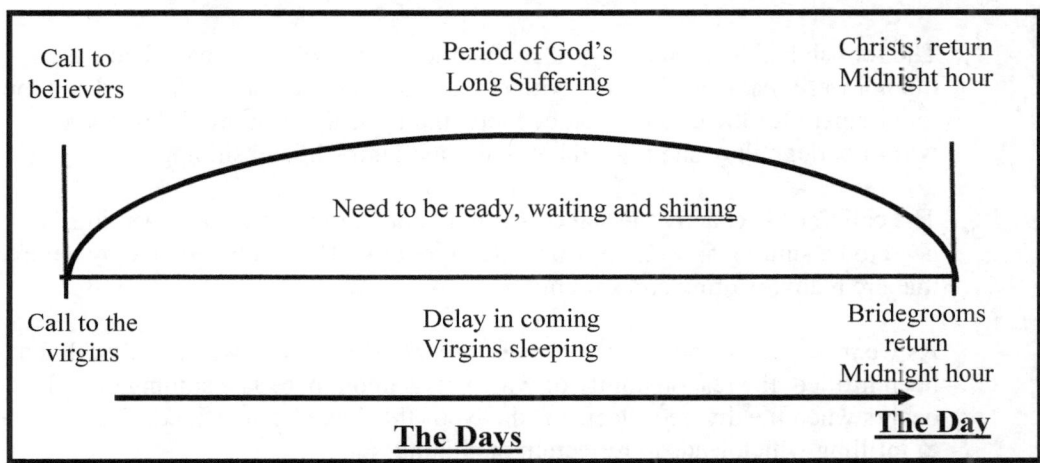

C. Application

From this there are a number of points of application for us as New Testament believers and ones that speak particularly to the theme of this section:

1. Waiting for the Return

   The ten virgins were all called to be ready and waiting for the coming of the bridegroom. They were to be in a state of anticipation of the coming bridegroom. There was one call to one group.

   The call of the Lord for believers is to be in the same state. We are called to be in a ready state, awaiting the return of Jesus. The great hope we look for is the coming of our King, and our call is to be ready and waiting for this.

2. Return Time

   The bridegroom seemed to delay in His coming, but He came at the midnight hour. There was a set time when the bridegroom would arrive.

   Ours is not to know the time of the arrival of Jesus, but our is to recognise the days leading up to this. What is clear from scripture is that we are in those days. We are not yet at the time of His return, but we are in the days leading up to it. The parable of the ten virgins is one that applies to the Church and believers in our days. Ours is not to focus on that day, but to make sure we are ready for it!

3. Call to Shine

   Through the waiting and up to the return of the bridegroom, the responsibility and obligation of the ten virgins was exactly the same. The call never changed! They were to be ready, waiting and shining. It was not enough for them to just be there, they had to be there ready, waiting and shining.

   The foolish had to go and buy oil so that they could fulfil this call. The wise though were ready and waiting with extra oil. They understood the need and the requirement for them to not just be there, but to be there shining! Attendance wasn't enough they had to be there with their lamps lit and shining.

   The call to us is exactly the same. It is not enough to be ready and waiting, we need to be shining as well. When the King returns, He will be greeted by believers that are ready, waiting and shining.

   As we have seen through this text, we can only shine when we have first dug and been infilled, the responsibility of which rests upon man. The shining or reflection occurs when the divine reflects off the wells that have been infilled. Digging leads to infilling which leads to reflection or shining.

If we are to be ready and shining on our King's return, we need to have fulfilled the steps that lead to this. We need to have pressed in and dug deep in those areas that we have been called to, so that the Lord can infill us with His oil. It is when we have been infilled that we are then ready and able to reflect His glory unto His return.

The call to 'Reflect His Glory, Revivals Call', is seen in this parable. The virgins were called to be ready, waiting and shining upon the bridegroom's coming. The wise were ready because they were shining. They were shining because their lamps had been infilled with oil. We, as churches and New Testament believers, are called to be as the five wise virgins. We are called to be to be ready and shining at our Bridegroom's return.

4. Need for continual Oil

We see from this parable that the only way a lamp is sustained is by the continual flow of oil. It is not enough to have a measure, there needs to be a flow. Light is sustained when the oil continues to flow.

Such reinforces the truths we discovered about the wells being maintained and the need for continual infilling. A measure of the Spirit is never enough for believers and His Church. As we wait for His return, we need a continual supply of oil so that we might shine brightly throughout the 'days' of His coming and be ready upon the 'day' of His return. We need to be tending and maintaining the wells so that He may continually infill and we may continually shine. Ours is to continually tend to the wells and make sure that we are continually receiving the infilling that the Lord has for us.

5. The Double Portion

The foolish virgins we are told took their lamps, but no extra oil with them. The foolish had a portion of oil. They had a single portion.

The wise virgins took their lamps as well as vessels with oil in them to sustain their lamps. The wise had two portions of oil or a double portion of oil. There was a portion in their lamps and a portion in the vessels. They had double that of the foolish.

A double portion is a scriptural theme and one that speaks of blessing on the recipient. The right of the firstborn was a double portion. Elisha asked for a double portion of the Spirit that was on Elijah. A portion is a blessing, a double portion sees that blessing expand.

The writer would put forth that in these days we are called to be a people that would hold a double portion of the Spirit of God. It was the double portion that allowed the wise virgins to be ready and shining and it was a double portion that separated them from the foolish. The distinguishing factor in the parable, that separates the wise from the foolish, the ready from the other, is the portion of oil that they carried. The wise carried a double portion!

The days of the virgins show the need that exists for a double portion of His Spirit in our days. We will examine this further in our next example and hopefully confirm these thoughts more fully. For now though, the writer would put forth that there exists a blessing for the people of God that the Lord is wanting to pour out. There is a double portion that is necessary for us to shine as brightly as we have been called to. It is not something that can be shared, but is something that each of us individually need to press in and seek the Lord for.

The mark of the wise was that they understood the need for the double portion in their days. They were prepared. The call for us is to take heed of the lesson of the wise virgins and see the need for the double portion in our days. If we are to be ready as the wise, then we need the double portion of His oil.

In the parable of the ten virgins we see Jesus put forth prophetic truth that has application to believers in the lead up to His return. This parable speaks of one class of individuals, believers, divided into two categories, the wise and the foolish. The differentiating factor between these two groups was in their supply of oil. The foolish had a portion, but the wise had a double portion. It was the double portion of the wise that allowed there to be a continual supply of oil to their lamps and allowed them to fulfil the call to be ready, waiting and shining when the day of the bridegroom's return came.

It was not enough to be ready! It was not enough to be waiting! They had to be ready, waiting and shining! The theme of this text is that 'Revivals Call' is for the people of God to be 'Reflecting His Glory'. We are called to shine, and we do this through the process of revival: digging, infilling and maintaining the flow. If we are to be as the ten virgins and shining upon our Bridegroom's return, then we too need to have prepared beforehand in the days leading up to His return. Now are the days to dig. Now are the days to press in and receive all that He has for us so that we may fully reflect His glory and be ready on the day that our Bridegroom, Jesus, returns. Ours is be ready as the five wise virgins, with a double portion of His Spirit, reflecting His glory brightly as the midnight hour approaches.

With these thoughts in mind, let us move onto our second example for consideration.

THE EARLY AND LATTER RAINS

The second example given for the reader's consideration is that of the early and the latter rains, otherwise known as the former and the latter rains. The early and latter rains form an interesting topic of study for any student of the Word and one that has been particularly placed upon the writer's heart in regard to the current topic we are considering. As we move through this section, the reader will hopefully not only see the application of the early and latter rains but also how they tie in and mesh with our previous example to confirm the call to revival that exists for the people of God in our times.

A. Understanding the rains

   The first question for us to explore, is what is actually meant by the term early and latter rains? The early and latter rains refer to two periods of rain that the Israelites would receive in the promised land. The terms in themselves are fairly self-explanatory. There were the early rains, or the rains that occurred early in the year and then there were the latter rains, or rains that occurred later in the year. These are two distinct periods of rain that Israel received in the promised land.

   In the book of Jeremiah we read:

   *Neither say they in their heart, Let us now fear the LORD our God, that giveth rain, both the **former and the latter**, in his season: he reserveth unto us the appointed weeks of the harvest.*
   (Jer 5:24)

Jeremiah here acknowledges that it was the Lord who gave the rain unto Israel. The Lord gave the early rain and He gave the latter rain unto the nation of Israel. The Lord gave Israel both of these periods of rain in their respective season. There was a season for the early rains and there was a season for the latter rains. Each or these rains had its own season. Whilst the two are linked, there is also distinction.

What we also see here in Jeremiah is the connection of rains and harvest.

> *that giveth rain, both the **former and the latter**, in his season: he reserveth unto us the **appointed weeks of the harvest**. (Jer 5:24)*

There were the rains and then there were the harvests that came from these rains. Just as the two periods of rain were distinct so too were the harvests that were associated with them. There was a harvest that the early rains would produce and there was a harvest that the latter rains would produce. This is a thought we see in Deuteronomy 11, where we read:

> *For the land, whither thou goest in to possess it, is not as the land of Egypt, from whence ye came out, where thou sowedst thy seed, and wateredst it with thy foot, as a garden of herbs: But the land, whither ye go to possess it, is a land of hills and valleys, and drinketh water of the rain of heaven: A land which the LORD thy God careth for: the eyes of the LORD thy God are always upon it, from the beginning of the year even unto the end of the year. And it shall come to pass, if ye shall hearken diligently unto my commandments which I command you this day, to love the LORD your God, and to serve him with all your heart and with all your soul, That I will give you **the rain of your land in his due season, the first rain and the latter rain**, that thou mayest **gather in thy corn, and thy wine, and thine oil.** And I will send grass in thy fields for thy cattle, that thou mayest eat and be full. (Deu 11:10-15)*

In the promised land, the Lord blessed the people of Israel with rain in its due season. There was the early season and there was the latter season. These were the seasons that the Lord had determined that the rain would fall upon the land. It was His due season. Again, connected to these rains we see the thought of harvest. Here we read that the rains in their due season would allow the Israelites to gather in their corn, their wine (from the grape) and their oil (from the olive).

For the nation of Israel, the early rains started in the first month and continued through to the third month. This period was when the Israelites would reap their grain harvests. This was the time of the harvest of corn, barley and wheat. This was the due season for these harvests and it was for this harvest that the early rains came. The early rains were tied to the grain harvest.

The latter rains on the other hand, came in the seventh month and with them came the fruit harvest. This is what is referred to in Deuteronomy where the Israelites would gather in their wine and oil. The wine harvest refers to grapes and the oil harvest refers to olives. These are the fruit harvests. These harvests are linked to the latter rains of the seventh month.

In between the early rains and the latter rains were what was known as the dry months. These were the fourth, fifth and sixth months respectively. This period of dryness separated the two rainy seasons and also the two harvests associated with them. In between these two rainy seasons was a period of no rain and no harvest.

As we consider the time of these rains and their harvests we see a direct link with the timing of the feasts of Israel. The nation of Israel had three great feasts that they celebrated annually. These were the feasts of Passover, Pentecost and Tabernacles.

The early rains came in the first month and continued through to the third month. These were the months of Passover and Pentecost respectively. Passover was the feast of the first month and fifty days after this, in the third month, the people of Israel would celebrate the feast of Pentecost.

The latter rains came in the seventh month, which was the time of the feast of Tabernacles.

From what we have seen so far, we see that the early/former and latter rains refer to two distinct periods of outpouring seen in the nation of Israel. These were two seasons of rain that the Lord had designated for the nation of Israel to receive. These rains were tied to the three feasts that the Lord had Israel celebrate. The early rains and their harvests were linked to Passover and Pentecost and the latter rains and their harvest were linked to the feast of Tabernacles. What we have discovered can be seen illustrated below:

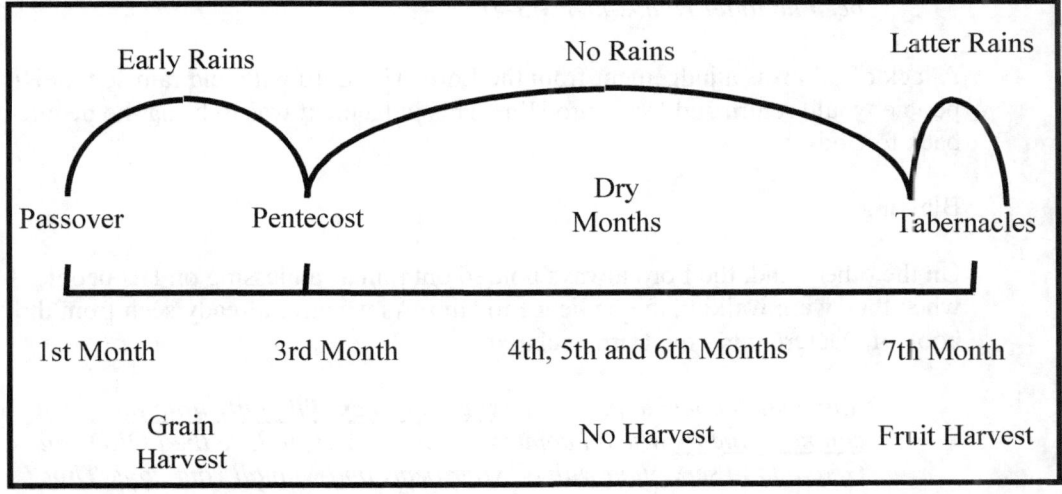

As we move forward here in our look at the rains, we will see that through all this the Lord was once again showing forth prophetic truth to His people. It is always first the natural and then the spiritual.

B. The purpose of the rains

Throughout the Word we find that rain had one of three purposes in regard to the people of God

1. Judgement

    Rain came in the form of judgement with the Ark of Noah, where God opened the heavens and this along with the fountains of the deep, caused the flood to cover the earth. This was the judgement of the Lord in the days of Noah.

    More commonly, throughout the Word, we see a lack of rain as a judgement from the Lord. The Lord would withhold His rain, or close the heavens, when His people were walking in disobedience. Solomon in praying unto the Lord declared this truth when he said:

    > *When heaven is shut up, and there is no rain, because they have sinned against thee;*
    > *(1Ki 8:35)*

    Jeremiah also echoed this sentiment.

    > *...and thou hast polluted the land with thy whoredoms and with thy wickedness. Therefore the showers have been withholden, and there hath been no latter rain;...(Jer 3:3-4)*

    A lack of rain was a judgement from the Lord. The Lord withheld rain so that His people would return and look unto Him. This judgement was to bring the people back to God.

2. Blessing

    On the other hand, the Lord always poured out rain as a blessing on His people when they were walking in obedience to Him. As we have already seen from the book of Deuteronomy the Lord declared:

    > *And it shall come to pass, if ye* **shall hearken diligently unto my commandments** *which I command you this day, to love the LORD your God, and to serve him with all your heart and with all your soul,* ***That I will give you the rain*** *of your land in his due season, the first rain and the latter rain, that thou mayest gather in thy corn, and thy wine, and thine oil (Deu 11:13-14)*

The Lord would always bless His people with rain when they were walking in obedience with Him. Part of the purpose of the rain was to bless His people for their obedience and faithfulness unto Him.

3. Fruitfulness

The third purpose of the rains was that of fruitfulness. The rains not only provided water for the Israelites, they also nourished the ground so that it could produce crops. The early and latter rains were what allowed the harvests to occur.

In the time of Elijah, the nation was greatly lacking provision because there had been no rain for three- and one-half years according to the Word of the Lord. The lack of rain led to a famine in the land. The ground had not been fruitful because there had been no rain upon it. (1 Kings 18:2). No rain meant no harvest.

When the Lord provided rain though, we see that it resulted in fruitfulness. The rain of the Lord caused the fruitfulness of the ground. As we saw in Deuteronomy, it was when the Lord provided the rain that the earth brought forth the corn, the wine and the oil.

> *That I will give you the rain of your land in his due season, the first rain and the latter rain*__**, that thou mayest gather in thy corn, and thy wine, and thine oil.**__ *(Deu 11:13-14)*

The purpose of the rain was to bring forth a harvest (Heb 6:7). The purpose of rain was not just the blessing of rain itself, as much of a blessing as that is, it was given with the intention of bringing forth harvest. The purpose of rain was for fruitfulness and harvest.

Having seen what the early and latter rains were and what their purpose was, we now want to look more specifically at what the Lord has to say about them. Scripture will always interpret scripture and we will spend some time here letting it do just that as we look at the mentions of the early and latter rains throughout the Word. We will start this by looking at what the Lord said through James in the New Testament regarding the early and latter rains. As we do this, the reader is encouraged to remember what we have learned above. As we move through these next points, the reader will hopefully see how the Lord weaves together His tapestry of truth regarding the rains, through His Word.

C. James and the rains.

Rain is mentioned approximately ten times in the New Testament, but the only book that specifically mentions the early and latter rains is the book of James. The latter rains are mentioned approximately six times through the Old Testament, but only once in the New. James is the only New Testament writer through whom the Lord spoke through regarding the latter rains, but within this short mention there is a wealth of truth for us to glean.

In James 5 we read:

> *Be patient therefore, brethren, unto the coming of the Lord. Behold, the husbandman waiteth for the precious fruit of the earth, and hath long patience for it, until he receive the **early and latter rain**. Be ye also patient; stablish your hearts: for the coming of the Lord draweth nigh. (Jas 5:7-8)*

James here started and finished with a focus on the coming of the Lord. That is where he was directing the focus too, the coming of the Lord.

James started off by exhorting the believers to remain patient unto the coming of the Lord. He then closed by telling them to again remain patient, for the coming of the Lord draws nigh, that is draws close or approaches. In between these two statements, James gave an analogy to try and communicate a spiritual truth to the reader and it is here that we see the reference to the latter rains.

James compared the coming of the Lord to a husbandman. A husbandman is a farmer or land worker. They are farmers who work the ground for crops. James stated that these farmers wait for the precious fruit of the earth. They don't reap their reward straight away, they wait for it. In fact they have long patience for it. The Greek word for patience, as used here, is also translated "long suffering or patiently enduring". These farmers wait for an extended period of time. There is a period of patience.

James then went on to say that the husbandmen were patient enough to wait for the early and latter rains. James here was writing to Jewish believers. He was writing to those who understood the seasons of the land of Israel. As we have seen above, Israel had two separate rain periods, each with their own unique harvests. The early rains brought the grain harvests of corn, wheat and barley whereas the latter rains brought the fruit harvest, the wine and the oil.

The point that James was making, was that a farmer would not be satisfied with only the first rains and first harvest. They patiently endure the dry months, waiting for the latter rains and the harvest associated with them. The farmers endure to receive the fulness of harvest.

So too is it with the coming of the Lord. The Lord is waiting until the early and latter rains have fallen on the earth. He is waiting until He has received the fulness of harvest. The day of the Lord comes, but not until the latter rains have fallen and the harvest has been reaped. Just as the husbandman waits for both the early and the latter rains so too does the Lord. The day of the Lord waits for the latter rains.

The message of James was for the Hebrew believers to be patient in this time. For the Jewish believers, the struggle with patience came because they were experiencing and living in the days of the early rains.

Jesus died upon the cross during the feast of Passover fulfilling all of the Old Testament truth typified in this great occasion. Fifty days later, on the Great Day of Pentecost, the Spirit descended as tongues of fire upon the one hundred and twenty gathered together in unity and obedience unto the Word of Jesus. Here, the early spiritual rains of the Lord fell, as the Spirit was poured out upon the people of God. It was here that Peter quoted the prophet Joel stating:

> *But Peter, standing up with the eleven, lifted up his voice, and said unto them, Ye men of Judaea, and all ye that dwell at Jerusalem, be this known unto you, and hearken to my words: For these are not drunken, as ye suppose, seeing it is but the third hour of the day. But this is that which was spoken by the prophet Joel; And it shall come to pass in the last days, saith God,* **_I will pour out of my Spirit_** *upon all flesh: and your sons and your daughters shall prophesy, and your young men shall see visions, and your old men shall dream dreams: And on my servants and on my handmaidens I will pour out in those days of my Spirit; and they shall prophesy: (Act 2:14-18)*

The Spirit was being poured out upon the people of God. The natural early rains of Pentecost were finding their spiritual fulfillment as the Spirit was being poured out upon the people of God. It was after this Spirit inspired speech of Peter, that on that very day, three thousand souls were added to the Church (Acts 2:41). The early spiritual rains were falling and with them a spiritual harvest was being reaped.

The Hebrew believers were living in and experiencing this early rain and the harvest from it and were looking for the return of Jesus. The words of the Lord through James to them though, was for them to be patient. That just as in the natural the farmer waits for the early rains and the latter rains with their respective harvests, so too does the Lord. Whilst the Church was experiencing the early rains and the harvest that came from these, there was still a latter rain period to come. During this time, or the gap between the two, the call for believers was to be patient. Just as the Lord is patient, so too were the New Testament believers called to be.

What we see from this example in James is illustrated on the next page:

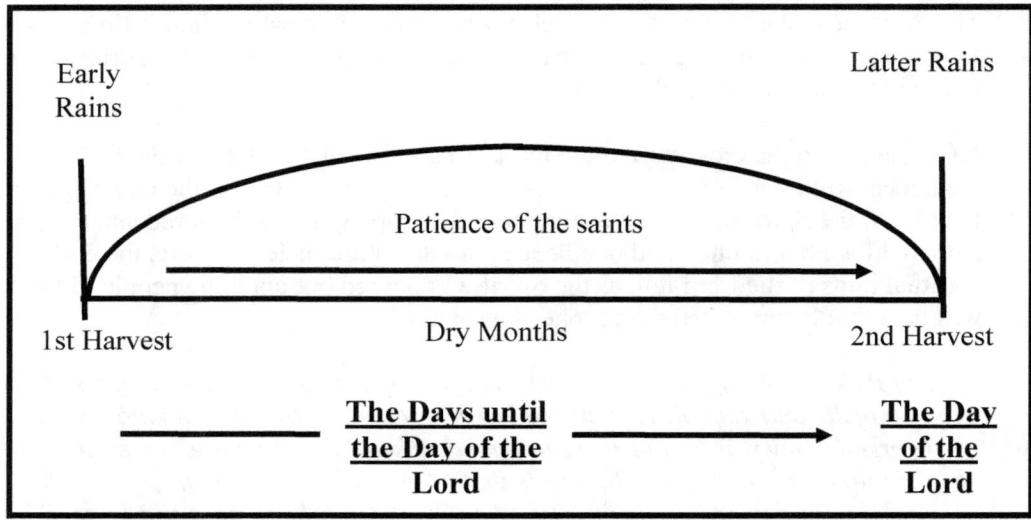

We see above that the coming of the Lord is likened by James to a farmer waiting for his crops. Whilst the farmer may receive the early rains and the harvest that comes from them, he patiently endures the dry months until he also receives the latter rains and the harvest that comes from them too. No farmer is satisfied with just one harvest! So too is it with the Lord. The early Church was looking for the coming of the Lord. James stated that whilst it is drawing nigh, before He comes again there must first be the latter rains and the harvest from these. Just as the Lord is patient to receive the fulness of harvest so too must the people of God be.

When we stop to consider the message of James here, we can start to see a link between this example and that of our earlier example of the ten virgins.

Both of these examples reference the day of the Lord. James calls it the coming of the Lord whereas in the parable of the ten virgins it is referred to as the return of the bridegroom.

Both reference a delay in the coming of this. In James it is the farmer waiting until he has received the early and latter rains (it is the time of the Lord's patience), in the parable it is called the delay in the bridegroom coming.

Finally, both also reference a point when He will come. In James it is after the early and latter rains have been received, in the parable it is at the midnight hour.

These thoughts are condensed in the table below:

	JAMES	10 VIRGINS
DAY OF THE LORD	The coming of the Lord	Return of the bridegroom
THE DELAY	Patience of the farmer	Delay in His coming
THE DAY OF RETURN	After both rains and harvests	The midnight hour

The similarities between these two examples can further be seen by the following diagram:

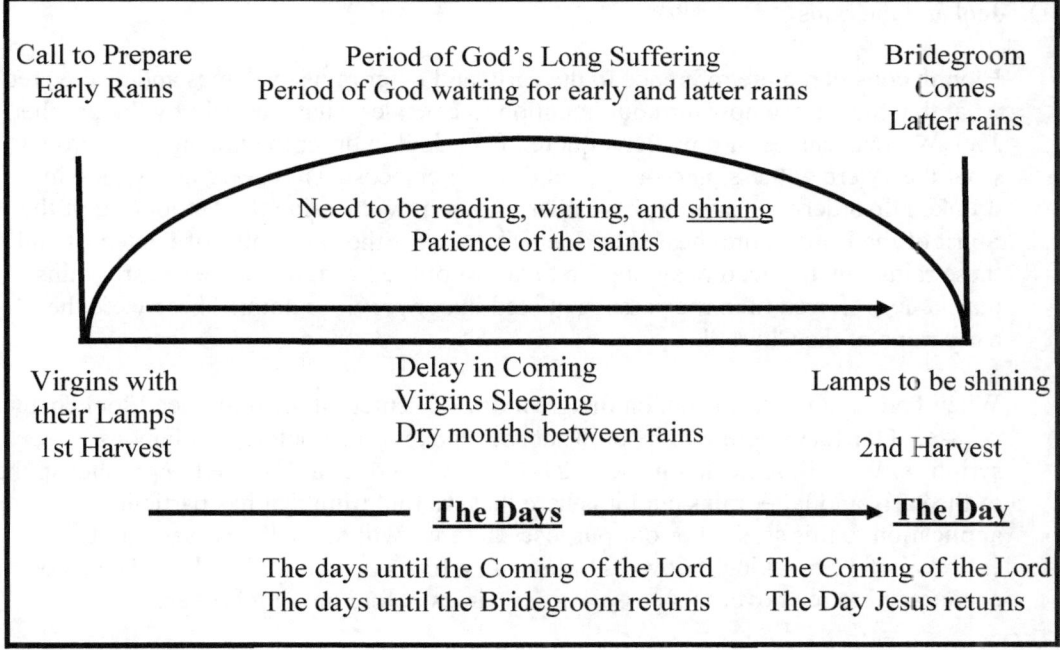

From this example of James we see that the message to the Hebrew believers was to be patient just as the Lord is being patient. The Lord is waiting for the fulness of the harvest from the early **and** the latter rains. Whilst the believers at the time of James' writing were experiencing the early rains, there was yet a time appointed for the latter rains. These rains would bring in the fulness of harvest and this time would be linked with the coming of the Lord.

As believers, we know that the day of the Lord has not yet come, but it is coming. The truth is, that we are in the days of His return. With the parable of the ten virgins, we noted that there exists a call for believers to be as the wise virgins and start preparing for the return of the King. The call has gone out and we need to be ready with the double portion of oil. When we add the thought of James to this, as illustrated above, we see that the time of His return, the time of the call to prepare, is also marked by the time of the latter rains. There is further truth added here by James. Whilst there is the call for believers to be ready, waiting and shining, scripture also shows forth that the time of the return of the bridegroom is also linked to the period of the latter rains.

Before the day of the Lord, according to the gospel of James the latter rains will fall and the Lord will receive the fulness of His harvest. He will not come until this occurs. He is waiting for the fulness of His precious fruit upon the earth. In the days just prior to His return there will be the latter rains and the harvest that these produce.

Scripture would point to the fact that we are in these days, and it is this thought that leads us to our next point.

D. Joel and the rains

Having considered the reference to the early and latter rains by James and discovered what that meant, we now turn our attention to consider what was said by the prophet Joel. We read earlier of how Peter quoted from Joel in order to explain to the crowd what they were witnessing on the great day of Pentecost. They were not witnessing drunken disorderly behaviour, but rather they were witnessing the outpouring of the Spirit of the Lord as prophesied by Joel. These were the early rains of Pentecost and these rains saw the accompanying first harvest of the Lord. It was these early rains that James referred to in the passage quoted in our previous point. These were the early rains of the Church!

When Peter quoted from Joel on the great day of Pentecost, he referenced Joel chapter 2:28-32. Our focus here will be on what Joel spoke of just before this famous scripture. We will focus in on Joel 2:21-27. It is here we find where the prophet spoke of the early and latter rains, and it is here that we find truth that has particular application to this study. For our purposes here we will quote the passage in its entirety before breaking it down a little, with a focus on verse 23 and 24. The reader is encouraged to read over this passage a few times before moving forward.

> *Fear not, O land; be glad and rejoice: for the LORD will do great things. Be not afraid, ye beasts of the field: for the pastures of the wilderness do spring, for the tree beareth her fruit, the fig tree and the vine do yield their strength. Be glad then, ye children of Zion, and rejoice in the LORD your God: for* **he hath given you the former rain moderately**, *and he will cause to come down for you the rain,* **the former rain, and the latter rain in the first month**. *And the floors shall be full of wheat, and the fats shall overflow with wine and oil. And I will restore to you the years that the locust hath eaten, the cankerworm, and the caterpiller, and the palmerworm, my great army which I sent among you. And ye shall eat in plenty, and be satisfied, and praise the name of the LORD your God, that hath dealt wondrously with you: and my people shall never be ashamed. And ye shall know that I am in the midst of Israel, and that I am the LORD your God, and none else: and my people shall never be ashamed. (Joe 2:21-27)*

Joel in this passage spoke of the Lord having mercy upon His people and returning unto them with favour. Within these few verses there are a number of points for us to glean. As we work through these, the reader should start to see the truths that we have discovered within this section start to come together.

1. The early rains

   Be glad then, ye children of Zion, and rejoice in the LORD your God: for he hath given you the former rain moderately (vs 23)

The prophet called the people to rejoice in the Lord for He had given them the former rains. This Hebrew word is also translated early rains and refers to the early rains that the nation of Israel received. If we consider the tense here, we can see that this refers to something that had been done. Note the language used:

> *rejoice in the LORD your God<u>**: for he hath given you**</u> the former rain moderately (vs 23)*

The former rains had been given and they had been given moderately. The rains had come from the Lord and He had given them to Israel. This an action that had already occurred.

2. The double portion of rain

and he will cause to come down for you the rain, the former rain, and the latter rain in the first month. (vs 23)

The tense then shifts as Joel said that the Lord will cause to come down for you the rain. This is not something that has happened, but something that will happen. The children of Zion were to rejoice for the former rain had been given, but there were rains still to be brought by the Lord. The former rain had come and had come moderately, **BUT** there was still future rains that were to occur. These future rains hadn't yet come.

If we consider this in light of the application of Joel 2:28-32 being quoted by Peter as applying to the great day of Pentecost, we understand that the Great Day of Pentecost was when the Lord had caused the early or former rains to come. As Peter quoted from Joel, he spoke of what the Lord was doing. The Lord was pouring out the early rain. On the day of Pentecost the early rains began falling on the early Church.

But just as with the husbandmen spoken of by James, there remains a future rain yet to occur. This was the time of patience that the early Church believers had to endure. Whilst the early rains had been given, there was still a future period of rain yet to come. The words of the Lord through James mirror the future rains spoken of by Joel here. The Lord had caused the early rains to fall, but there remained future rains that "He will cause to come down". Again we see the Word confirm two distinct periods of rain.

Joel then went on to describe these future rains. He said that the Lord would cause to come down the former rains and the latter rains together. The rains that the Lord would cause to come down, would not just be the latter rains, but the latter and the former rains together. This would be a double potion of outpouring. This would be two groups of rain at once. It is a double portion. This would be a supernatural event caused by the Lord as He would pour out a double portion of

His Spirit upon His people. This season would see the former and the latter rains fall together.

We see the truth of this double portion align with the truth of the double portion of oil from the parable of the ten virgins. The last days require a double portion of oil and as we have seen throughout this text, infilling always comes from the Lord. The latter rains are going to be rains of a double portion for the people of God. There will be a double portion available for the wise believers, so that they are ready, waiting and shining for the Lord's return. The Word of the Lord shows us that the rains are coming, ours is to dig in preparation that we might receive them. We recognise our need, but He supplies the double portion of rain.

3. The first month

in the first month (vs 23)

Joel stated that the former rains and the latter rains would fall together in the first month. Upon first reading this we can be a little thrown off, because as we have already discussed in this study it was the early rains that fell in the first and third months. If Joel is referring to the first month, then isn't he referring to the period of the early rains?

To properly interpret this there are two things for us to take note of. Firstly, Joel had already addressed the early rains in this passage. He had said that they had already fallen. That part had been completed. The early or former rains had been given moderately. It is a completed action. Having looked at the spiritual interpretation of this we see the truth that the early rains fell on the Great Day of Pentecost. The rains of the first month have already fallen upon the Church of God. Joel, having spoken of these former rains having already occurred then stated that there were future rains to come. What then does he mean by the former and latter rains falling in the first month?

The second thing for us to be mindful of is that the Jewish calendar actually consisted of two simultaneous years. There was the civil year and the sacred year. The first month of the sacred year was actually the seventh month of the civil year and the first month of the civil year was actually the seventh month of the sacred year. To break this down a little bit further and hopefully explain it further, if we consider the feasts of the Lord we see:

> Passover occurred in the first month of the sacred year and the seventh month of the civil year.
>
> Pentecost happened in the third month of the sacred year and the ninth month of the civil year.

Tabernacles occurred in the seventh month of the sacred year and first month of the civil year.

Joel as we have already seen, had spoken of the early rains as having happened. These were the rains of Passover and Pentecost, so he was not speaking of the first month of the sacred year.

Joel spoke of these rains as yet to come. These would be the former rains and the latter rains together and these would fall in the feast of Tabernacles in the seventh month of the sacred year **BUT** the first month of the civil year. This is what Joel referred to as the first month. He was referring to the first month of the civil year. This double portion of rain would fall in the first month of the civil year, which was also the seventh month of the sacred year and linked with the feast of Tabernacles.

Throughout our study thus far we have seen that the early and latter rains are two distinct periods and between them exists a gap. This is the period of the dry months, the delay of the bridegroom, the period of the patience of the saints and the period of God's longsuffering. This same truth was emphasised by Joel. The early rains have fallen, but there remains the time of the latter rains yet to come. There exists a gap between the rains that have fallen and those that are yet to fall. When these rains come though, it will be a period of a double portion, the former and the latter together.

4. The double portion of harvest

And the floors shall be full of wheat, and the fats shall overflow with wine and oil. (Joe 2:24)

When we looked at what the early and latter rains were, we discovered that they were two separate periods of rain linked to two separate harvests. The early rains brought the grain harvest of wheat, barley and corn. The latter rains brought the fruit harvest, the wine from the grape and the oil from the olive.

What we see here with Joel is that the double portion of rain that is to fall brings with it a double portion of harvest. The prophet said that the floors will be full of wheat, wine and oil. These are separate harvests, separated by a period of dry months, yet here united. As the Lord pours out a double portion of His rain, the former and latter together. we will see a double portion of harvest. This is two harvests in one. It will be a double portion of harvest. The double portion of rains that are to fall will see a double portion of harvest reaped.

5. The restoration

And I will restore to you the years that the locust hath eaten, the cankerworm, and the caterpiller, and the palmerworm, my great army which I sent among you. (Joe 2:25)

The words of the Lord through Joel finished with a promise of restoration. The double portion of rains which will produce the double portion of harvest will also bring a restoration of that which had been lost.

In the natural, the produce of the harvest from the former rains would have been stored for gradual use in the future. This was a reserve that was to be used until the next harvest of grain. This was a common farming practice. Joseph did this in Egypt when he stored up the seven good years produce to get the nation through the seven bad years that were prophesied. The harvest was stored for future provision.

The implication here is that this reserve had been plundered by the locust, the cankerworm, the caterpillar and the palmerworm. All that had been reaped from the harvest of the former rains had been lost. The provision that had been stored for the people had been devoured in the period between the rains.

The Lord here states that it was He who sent these armies which had devoured the produce of the harvest. Throughout scripture the plagues referenced by Joel here, always come as a judgement of the Lord to a people who have turned away from Him. They are a prompt from the Lord to grab His people's attention and cause them to turn back to Him.

As we have moved through this section, we have seen how the former rains apply to the birth of the early Church on the day of Pentecost and the harvest that accompanied this and continued through the days of the early Church. From history we know that after this time the Church would enter what is now known as the dark ages of the Church. These were indeed periods of dryness, and it was during these dry months that the harvest of truths from the former rains were eaten away and lost. Much was lost as the Church went through the dry days that followed the early rains.

The promise we have in Joel though, is that not only will there be a double portion of rain in the latter days, but there will also be a double portion of harvest **AND** a restoration of all the years that have been lost. There is indeed to be a great move of the Spirit and one that we possibly can't quite grasp the magnitude of. As the people of the Lord return unto Him, there is going to be a blessing and restoration such as there has never been seen in Church history. There will be an outpouring, a harvest and a restoration of lost years. The Lord in the period of the latter rains will bring restoration of truth to His people.

This portion of scripture from Joel contains so much prophetic truth for believers and the Church of today. That which we have discovered is illustrated below:

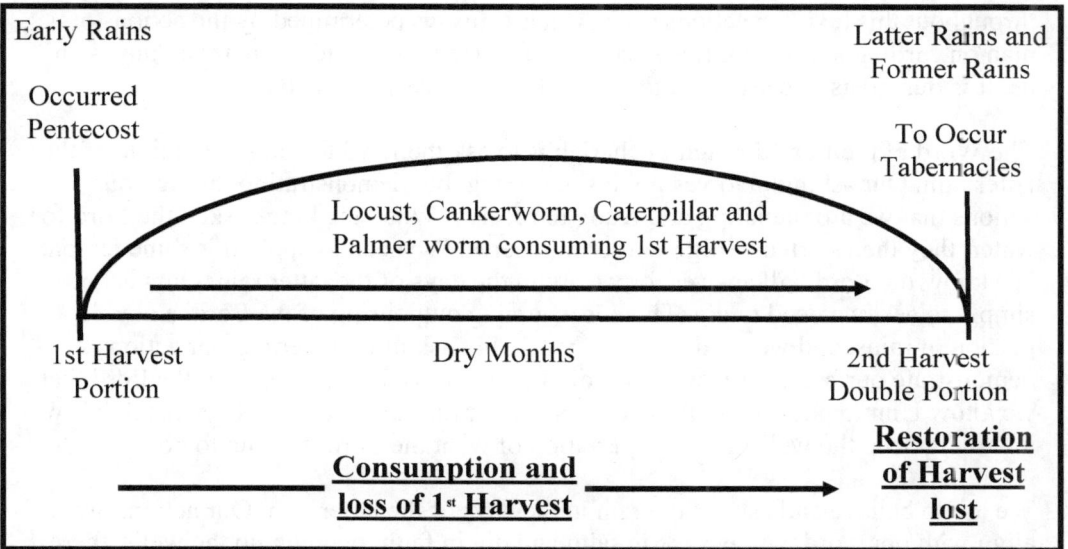

Through the prophet Joel, the Word of the Lord tells us that the former rains have already come and that they were given moderately. Joel stated that there was a period of rain that was yet to come. This is the period of latter rain. The latter rains for the Church and the people of God will not be like the former. Whilst we see in scripture the magnificent things that happened and how the Church grew in the period of the early rains, the Word of the Lord through Joel is that the former rains were given moderately. This will not be the case with the latter rains! The latter rains will see a great outpouring. There will be a double portion of rain that will see a double portion of harvest and a restoration of things that were lost in between the rains. Much harvest will be reaped under the outpouring of the latter rains!

E. Zechariah and the rains

The final mention of latter rains that we will consider in this section is found in the book of Zechariah. There the prophets said:

> *Ask ye of the LORD rain in the **time of the latter rain**; so the LORD shall make bright clouds, and give them showers of rain, to every one grass in the field. (Zec 10:1)*

The words of the Lord through Zechariah here are that the people of the Lord are to ask the Lord for the rains in the time of the latter rain. We are not to just sit back and expect the rains to come. We are to ask the Lord for them. It is when we ask, in the time of the latter rain, that the Lord then sends the showers of rain.

The promise of the Lord is that in the time of the latter rain, if His people ask, He will provide. If we ask, the Lord will provide and there will be a harvest. We see again here that there is a responsibility that lies on the part of man. As we have said throughout this text, the actions of heaven are always determined by the actions of man on earth, good or bad. If we seek the rain, He will provide it, but the onus is on us. It is ours to ask, to seek and to knock that we may then receive.

The Word of the Lord through Zechariah is to ask the Lord for rain in the time of the latter rain. Our asking involves not just speaking, but demonstrating through our actions that we are preparing and ready to receive. When the kings asked the Lord for water, they then started to dig in order to receive. We need to apply this same lesson. We know the Lord will answer for we are in the days of the latter rain. Ours is not simply to ask, we need to dig. There is a coming outpouring of the Lord, a double portion of rains, and we need to not only ask, but ask in faith, letting our actions demonstrate our belief. It is when we dig the seven wells and press into the Lord that we allow Him to pour out in these days a greater rain than has ever been received. We are to dig deep the wells in full expectation of what the Lord is going to do!

We are to believe and ask for the rain in the days of the latter rain. Our actions are to align with our words. As we ask in faith and dig in faith, opening up the wells, there will come a great outpouring upon the people of the Lord.

F. Summary

In this section we have considered the Biblical theme of the early and latter rains. In doing this we have discovered that these rains refer to two distinct periods of rainfall in the nation of Israel. The early rains fell in the early part of the year and supported the grain harvest of wheat, barley and corn. These rains were associated with the feasts of Passover and Pentecost. The latter rains fell midway through the year and were associated with the fruit harvest and the feast of Tabernacles. Between these two periods of rain were the dry months, where there was no rain and the nation lived off the gleanings of their harvests.

As we have considered all of this, we have come to understand the spiritual application. The early rains point spiritually to the rains of Pentecost when the Church was born, and a great harvest was reaped. These were the early spiritual rains that saw the Church birthed. The latter rains point to a time yet to come and a harvest that is yet to come. Just as certainly as there were former rains, so too will there be latter rains. These are the rains that the farmer waits for. The period in between these two rains, the dry months, is the period that James tells us is for the patience of the saints. The Lord, in this time waits patiently as the husbandmen, until He has received the early and latter rains and the fulness of harvest.

Spiritually the latter are rains still to come. The Church has experienced the early rains at Pentecost, but we are yet to experience the fulness of the latter rains. These will not be normal rains, but rather a double portion of rain. These will be the former and the latter rains together and they will bring with them a double portion of harvest. Just before the coming of the Lord we will see a double portion of rain and a double portion of harvest. Again we see a double portion associated with the Day of the Lord. Hopefully enough has been said so far for the reader to understand the days that we are in. The writer is not saying that we are at the day of the Lord, but we are nearing its approach. Such is not said to put fear into the heart of the reader, but rather as a call to understand the urgency of the days we are in. We are in the period of the latter rains, and it is a period where God is going to pour out the former and the latter rains together. There is going to be a double portion of rain and a double portion of harvest that will see the lost harvest restored.

The call to believers and the Church in this time is to dig. Just as the Lord promised rain through the prophet Elisha to the united armies, so too is there a promise of rain to the people of God. Our call is the same as that of the armies, we need to dig. Zechariah's words were to ask the Lord for rain in the time of the latter rain. Through this study we have seen that the Lord always responds to the actions of man. If we are truly wanting the double portion of rain then we need to be digging and maintaining the wells that the Lord has directed us to dig.

The united armies had to be prepared for the blessing of the Lord that was coming. The Lord told them it was coming, but it was their choice to be obedient and dig. If they would dig then they would receive a blessing that would infill, sustain and bring victory. Our call is no less and no different. The Lord has promised the rains. He has laid out in His Word that there is going to be an outpouring of His Spirit before His return. The rains are coming! As Elijah saw the small cloud the size of a man's fist and in faith declared the mighty downpour that was coming, so too is the case for believers and the Church today. The clouds are forming, the rain is coming, His people need to dig.

The message of the early and the latter rains to the people of God is to dig. If we truly want all that He has for us and all that comes from His outpouring, then we need to be pressing into the Lord as never before. We need to dig the wells! Now is the time. His Spirit is stirring in His people and calling them to go deeper than they have before. It is time to shake of lethargy and the cares of the world and press into the Lord, placing Him as the primary focus of our lives.

The victory comes when His glory reflects. His glory reflects when His people and churches are infilled. His people and churches are infilled when they dig and press into the Lord. It all starts with us. If we are to reflect His glory and see revival overtake our streets, towns, states and countries then it is up to us to seek Him with a depth we possibly haven't had before. The Lord is calling. Revivals Call is in the air. Our choice is whether we will respond or not! We are to be a people who in faith seek the Lord for His rain in the time of the latter rain.

G. The warning of Jeremiah

Whilst not on the topic of the early and latter rains, there is a verse in Jeremiah that the writer was prompted on as he mediated on the call for the people of God to dig in order to receive the blessing of the coming latter rains.
We read in Jeremiah 2 of one of the great concerns for the people of God today:

> *For my people have committed two evils; they have forsaken me the fountain of living waters, and hewed them out cisterns, broken cisterns, that can hold no water. (Jer 2:13)*

Here the prophet, spoke of the nation of Israel, and told them that they had committed two sins. The first is that they had forsaken the Lord, the fountain of living waters. The nation had turned their back on the Lord and no longer looked to Him. They had forsaken the Lord. They had turned from Him who was their source and supply.

Their second sin was that they had hewed out their own cisterns. The people had not only forsaken the Lord as their fountain of living water, but they had also sought their own supply of water. The nation of Israel had turned their back on the Lord and fallen into idolatrous practices, hewing out their own ways of worshipping rather than seeking the Lord according to His Word.

The writer is not saying that the Church has fallen into an idolatrous state, or that it has turned its back on the Lord. Within this verse of Jeremiah though there is a warning to us that we need to take heed of.

Earlier in our study, when we investigated the vision of Zechariah and the Golden Lampstand, we covered seven scriptural wells that allow us as believers and Churches to receive the infilling of the Spirit. These were:

1. The well of prayer.
2. The well of reading and meditating on the Word.
3. The well of sensitivity to the Holy Spirit.
4. The well of faith.
5. The well of obedience.
6. The well of tongues.
7. The well of praise and worship.

When we look over this list, none of these things should strike us as being out of place. One of the questions we need to ask ourselves though is how much place or priority do these have in our individual lives and services? Are we pressing into the fountain of living water to receive all that He has, or do we scale these down to an acceptable level, hewing out our own cisterns that fit our life and promote a service we think people will want to come to? Is it His wells, or our cisterns that are evident? One of the great dangers that exists for us as individuals and corporately as the Church is when we try to turn down the dimmer switch on the spiritual truths we are called to proclaim in order to make people feel more comfortable. We have wrongly assumed that it is the responsibility of humans to convert individuals when it is in fact the function of the Holy Spirit. The Holy Spirit can only work effectively though if we allow Him. If we are not allowing a full flow of His Oil into our wells and allowing His light to shine as brightly as it should, how can we expect the lives of people to be dramatically changed?

Again, the reader is asked to understand that the writer is not judging anyone or any Church, but as the writer has been preparing this study the Lord has constantly prompted him on the vital importance of the above-mentioned wells. If we are truly wanting to receive the fulness of the latter rains and all that comes with them, we cannot afford to be in a place where we have our own cisterns, broken cisterns that hold no water. The words of Jeremiah are a warning for us all to make sure that we are focused on the fountain of living waters and His wells. It is a warning to check that we haven't veered off the path in any degree and made for ourselves cisterns of convenience that fit our lives better.

Victory comes when His glory reflects off the wells that are full. Broken cisterns can't hold water! There can be no reflection off a broken cistern. We need the fountain of living water and His wells. Any time we try and replace the wells of the Lord, we end up with an inferior product that can't fulfill the role of a well. Any time we try and scale these down to make them fit our lives better or appear more acceptable we end up with broken cisterns, that though they may look similar, they cannot fulfill the role of a well. We end up with broken cisterns, that hold no water.

The only way that we can reflect His Glory is by seeking Him through the wells that allow His infilling. It is only as we dig deep into the above-mentioned wells, giving them priority in our lives and services, that we can then receive the fulness of infilling from the fountain of living waters. If we are going to receive the double portion of the latter rains, then we need to be digging deep into His wells. In these days, as we ask the Lord for His rain, we need to make sure that we are attending to His wells. We are to embrace those wells, dig them deep and maintain them. They need to be an ever-present feature of our lives and services.

The warning of Jeremiah is one for us to take hold of. If we aren't following His process of revival, we can't expect His fruit of revival. Revival starts when we focus on the Lord and dig His wells. It does not start when we attend to our own cisterns. We need to look to the source of the rains, the fountain of living water, and ask Him for His rain in these latter days!

CORRELATION OF THE VIRGINS AND THE RAINS

In this section we have considered the parable of the ten virgins and the topic of the early and latter rains. As we have progressed, we have at times mentioned the correlation of the two. We saw this particularly when we considered the parable of the ten virgins and that which James said about the early and latter rains. Here we will spend some time reemphasising the truths we discovered in each example and show the correlation that exists, so that the reader may fully see and appreciate the relationship between both of these examples. As we do this, the reader should start to see the picture that the Lord reveals in each of these examples, and how they speak of one and the same time. These references show revivals call to believers and the Church of today.

In order to do this, we will focus in on the key timeframes described in both examples. In each example we find that there is a starting point, an end point and a gap in between. Whilst different descriptions and language is used in each example, nevertheless the correlation is there for us to observe.

A. The Starting Point

   We noted with the early or former rains, that these were the rains associated with the grain harvest and occurred during the time of Passover and Pentecost. These were the early rains of the sacred year. We noted how Peter on the great day of Pentecost revealed the spiritual reality of this when he declared that God was outpouring the rain of His Spirit upon His people. According to the prophet Joel these were the former rains that had been given moderately. The early rains were the starting rains, the starting point.

The parable of the ten virgins started with the virgins going out to meet their bridegroom. There was a call to be ready to meet. The starting point in the parable was the virgins going to meet the bridegroom.

In relation to this, in Acts chapter 1 where it describes Jesus' ascension we read:

> *And when he had spoken these things, while they beheld, he was taken up; and a cloud received him out of their sight. And while they looked stedfastly toward heaven as he went up, behold, two men stood by them in white apparel; Which also said, Ye men of Galilee, why stand ye gazing up into heaven? this same Jesus, which is taken up from you into heaven,* **shall so come in like manner as ye have seen him go into heaven**. *(Act 1:9-11)*

The message here was that Jesus would return. Just as He left so also would He come again. The disciples here received the call of the return of Jesus, the return of the Bridegroom, by the two heavenly messengers. The call was that He is coming back. This was the call to be ready and this occurred in the time of the early rains, between Passover and Pentecost. From this point forward the disciples set about preparing His Church for His return.

So we see that the early rains and the call to the virgins both have the same starting point. They are both in that Passover/Pentecost period surrounding the birth of the early Church. Both have the same starting point.

B. The Gap

In the natural we discovered that there was a gap between the early and latter rains. The fourth, fifth and sixth months were dry months that separated the early rains from the latter rains. This gap between the rains is a period where God is waiting for the latter rains to come and the fulness of harvest that comes with them.

James referred to this same period as the period of Gods long patience or longsuffering, a sentiment echoed by Peter in 2 Peter 3:9. In between the rains, the Lord as the farmer, waits patiently. Joel in referencing the same period told us that this is a period where the locust, cankerworm, caterpillar and palmerworm had eaten the fruit from the harvest of the early rains.

In the parable of the virgins, this gap is referred to as the time of the bridegroom tarrying. The Greek word for tarrying here means to take one's time. The writer of Hebrews uses this same Greek word to describe that when Jesus returns, the time of tarrying will be over. The thought in Matthew of the bridegroom tarrying very much lines up with the thought of James where the Lord waits for the latter rains as the husbandmen. Just as the bridegroom tarries in coming so too does the farmer as he waits for the latter rains.

After the starting point we see that there is a gap in both examples which also correlate. They again speak of one and the same time. Between the rains is a period of tarrying.

C. The End Point

The end point is seen with the words of James that the Lord is waiting for the fruit of the earth produced by the latter rains. His coming draws nigh, He is just waiting for the rains and their harvest. Not just any rains though, but a double portion of rains and a double portion of harvest. Once that day comes, He comes.

With the virgins we see that at the midnight hour, the bridegroom came and the virgins needed to be ready to meet Him. There was no more waiting and no more gap. The day had arrived and those that weren't ready missed out. The key for the virgins in the day of the bridegroom's coming was the double portion of oil.

Whilst we have detailed this previously, we will repeat our illustration here so that the reader may see the alignment of what has been laid out.

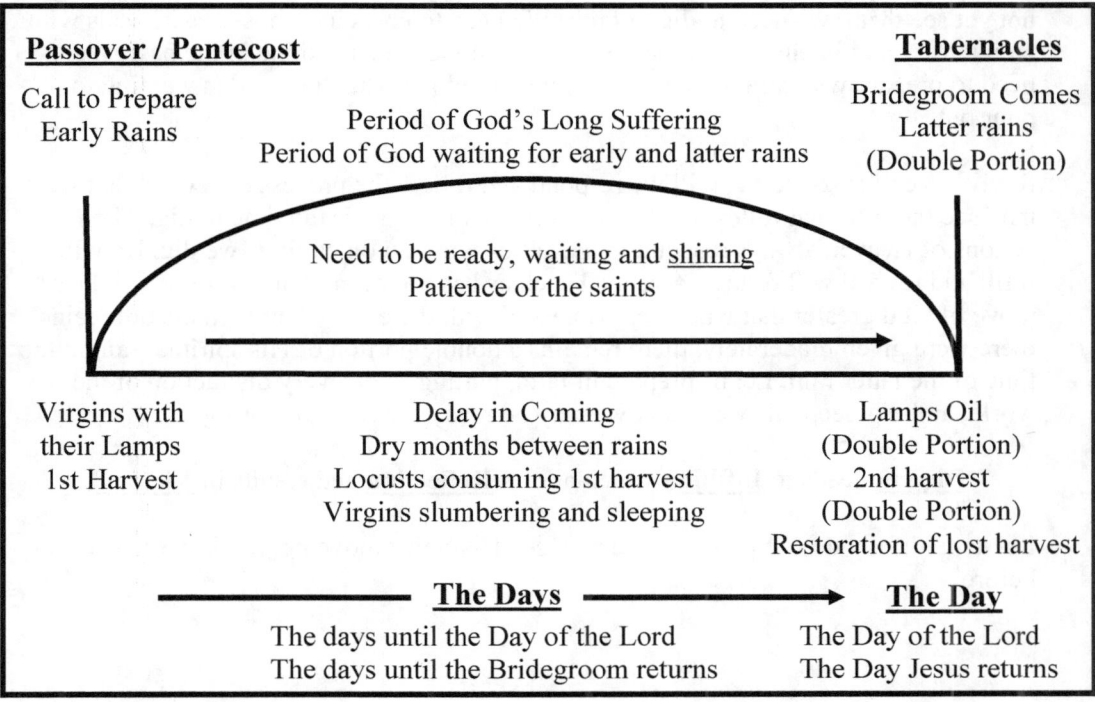

We are in the last of the last days and the call is going out for the bridegroom's return. We see here the linkages of the timeframes mentioned in the above points. Both refer to the same starting time, both have gaps of tarrying and waiting and both finish at the return of the Lord. What we also see is that whilst we are in the days of needing the double portion as the wise virgins, the supply for this comes through the double portion of rains in the time of the latter rain. The double portion of oil needed in the last days is supplied as the Lord pours out the former and the latter rains together. This sees not only a double portion of harvest, but also a restoration of all that has been lost in the 'dry months.' As believers and the Church, we are to seek the Lord for the rain in the time of the latter rain. We are to dig deep the wells in faith, believing for the promised outpouring of the Lord.

When Elisha gave the Word of the Lord to the three kings, they responded in faith, filling the valley full of wells for the promised outpouring of the Lord. At the time of digging there was no indication of water being provided. No rain had come, no water flowed. Their digging was an act of faith, believing that God would be true to His Word. They stepped out in faith, believing that their reviving would come as they were obedient unto the Lord.

As believers and churches, we are to mirror that same faith that we see evidenced in the Kings account. The truth of the Word shows us the promised rains of the Lord in the days before His return. He has declared that they are coming, and whilst we might not yet see them, we need to dig in faith. We need to press into those seven wells with an intensity and intentionality that exceeds anything we have done in the past. We need to prepare with a faith that sees the magnitude of what the Lord is wanting to pour out.

Revival's call is sounding, will we respond and follow the process of revival that we may see the fruit that follows? The rains are coming, now is the time to dig! The actions of Heaven always respond to the actions of man on earth. If we dig, He will infill and revival will follow. A revival such as has not been seen before. It will be a move of God greater that what was witnessed with the early Church. Whilst the rains there were given moderately, there remains a double portion of His spiritual rain in the time of the latter rain. Let us prepare in faith, putting aside every distraction of the world, and dig deep His wells that we may be ready for His outpouring.

<u>Digging</u> leads to **<u>Infilling</u>** which allows **<u>Reflection</u>** and results in **<u>Victory!</u>**

Let us faithfully do our part, that we may see His Spirit move upon this earth as never before.

.

PART C SUMMARY

Hopefully as we have gone through this section the writer has been able to effectively communicate the call of revival that the Lord has placed on his heart. Whilst scripture clearly tells us that no one knows the day of the Lord's return, it does describe what the days will be like in the period preceding this. Whilst we are not yet at the day of His return, we are nearing it!

From the examples we have considered in this section we can observe two things:

> Firstly, if we are to be ready and waiting as the wise virgins we need to have a double portion of oil. To be waiting is not enough. To have a portion of oil is not enough. We need to be ready and waiting with a double portion of oil. This is what separated the wise from the foolish.

> Secondly, we need to start digging! There is a double portion of spiritual rain coming and if we are to receive that and be ready with our double portion of oil, then we need to be digging the wells now. The foolish virgins missed out because they were not ready. Let us not make the same mistake! The armies couldn't wait until the rains came to start digging, they had to dig in faith before the rains came. The rains were promised, but it required man to step out in faith and believe that which God had said.

The day of the Lord is coming, but before that day comes there is a period of double portion. The Lord has told us that this is coming. He is waiting for these rains and the harvest they produce. Ours is to do our part and like the united armies, dig the wells so that we may receive the fulness of what He has for us. Victory comes when His people press in.

Revivals Call has sounded. It is calling the people of God across the world to a new depth of relationship. We are being called back to truths that the locust and cankerworm have

Part C Summary

eaten. We are being called to a place of intimacy that the early Church had, where Christ took precedence and life fitted in around Him. We are being called to a place where we look unto the Lord as our only fountain of living water and realise the need we have of Him if we are to truly see our world change.

There is coming an incredible time for believers and the Church. A time when His glory will reflect off all those He has infilled and we will see His Kingdom of light push back the kingdom of darkness. The time is coming, the cloud is on the horizon, the rains are coming and the responsibility is on us to prepare. Let us dig and maintain that which we have dug as we never have before, waiting for the coming of our beloved Saviour.

FINAL THOUGHTS

Final Thoughts

So concludes our study of "Reflecting His Glory, Revival's Call". It is the writer's sincere hope that the reader has been blessed through reading this and that the Lord has spoken to them through it.

This study has been a journey for the writer. In one sense the writer's heart has felt challenged by the Lord, seeing the need in his own life to attend to the wells and address areas that he has possibly neglected. In that sense this study has been a challenge not only to write but also to live out and apply. Throughout the preparation of this study the writer has felt the Lord calling him to a new depth of relationship.

On the other hand, the writer has been stirred with a spiritual excitement for what the Lord is wanting to do in His people and in His Church. There is such a magnificent promise awaiting the people of God if we can apply the truths from the account of 2 Kings 3. Those four simple steps have such a profound outworking. We open the wells, and the Lord responds and infills. He then shines and brings about the victory as His light pushes back the spiritual darkness that has infiltrated our lives, towns, states and countries. We attend to the process of revival, and He then brings forth the fruit of revival. Revival is coming, a mighty revival, but we have to dig. The Lord is wanting us to fill the valleys full of diches that His Spirit may flow freely and fully into our lives that we may reflect His glory to a world that desperately needs to see it.

There is a double portion of rain coming. We are coming to a period when the early and the latter rains will fall together and with them will be a double portion of harvest and a restoration of that which has been lost. It will be a move of God such as has never been seen. It is one that should stir the spiritual hunger within us. But we cannot afford to wait until we see the clouds. Like the kings and their armies, we have to step out in faith, believing the Lord for His promised rains and start digging. Now is the time to dig that we might receive His double portion of oil and be ready, waiting and shining upon our Bridegroom's return.

We as the people of God are called to reflect His glory. Revivals call has sounded, do we have an ear to hear what the Spirit is saying to His Church? Will we answer the call?

May we ever seek Him deeper and have Him as the absolute priority of our lives.

Blessings in Christ,

Courtney A Laird.

SUPPLEMENTAL

Supplemental

Throughout this text, the writer has put forth a number of diagrams, with the purpose of trying to communicate further that which has been discussed. Our aim here is to bring all of these diagrams together so that the reader may see how those things we have looked at interlock with each other. Scripture at times is a divine jigsaw. Ours is not to ever force the pieces, but as we study the Word and rely on sound interpretation, the pieces should naturally start to fit.

As a reminder to the reader, the following thoughts have been looked at in diagrammatic form:

A. We started with a consideration of the Tabernacle of Moses and considered its layout concerning the Outer Court, the Holy Place, the Most Holy Place and their respective light sources.

B. We then looked at how the areas of the Tabernacle point to the three distinct ages, i.e. the age of sacrifice, the Church age and the Kingdom age. Further to this we then saw that there are also three distinct dispensations of time in relation to God's dealing with man. There is the dispensation of the Father, the dispensation of the Son and the dispensation of the Holy Spirit. In our consideration of these we saw that the dispensation of the Holy Spirit and the Church age are intrinsically linked.

C. We then considered the vision of Zechariah and the Golden Lampstand and saw that this vision contained a Golden Bowl with seven pipes coming out of it that led to the lamps of the Lampstand. It is through these seven pipes that the oil flows and enables the Lampstand to function.

D. Finally, we looked at the parable of the 10 virgins and the example of the early and latter rains. We saw that these speak of one and the same time, with a focus on the return of Jesus.

When we place the pieces of this study together, we see the below:

Supplemental

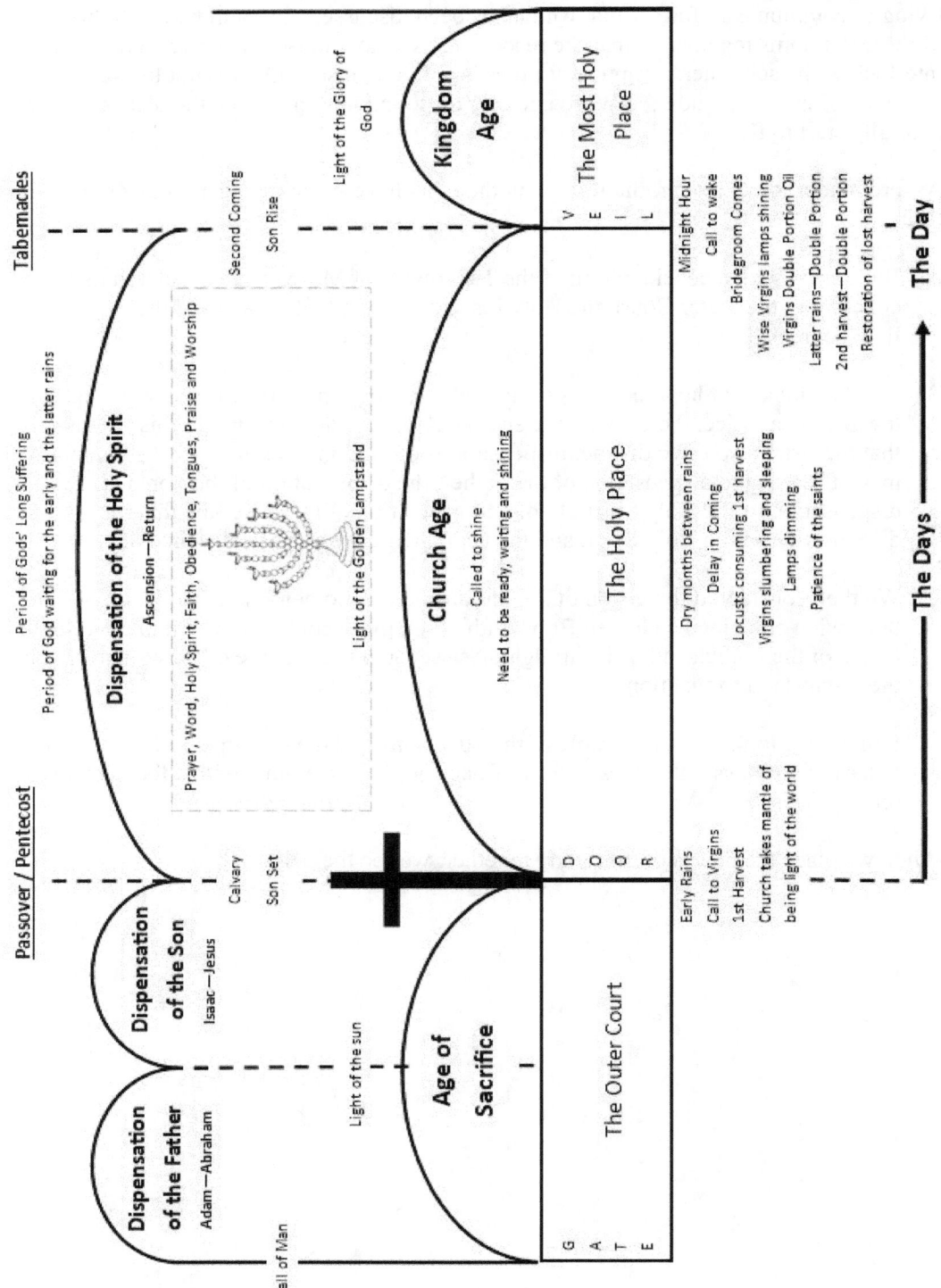

Supplemental

Hopefully in bringing all of the pieces together in visual form, the reader may more readily understand the fulness of that which the Lord has placed on the writer's heart. For any questions that remain the reader is encouraged to look back at the parts of this text that deal with the area of concern.

Arise, shine; for thy light is come, and the glory of the LORD is risen upon thee. For, behold, the darkness shall cover the earth, and gross darkness the people: but the LORD shall arise upon thee, and his glory shall be seen upon thee. And the Gentiles shall come to thy light, and kings to the brightness of thy rising. Lift up thine eyes round about, and see: all they gather themselves together, they come to thee: thy sons shall come from far, and thy daughters shall be nursed at thy side.
(Isa 60:1-4)

OTHER BOOKS BY THE AUTHOR

If my people, which are called by my name, shall humble themselves, and pray, and seek my face, and turn from their wicked ways; then will I hear from heaven, and will forgive their sin, and will heal their land. (2Ch 7:14)

In 2 Chronicles we read of the temple of the Lord being built by King Solomon after many years of planning and preparation by King David. Just after the Temple's dedication, we read in 2 Chronicles 7:11-16 that the Lord spoke to Solomon through a dream. It is the words of the Lord to Solomon in this dream that form the basis of this study. As we examine this dialogue, we discover that there are a number of biblical truths that flow from this encounter.

If My People examines what these truths are and follows them through scripture before considering their application to the Church. The call of the Lord in 2 Chronicles is one that echoes to the Church of today. The precedent that the Lord set forth to Solomon has application to us as believers. Within the pages of this study we well discover how the call of "If My People" applies to the Church of today and the responsibilities that come with it. The Lord has much for His Church and His people if they can fulfill His call of "If My People'.

www.ingramcontent.com/pod-product-compliance
Lightning Source LLC
Chambersburg PA
CBHW060527010526
44107CB00059B/2615